WITHDRAWN

TWO CHINESE POETS

Vignettes of Han Life and Thought

TWO CHINESE POETS

POETS

Vignettes of Han Life and Thought

BY E. R. HUGHES

PRINCETON, NEW JERSEY
PRINCETON UNIVERSITY PRESS
1960

Publication of this book has been aided by
a grant from the Bollingen Foundation

◊

Printed in the United States of America
by Princeton University Press, Princeton, N.J.

PUBLISHER'S FOREWORD

ERNEST R. HUGHES was for many years Reader in Chinese Philosophy and Religion at Oxford University. He was the author of a number of Sinological studies, including *Religion in China* (with Katharine Hughes), *Chinese Philosophy in Classical Times*, and *The Art of Letters: Lu Chi's "Wen Fu,"* A.D. *302.* Mr. Hughes was working on the manuscript of the present book at the time of his death in October 1956. It is regrettable that the work has not received the finishing touches that Professor Hughes would no doubt have wanted to make had he remained alive. Princeton University Press is profoundly indebted, however, to Dr. David Hawkes, a former pupil of Professor Hughes and now Professor of Chinese at Oxford University, who generously undertook the necessary revision of the manuscript before publication. The Press also wishes to express its thanks to the Bollingen Foundation for its generous assistance in support of publication.

PREFATORY NOTE

Mr. Hughes began this comparative study of the poems of Pan Ku and Chang Heng after the publication of his book on the *Wen Fu* of Lu Chi (*The Art of Letters*, Bollingen Series No. xxix, New York, 1951). He finished it in June 1956 when he was already suffering from the disease from which he died in October. The Princeton University Press had earlier agreed to look at the book, so it was sent to them. It was returned after Mr. Hughes's death, with the recommendation that considerable revision and additions in the way of notes and bibliography were required. His former pupil, Dr. David Hawkes (now Professor in Oxford University) undertook this task, and the book as now published is the result of his work.

I am deeply grateful to Dr. Hawkes for the trouble he has taken and the time given which he could ill spare from his own work, and also to Mr. Wu Shih Chang for his advice and help. Without these two friends my husband's last contribution to the study of Chinese literature could not have been put into a form in which it could be available for those interested in the literature of the Han period. He also hoped that this study of history as seen through the eyes of two poets would appeal to historians.

KATHARINE HUGHES

PREFACE

◇◇◇

SOME readers skip prefaces; others, perhaps advisedly, read them carefully. For a man like myself who has benefited greatly from explanatory prefaces, it seems that a debt of honor claims his laggard energies to write one now. In brief, then, in my last period of research in Peking (1933-34) there was a haunting feeling that for me chiseling away at "the Classics"—my main center of interest in Sinological studies— was a Sisyphean task. Each Classic had its own insoluble problems. To a historian in search of dateable material on ideological development, although a number of miscellaneous dates were to be found, they did not afford a basis on which to build: follow one main clue derived from one Classic, follow another from another Classic, and the two clues compared did not make historical sense. . . . It became clear that a purely linguistic approach to the problems was the more profitable course. Some first-rank scholars were working in this field. Could I do anything there? An experiment or two demonstrated that for a lone worker in his Oxford hermitage, even to "settle the enclitic δέ" was practically unachievable.

In the forties I went on to the study of what the Ch'ing litterateurs so happily called "*p'ien wen*," literally "double-harness style," first in Later Han prose compositions, then in the mid-Han *fu* (prose poems). Their attraction lay in the fact that in the first-century-B.C. compendium, the *Li Chi* ("Record of Rites"), there were lengthy passages, and even whole essays, in which there was continuous complementation of sentences and clauses, together with tighter forms of sentence structure. The study was encouraging, but doubts assailed me when I discovered that in post-Han literature the acknowledged masters of style were not so much concerned with clear statement and accurate description as with making "delicious hanging clusters of words." I then went to the Han scholiasts and the historical recorders to see what their respective styles revealed. This study on the whole re-assured me. I came to the tentative conclusion that by the first century A.D. able writers had a command of ordered communication which earlier ages of writers had not possessed.

In order to check on these various impressions I made a special study of Lu Chi's *Wen Fu* ("Prose-poem on the Art of Letters") written in A.D. 301-302. That study proved highly illuminating as to methods of approach to the classical literature: first, find a document of manageable proportions, of certain authorship, certain date, and practically indubitable text, and then follow where it leads. This conclusion lies behind my book on the *Wen Fu* published in 1951 (Bollingen Series, No. xxix, New York, Pantheon Press).

The next step was then clear. Two acknowledged masters of double-harness description of objects (*wu*) were Pan Ku and Chang Heng, and within twenty to thirty years of each other they had composed their respective "*Fu* on the Two Capitals." Here were dateable documents by well-known authors, the extant texts in most admirable condition. Further, the two authors had under contemplation the previous Han regime in contrast to their own. What more could an ideological historian want in the way of reliable and illuminating data? In this fashion I came to these special studies, came to write this book. Three considerations dominate its method: (1) to get at the texture of the minds of the two authors and their contemporaries; (2) placing the authors in the witness box as to Han beliefs and institutions, to estimate their reliability; (3) to explicate the particular matters on which they gave evidence.

With regard to the style of composition, it has to a large extent been dictated by my aim to reach not one but two kinds of readers: the Sinologists whose familiarity with names and places makes explanation unnecessary, and also a certain particular Western type of experienced historian who desires to include the Far East within his purview. That there are such, long association with historians has demonstrated to me. I gather they have a suspicion that, apart from the desirability of excursions outside their cultural habitat, there is something to be learnt from that most historically-minded of all peoples, the Chinese. Since I have profited so much in my studies by exploring these historians' minds, I cannot but attempt to serve their interests. Not only so: surely the next step in historiographical research is by appreciation of the merits and demerits of Chinese historiography. Also, since it was in the Han era that "China" first saw itself as a world civilization, that era above all is relevant to the world-conscious historian.

Therefore, in these pages, the form of presentation involves an admixture of ABC information which the Sinologist does not require. Also, the more specialized documentation has been relegated to footnotes which in nine cases out of ten do not concern the general reader. One matter, which is possibly a moot point in discussion, is whether the Chinese historic culture is so unique that it stands in a class by itself. I have taken it for granted that in no sense is "China" a *lusus naturae*, but a phenomenon which is in all respects comparable to other such large-scale phenomena. My book seems to me to convey information which strengthens this impression. As a corollary stands the belief that the time-schedule of European and American cultural advance is not the archtype on the basis of which value judgements can reliably be made.

It remains to make grateful acknowledgement of outstanding help which I have received. First come the Chinese libraries: the Tsing Hua University Library and that of the Provincial University of Yunnan (1942-44). Then come the Western libraries: the Library of Congress in Washington (1947), the Harvard-Yenching Institute Library (1948), the University of California Library, Berkeley (1949), the Claremont Colleges Library (1950-52), the Oxford Chinese Faculty Library, and the Cambridge University Library. I welcome this opportunity of apologizing to the librarians concerned for straining their patience from time to time.

Then there are Dr. Ch'en Shou-yi, in the earlier stages, and Mr. Wu Shih-chang in the later stages. Both these savants have rescued me from various serious interpretational errors. I am also indebted to Mr. Wu for his critical interest in my problems. It has been the more generous of him because his own book on the history of Chinese prose is still in the making. To Madame Maspero I am indebted for her gift of a copy of Henri Maspero's *Les Instruments Astronomiques des Chinois au Temps des Han*,[1] to Dr. Joseph Needham for his illuminating reactions to my questions on Chang Heng's type of mind and other such scientific problems.

I regret that Dr. Hulsewé's *Remnants of Han Law*, Vol. I (Leiden, 1955) reached me so late that its influence on my thinking has been only a tithe of what it doubtless will be. Professor Dubs' *History of the Former Han Dynasty*, Vol. III reached me too late even to be skimmed. In regard to his Vols. I and II (Baltimore, 1938 and 1944), I am under a debt, as all students of classical China are, to him and his colleagues for the valuable fruits of their labors. Yet more am I under a debt to Dr. Tjan Tjoe-som for his *Po Hu T'ung* (Leiden, 1949 and 1952).

E.R.H.

Dorn Cottage
Blockley
Moreton-in-Marsh
Gloucester, England

June 1956

---

[1] *Mélanges Chinois et Bouddhiques*, VI, Bruges, 1939, pp. 183-370.

CONTENTS

◇◇

Preface. 1. Introduction of the *Dramatis Personae*. 2. The Topography and Geography of the Site. 3. The City and Its Suburbs. 4. The Imperial Demesne. 5. The Emperor's Personal Dwelling-Places. 6. The Rear Palaces. 7. The Administration Offices, the Archives, and Other Buildings. 8. The Chien Chang Palace and Its Appurtenances. 9. The Imperial Hunt. 10. After the Hunt. 11. The Western Capital Guest Sums Up.

1. The Introduction of Two Interlocutors. 2. The Topography and Geography of Ch'ang-an. 3. The Palace Buildings. 4. The Rear Apartments. 5. The Outbreak of Megalomania. 6. The Chien Chang Palace Area, with Its Spirit-Revealing Tower. 7. The Chien Chang Area (continued). 8. The City and Its Suburbs with Their Inhabitants. 9. The Hunting Park. 10. The Imperial Hunt. 11. After the Hunt. 12. The Emperor's Undignified Amour. 13. Final Conclusions. 14. The Nobleman Makes His Bow.

[xiii]

CONTENTS

CONTENTS

TWO CHINESE POETS

Vignettes of Han Life and Thought

CHRONOLOGICAL TABLE

THE SHANG DYNASTY
(founded by T'ang the Victorious)
traditional dates 1766-1122 B.C.

THE CHOU DYNASTY
(founded by King Wu)   traditional dates 1122-256 B.C.

THE CH'IN DYNASTY
(founded by King Cheng of Ch'in)   221-207 B.C.

THE FORMER HAN DYNASTY (founded by Liu Pang)
206 B.C. - A.D. 8

Emperor Kao..........206-195	Emperor Chao...........86-74
Emperor Hui..........194-188	Emperor Hsüan..........73-49
Empress Lü............187-180	Emperor Yüan............48-33
Emperor Wen........179-157	Emperor Ch'eng........32-7
Emperor Ching.....156-141	Emperor Ai............... 6-1
Emperor Wu..........140-87	Emperor P'ing..........1 B.C. - A.D. 5

The Infant Emperor A.D. 6-8

THE "NEW" DYNASTY
(Wang Mang the Usurper)   A.D. 9-22

THE LATER HAN DYNASTY
(founded by Liu Hsiu)   23-219

Emperor Kuang Wu 25-57	Emperor Shun........126-144
Emperor Ming....... 58-75	Emperor Ch'ung.... 145
Emperor Chang...... 76-88	Emperor Chih........ 146
Emperor Ho.......... 89-105	Emperor Huan........147-167
Emperor Shang......106	Emperor Ling........168-189
Emperor An...........107-125	Emperor Hsien 190-219

Chapter I

INTRODUCTION

◇◇

THERE is some danger attached to the use of the word "vignette" in the title of this book. "Vignette" has long been used to denote those little floral patternings that, notably in nineteenth-century publications, fill up the blank spaces on the opening and closing pages of the chapters. They can be pleasing enough to the eye, but in so many cases they have nothing to do with the meaning of the book. They are, therefore, in the full sense of the modern opprobious term "extraneous ornament." "Vignette" has, however, of late years acquired more reputable nuances of meaning, as, for example, a photographic vignette in which the attention is focussed on the subject in a characteristic pose and the non-characteristic outlying parts of the figure are deliberately blurred. Since the main part of this book is to present Pan Ku (A.D. 32-92) and Chang Heng (A.D. 78-139) as they appear in their respective two prose-poems on the Two Capitals,[1] "vignette" in this sense would seem appropriate.

Further, in the eighteen-eighties George Saintsbury wrote "to finish off and vignette isolated sketches of manner, character, and thought with more precision . . . than is possible and suitable in prose" (see *Oxford Dictionary*, ad loc.). That usage also validates the term in connection with this book, written primarily for Western readers.

For the benefit of the general reader who may be unfamiliar with the early history of China, it is perhaps desira-

---

[1] An annotated French translation of the two prose-poems by Pan Ku may be found in G. Margouliès *Le "Fou" dans le Wen-siuan*, Paris, 1926, pp. 31-74, and a German translation of the two by Chang Heng in E. von Zach, *Die Chinesischen Anthologie, Übersetzungen aus dem Wen Hsüan*, ed. I. M. Fang, Harvard-Yenching Institute Studies XVIII, 1958, vol. I, pp. 1-37. The von Zach translation was first published in *Sinologische Beiträge* 2 (1936).

ble at this point to supplement the chronological chart at the beginning of this volume with a brief outline of the historical developments which led up to the creation of the LATER HAN society in which Pan Ku and Chang Heng, the two writers with whom this book is chiefly concerned, both lived.

The immensely long period known as the CHOU DYNASTY began with the conquest of the SHANG kings in Honan by powerful vassal chieftains from the west. The traditional date of conquest, 1122 B.C., is probably about a century too early. The Chou kings ruled in Shensi and exercised some sort of control over a large number of small vassal states scattered over the whole of northern China. The nobles who governed these states were generally related to the Chou kings either by blood or marriage. In 771 B.C. the Chou capital was sacked and the Chou king slain by barbarian invaders, and a remnant of the royal house set up a new capital farther east in LOYANG. From this circumstance the era ending in 771 B.C. is known as WESTERN CHOU and the era following the removal of the capital EASTERN CHOU. It will be seen that there is a parallel in the Han dynasty when the capital was moved from Ch'ang-an to Loyang in A.D. 24.

After the transfer of the capital, the control of the Chou kings over their vassals became more and more ineffectual. The vassal princes enlarged their states by opening up new lands, by the elimination of the "barbarian" peoples who had formerly lived side by side with the Chou settlements, and by the conquest of weaker rivals. But since no single state was strong enough to withstand unaided the onslaught of powerful external enemies like the barbarians of the north or the peoples of the Huai and Yangtze river valleys, a succession of HEGEMONS arose—rulers of outstandingly rich and powerful states who, acting nominally on behalf of the effete Chou kings, led confederacies of the Chou states in war and exacted tribute from them. This period (722-481 B.C.) is called the SPRING AND AUTUMN period after the name of the chronicles of the state of Lu which are our chief source for its history.

The last two centuries of the Chou dynasty, from 403 B.C. to the end of the dynasty, are known as the WARRING STATES period. In this era the Chou kings ceased to exercise even a nominal control over the other states. The rulers of the seven most powerful states called themselves kings and each aspired to unify China under his own sway. They ruled over territories as large as European countries with large populations which economic, technological, and cultural advances had raised to a level of civilisation vastly superior to that of Chou society in the early days of the dynasty. These great states were almost continuously engaged in war and diplomatic intrigue against each other. Finally the powerful western state of Ch'in eliminated all the other states, and in 221 B.C. the king of Ch'in became emperor of a unified China and founded the CH'IN DYNASTY. He abolished the feudal nobility, set up a great bureaucracy, standardised weights and measures and the Chinese script, built roads, canals, and the Great Wall of China, and extended his conquests into Korea and Indo-China. His dynasty did not long survive him, however, since these immense achievements were based on a ruthless and tyrannical oppression of the people, who quickly disposed of his incompetent and weakly successors. Of the various adventurers who strove for control in the ensuing anarchy, a soldier of humble origin called Liu Pang (later known as KAO TSU, the "August Founder" of the Han dynasty) eventually succeeded in establishing a new dynasty. This HAN DYNASTY had its capital at CH'ANG-AN,[2] near the modern Sian in Shensi.

Of the emperors who succeeded Kao Tsu, the most remarkable was the EMPEROR WU (140-87 B.C.), both for the

---

[2] The spelling adopted here and elsewhere for the name of this city is in accordance with the Wade-Giles system of romanisation. The name is no longer current, having been replaced, in modern times, by Sian. In the case of the other capital, Loyang, the name still exists today and so the conventional Western spelling has been employed.

length of his reign and for the remarkable expansion of Chinese power and influence in Asia which took place during it. In the steppes north of China a nomad empire of the HUNS had come into being at about the same time as the Ch'in emperor's establishment of a unified empire in China. The exploits of Emperor Wu's armies drove back the Huns and ended for a time the hitherto constant threat of their incursions into Chinese territory. Chinese armies penetrated far into Central Asia, and the Ch'in conquests in Korea and in the south were renewed.

The splendours of Emperor Wu's reign resulted in considerable impoverishment of the economy, and the emperors following him were mostly incompetent. In A.D. 9 a member of the Empress' clan called WANG MANG overthrew the dynasty and usurped the imperial title. Wang Mang's ill-judged reforms of the economy led to great confusion and distress resulting in a great peasant uprising called the Red Eyebrows rebellion. This was closely followed by further risings led by various Han nobles. One of them, Liu Hsiu, eventually prevailed and became Emperor of a restored Han dynasty in A.D. 23. Wang Mang was killed and the imperial palaces burnt to the ground when Liu Hsiu's soldiery sacked Ch'ang-an. Millions are said to have perished in the fighting and massacres which took place during these disorders. This restored Han dynasty is usually called LATER HAN to distinguish it from the FORMER HAN dynasty deposed by Wang Mang. The capital was removed to Loyang. The first half-century of the Later Han period was a time of economic recovery and expansion. This was the period in which the first of the two authors with whom we are concerned lived. From about A.D. 80, however, there was a steady deterioration in the internal political situation, notably in the struggles between the powerful eunuch party at court and the scholar bureaucrats in the provinces, which ultimately led to the dynasty's overthrow.

Apart perhaps from one or two Western historians of the calibre of Chavannes and Henri Maspero, the distinctive features of the Later Han regime about A.D. 100 are for the most part blurred and haphazardly distinguishable from those of a century earlier when Former Han was on its last legs. Yet it is common knowledge today that in the half-dozen generations from 100 B.C. to A.D. 100 something of extraordinary moment happened to the ideologically inchoate peoples who inhabited the vast continental region east of the Himalayas. That "something" has been traditionally denoted as the triumph of the *Ju T'ao*, the doctrines upheld by the main bulk of the literates of that age. Recently the development of a more critical study of the records has led to the coining of a new term among Sinologists, "State Confucianism." The term is useful, as far as it goes, but it is submitted here that there is still a considerable blur in Sinologists' minds as to what actually happened.

Since those half-dozen generations were, in the fullest sense of the term, epoch-making in the history of the Chinese people, there is crying need for vignetting "sketches of manner, character, and thought," and for doing this on the basis of documents identifiable as to date and authorship. For this reason I came to a somewhat dangerous decision. Instead of giving complete translations of Pan Ku's and Chang Heng's respective prose-poems on Ch'ang-an, the old capital, and Loyang, the new capital, I summarized those parts of the texts where it seemed least damage would be done to the full explication of the authors' minds. (See Chapters III-VI. The indented material is direct translation; the remainder is summary and paraphrase.) Thus room was made within the bounds of one volume for four considerable chapters of critique (Chapters VII-X). In these the raw materials for vignettes of characteristic manners and modes of thought have been set down just as they emerged to view when the sentiments expressed in the poems were related to such other documents as appeared relevant. In the last chapter, after a final scrutiny of Pan Ku's and Chang Heng's reliability as contemporary witnesses, the more important of these vignettes-in-the-rough have been examined under systematic headings.

The quotation from Saintsbury contained these words: "sketches . . . with more precision . . . than is possible and suitable in prose." A provocative sentiment, calculated to surprise and even to arouse dissent from the research type of historian. Now, whatever may have been in Saintsbury's mind when he wrote those words, the reference to poetry as being more precise than prose can and should be is highly relevant to the subject matter in Chapters III to XI. The whole of this book centers round the four poems: very lengthy poems, containing prose elements but nonetheless highly poetical with their rhymes and their studied patterns of rhythmic sentence structure. In a word they are descriptive poems in which the authors' dominant aim was to depict certain objects (*wu*) of contemporary interest, not to explore the ramifications of their own emotions. Yet emotion comes in from time to time.

To the would-be reader in search of facts this feature of the documents under scrutiny may damn the book right away. Yet the rigorist historian, before turning his back on the evidence to be found in these poems, might do well to pause and consider three indisputable facts: (1) The two authors, Pan Ku and Chang Heng, were noted men in their day, their births and deaths are on record, as also considerable information about their careers. (2) Pan Ku was a historian by training and profession, of the highest repute in the annals of Chinese historiography; Chang Heng was a mathematically-minded astronomer, eminent as a trail-blazer in the scientific study of the heavens. (3) Both men wrote much in prose, but they elected to embody their respective depictions of the Two Capitals and the accompanying regimes in that new *fu* genre[3]

---

[3] The *fu*, a literary medium which became very popular during the Han dynasty, was a sort of poetic essay, generally descriptive, in which prose and verse were mixed. Its most characteristic features are the consistent use of parallelism and a highly ornate vocabulary.

to which the genius of Ssŭ-ma Hsiang-ju had given so sharp a dialectical edge.

Since external and internal evidence demonstrate that the two authors took immense pains to make their compositions effective appeals to their age, it would seem rather hazardous to assume that the precisional quality which characterized their professional studies should not inform their poetical efforts. Each had an axe to grind—possibly a personal one, possibly a nobly patriotic one—but since when did research historians refrain from examining documents because they showed signs of prejudice and *tendenz*? Does not the scientific approach to history take it as inevitable that every writer on his own period, even the recorder of statistics, has some particular conscious or unconscious slant to his mind?

The emphasis on these three facts has, it is hoped, given assurance on the evidential value of the four documents proposed for examination. There is a fourth consideration arising out of the epistemological axiom that rational knowledge comes by comparison, and the more clearly the compared objects can be envisaged the more precise and more reliable the results in knowledge. In the case under consideration the first object was the capital, Ch'ang-an, which had been looted and largely burnt some sixty years before Pan Ku wrote, and the Former Han regime which expired twenty-one years before that looting and burning. The second contrasted object was Loyang, capital of the Later Han regime of which Pan Ku was a court official. Some years after Pan Ku died, Chang Heng, having read Pan Ku's detailed descriptions of the Two Capitals, wrote a considerably longer comparison of them. Both Pan Ku and Chang Heng had each his own angle of vision, made his own particular emphases, but had his own inner compulsion to state his definite impressions. The results, the four poems, reveal agreements and disagreements. At numberless points the narratives give details which supplement the information given in one or the other document. The reflections on the varied phenomena treated are often strikingly individual. Comparison, however, cannot be completely *pari passu*, for Chang Heng was cognizant of events which occurred between A.D. 89, the last possible date for the completion of Pan Ku's poems, and A.D. 126, the year in which Chang Heng presented his poems to the throne. (See Chapter II for a discussion on the two dates.)

The conclusion stares us in the face that these four poems might well contain a considerable store of information. What is more, the store is a unique one, since nowhere else in the literature of the Han era can we find two such near-contemporary authors dealing with the same subjects of discourse in so intimately comparable a fashion. As to the relative intelligence and rational acumen of the two authors, that will be one line of enquiry in the critiques on the poems. But it is as well to make clear in an introductory chapter that their epistemological consciousness was not so naive as it is tempting to suppose with men belonging to so superstitious an age as that of Later Han. For example, in the language current in their day there was the term *"hsiang"* (representational image) standing in contrast to a *"wu"* (a concrete object of sense perception). Behind this distinction lay the recognition of the part played by the five senses in creating mental images. There was also the recognition that knowledge derived from hearsay had less veridical value than knowledge gained by direct observation. The poems reveal that Pan Ku and Chang Heng were mindful of this—although whether they and their contemporaries were consistent in their application of the distinction is open to question.

With regard to such scaffoldings to thought on concrete matters, no attempt is made here to list them in relation to the mid-Han literates: helpful as Fung's *History of Chinese Philosophy* and Bodde's translation of it are,[4] the necessary data are still far from being classifiable on reliable semantic

---

[4] Fung Yu-lan, *Chung-kuo chê-hsüeh shih* (2 vols.), Commercial Press, Shanghai, 1946. Fung Yu-lan, *A History of Chinese Philosophy*, Vols. I & II, tr. D. Bodde, Princeton University Press, 1952-53.

foundations. But they are of the utmost importance, and it is hoped that this present study of two outstanding mid-Han minds may throw some light on the problems involved. The chief of these problems is, as all Sinologists are so painfully aware, to date with anything approaching certainty or precision the Five so-called "Confucian" Classics.[5] They constitute the largest and most important, although by no means the only important, source of ideological information for the period. Historians can agree that their existence in recognizable shape is guaranteed by the listing of them in Liu Hsin's "Catalogue"[6] of the date A.D. 1 or thereabouts. But the same passage reveals that there were variant texts of these Scriptures in the imperial library, whilst the researches of the Ch'ing scholars and modern critics have driven home the fact that for these "Five Scriptures" (with the possible exception of the "Spring and Autumn Annals") there is no conclusive evidence as to who the authors and compilers were, and how few or how many redactors and amplifiers had a hand in bringing these texts to the uncorrelated condition disclosed by Liu Hsin's "Catalogue." Since the inception of these documents dates far back in the Chou Dynasty, the vast bulk of the statements in them is only hypothetically dateable. Yet their influence in mid-Han times is writ large in every phase of thought and social observance, so that the historian today cannot afford to ignore them. When he tackles this problem, he finds himself in the situation of Gilbert and Sullivan's billiard sharper, "playing extravagant matches with a twisted cue on a cloth untrue and elliptical billiard balls."

From the point of view of the ideological historian here is perhaps the paramount incentive to the student to break

---

[5] i.e. (1) the "Changes" (*I Ching*), (2) "History" (*Shu Ching*), (3) "Odes" (*Shih Ching*), (4) "Rituals" (*Li Chi*, etc.), and (5) "Spring and Autumn Annals" (*Ch'un Ch'iu*). In this book these five are collectively referred to as the Scriptures.

[6] The "Monograph on Bibliography" (*I Wen Chih*) in Pan Ku's "History of the Former Han Dynasty" (*Han Shu*). The monograph was mostly written by Liu Hsin.

out of that charmed Scripture circle and be content for a
time to concentrate on dateable documents by well-known
authors late in that key mid-Han age. In their four poems
Pan Ku and Chang Heng make one or two references to "the
Scriptures" in general. They do so in the respectful language
one would expect from members of the Later Han court,
but their outlook on life is by no means restricted to guidance
from Scripture texts. Pan Ku, indeed, expresses his disgust
at the benighted practice of proving by proof-texts. On the
other hand, there is the fact that throughout the 2360 verses
which make up the four poems[7] the phrasing is constantly
remindful of Scripture sentences.[8] This, of course, is what
one would expect from men whose education consisted mainly
in learning to read and understand the Scriptures. But the
research mind can hardly be content to be stopped by that
reflection. New light on meaning comes from seeing those
phrases caught out of their Scripture contexts, adapted to the
poet's use in metrically formed sentences, sometimes in ways
which might stagger the original authors.

The profit, however, goes beyond that. The vivid personality of each author is constantly in evidence, and by his
mastery of language we are able to see things through his
eyes: emperors and their palaces and entourages, their duties
and amusements, as also the busy life of the city streets, the
merchants and pedlars, the street-corner arguers, the gangsters in the suburbs lying in wait for the unwary, and the children in procession expelling the demons of disease. At the
very least the people of that far-back age become more nearly
alive as human beings, cease in a measure to be lay figures
in the mass, vague representational images created in the

---

[7] A small margin of error must be allowed for in this assessment. With
Pan Ku's Preface (304 characters), the total number of characters comes
at a rough estimate to well over 12,400.

[8] The seventh-century commentary on *Wen Hsüan* by Li Shan consists
mostly of illustration of the text by means of citations from the Scriptures
and other works. In the case of Chang Heng's "*Fu* on the Eastern Capital"
many of the citations are taken from *Chou Li*, suggesting that Chang Heng
may have been familiar with that work.

modern's unconscious imagination. There is even more than that: dateable descriptions of imperial sacrifices, of a great durbar for foreign potentates and domestic princes and nobles, pictures in concrete detail of the throne as it functioned in Later Han. Also here are examples of what could be said to Later Han ancestor-worshipping emperors in criticism of earlier occupants of their dynastic throne.

With regard to those Scripture parallels, it is urged that the linguistic researcher would do well to tread warily. He dare not blindly assume that in all cases here is evidence guaranteeing that such and such a passage was in such and such a Scripture at such and such a point. It is quite possible that a certain phrase might have come into quite recent circulation, a newly coined idea, outcome of the intellectual *éclaircissement* which characterized the mid-Han age, and then either by addition of some amplification to a Scripture or by way of being an elucidatory redaction have crept into the sacred text. Three considerations demonstrate the need for caution. One is that although after Emperor Wu's reign (140-87 B.C.) it may have been difficult for a group of official expositors to insert additions, yet Liu Hsiang found the tablets and scrolls in the imperial library imperfect and out of their proper order; and we do not know what he and his colleagues did to make order out of disorder and sense out of non-sense. The second is that during the two decades of the Wang Mang regime (A.D. 9-22) the propagandist mind was strong in court circles, and also that whilst Kuang Wu (A.D. 25-57) was desperately engaged in establishing his supremacy, his Erudites were both guardians of the sacred texts and propagandists for their master's cause. Thirdly, the Ts'ai Yung inscription of some sort of *textus receptus*[9] on pillars of stone in A.D. 175 was sanctioned because there was doubt as to what the authentic texts did or did not contain. In Chap-

---

[9] Now known only from fragmentary references in the writings of later scholars.

ters VII-X this state of affairs crops up here and there for consideration in passing. In Chapter XI is an attempt to draw the earlier suggestions together and clarify their significance, but no attempt is made to do more than set down one student's reflections.

I make no apology for the microscopic attention to detail. As the late R. G. Collingwood, a brilliant archaeologist and student of history as well as an Oxford professor of metaphysics, maintained in his inaugural lecture, the study of history is in the last resort a study of the individual and concrete.[10] To this I would add this amplification: those fractional yet at times highly revealing concrete bits of information which have survived the wrack of time till now. The only question with regard to a particular culture and period of history is whether it is sufficiently in the main stream of world history to warrant the labor of envisaging. From that angle of approach, in this "Year of Grace" 1956, a quite impressive case may be made out for the history of the Han era. To take only the history of Western civilization for comparison, the Greek ideological and institutional achievements were followed by the Roman; and it was Rome which first envisaged the prerogatives and duties of world-dominion and started to integrate the various races under its influence. The power of Rome crashed eventually, but not before a new mysteriously energising force, known as "Christianity," had become a re-integrating influence from which sprang a new distinctive Western culture which throughout its succeeding phases has more and more become relevant to other races besides those of Europe. If "Rome" had not succeeded

---

[10] R. G. Collingwood, *The Historical Imagination* (Clarendon Press, 1935). E.g. p. 5: "No doubt, historical thought is in one way like perception. Each has for its proper object something individual. What I perceive is this room, this table, this paper. What the historian thinks about is Elizabeth or Marlborough, the Peloponnesian War or the policy of Ferdinand and Elizabeth. But what we perceive is always the this, the here, the now . . . the things about which the historian reasons are not abstract but concrete, not universal but individual, not indifferent to space and time but having a where and a when of their own." See also Collingwood's *The Idea of History* (Clarendon Press, 1946), a posthumous production of his uncompleted work.

"Greece" and "Christendom" not succeeded "Rome," what then?

The "China" of the Han era, with its envisagement of the prerogatives and duties of world-dominion, constitutes a Far Eastern phenomenon comparable to Rome, particularly as the Han alertness to philosophical values stemmed from the Chou thinkers, as Rome did from Greece. Pan Ku optimistically, Chang Heng less optimistically, believed that the civilisation of Great Han would endure for a thousand ages. In that belief Pan Ku was mistaken and Later Han crashed a hundred years after Chang Heng's death. Yet after five centuries of almost continual disruption and barbarian infiltration a unified China of more than Han integral dimensions re-emerged, to be followed by periodic effectual assertions of cultural cohesion and civilizing power. The Chinese of these later ages have had a synonym for their cultural unity, "sons of Han." *If* "Great Han" had not supervened on the finally disrupted Chou order, and *if* what "Great Han" achieved in cultural integration had not been strong enough to survive the strains and stresses of the following five centuries, to be followed by "T'ang China" and "Sung China" . . . , what then? The "ifs of history" when categorically set forth admit of no categorical answer. They remain question marks and very dangerous ones. But as such they are useful in driving the historian to pursue his dedicated task of ascertaining such concrete facts as may illumine the interplay of the great cultural forces which in their contemporary forms are today shaping the course of world events. That "Great China" is one of those forces is self-evident, as much as "Great America," "Great Britain." In Henry Steele Commager's impressive *The American Mind*[11] there stands in the forefront Santayana's pregnant dictum, "to be an American is of itself almost a moral condition, an education and a career." To Pan Ku and Chang Heng at the turn of the first century A.D., to be a Han Chinese had very much the same portentous meaning.

[11] H. S. Commager, *The American Mind, An Interpretation of American Thought and Character since the 1880's*, London, 1950.

Chapter II

BIOGRAPHICAL DETAILS

NOTE: The following two accounts are constructed mainly from information given in the biographies of Pan Ku and Chang Heng, chs. 70 and 89, respectively, in the "History of the Later Han Dynasty" (*Hou Han Shu*), the biographical section of which was composed by Fan Yeh (398-446) of the (Liu) Sung Dynasty. Pan Ku's story has been supplemented with information from the biographies of his father, Pan Piao, his brother, Pan Ch'ao, and his sister, Pan Chao; also from his autobiographical preface (*Hsü Chuan*), the last chapter of the "History of the Former Han Dynasty" (*Han Shu*). A few details come from other parts of the "History of the Later Han Dynasty" in which references to Pan Ku occur. Chang Heng's story is almost entirely from his biography, but certain details are derived from modern histories of mathematics, notably that by Professor Li Yen (*Chung-kuo Ku-tai Shu-hsüeh Shih-liao*, Chung-kuo K'o-hsüeh T'u-shu I-ch'i Kung-ssŭ, Shanghai, 1954).

Fan Yeh depended on records in the archives at Chien-yeh (Nanking), the Chin capital, amongst them the *Tung Kuan Han Chi*, which was compiled more or less contemporaneously by imperial orders. How much of this document was in existence in the fifth century is in question, but some of it is still extant. Fan Yeh died before his projected work was completed, and the *Chih* (monographs) he had in mind to write were later supplied by the commentator Liu Chao (flor. 502-519) from the *Hsü Han Shu* of Ssŭ-ma Piao (240-306) and incorporated in Fan Yeh's work. Today, therefore, we are unable to estimate what Fan Yeh's final word would have been, e.g. in regard to the biographies he compiled. But in a letter he wrote to his family just before his execution (printed in Wang Hsien-ch'ien, *Hou Han Shu Chi-chieh*, Introduction) he referred to his aims in compiling them; and in the light of that highly illuminating document—a landmark in Chinese historiographical acumen—his biographies of Pan Ku and Chang Heng are assumed here to be generally trustworthy.

[16]

Pan Ku (*tzŭ* Meng-chien), born A.D. 32, died A.D. 92, came of a family of considerable distinction in the service of the state. Its fame in this respect dated from the last decades of the Former Han regime, but the family tradition was that they were descended from the royal house of Ch'u State. In the Ch'in First Emperor's time an ancestor packed up and went off to the frontier lands in the northwest where he made money in sheep and cattle. Two of Pan Ku's great-uncles had careers at court, and one of them, Pan Yu, was ennobled and finally became collaborator with Liu Hsiang in the task of putting the imperial library in order. The Emperor presented him with books from his store, thus adding to the family library which scholars came from far to see. One member of the family was an authority on Taoist books. At that time the Pans were affluent, although whether they continued to be so is doubtful. Pan Yu "died untimely" when Wang Mang began his usurpation. Pan Piao, Pan Ku's father, remained loyal to the Han house and retired into the west. Being badgered by the war-lord where he was to assist in his rebellious plans, Piao went elsewhere and took service with a loyal general. When Emperor Kuang Wu came to power, Pan Piao was appointed Governor of Hsü (North Kiangsu), but after a time was released from office owing to ill health. Later he was summoned to court and held a succession of posts, all of them a source of discomfort to him. He did not achieve the distinction of ennoblement. At the age of fifty-two he died while magistrate of a district. "His officers and people loved him."

The upper-class way at that time was for lads of promise to be sent for schooling in the capital. Pan Ku, although clearly blest with brains, was for some unknown reason trained at home. His father cherished a scheme for writing a history of the Former Han dynasty, and it was in this austerely studious atmosphere that Pan Ku developed his intellectual powers. When his father died he continued with the history-writing project. Before long he ran into trouble. A report reached the court that a private person was engaged in writing a history—a punishable offence. His brother, Pan Ch'ao, was in Loyang at the time, being engaged in some minor copyist capacity. Pan Ch'ao immediately took steps to protect his brother's name, and the result was that Pan Ku was summoned for interrogation by Emperor Ming (A.D. 58-75). The Emperor not only decided in his favor, but also gave him access to the palace archives.

Thus the prospect of a successful court career opened before Pan Ku's eyes. Yet, although he was near to his fortieth year, his official standing was only that of a *lang* (a cadet awaiting appointment), his allowance a mere few hundred piculs of grain a year.[1] His brother also was finding no scope for his abilities in the capital. For Pan Ku the only course was to put on all speed and complete his Han history. There is no external evidence by which to date his beginning of the "*Fu* on the Two Capitals," but it seems probable that the theme began to take shape in his mind during his first impressionable years at Emperor Ming's court.[2] Some time in Emperor Chang's first reign-period (76-83) the task of over twenty years was completed and the "History of the Former Han Dynasty" was submitted to the throne, all, that is, except the monograph on *T'ien Wen* (astronomical observations).[3] It was accepted with approval and among the scholars received with enthusiastic welcome. Yet no well-paid post came to him. All that the Emperor did was to employ Pan Ku in

---

[1] From Chia K'uei's biography (*Hou Han Shu*, ch. 66) it appears that Pan Ku was associated with the intimates of the imperial circle, and he may have had a hand in preparing the "Acts of Emperor Kuang Wu" (see *Tung Han Hui Yao*, ch. 12). Conceivably his apparent failure to obtain any substantial sign of imperial approval was due to the jealousy of Chia K'uei.

[2] Cf. Pan Ku's *Tien Yin* (*Wen Hsüan*, ch. 48) written in collaboration with Chia K'uei and others at Emperor Ming's instigation. Some of the emphases characteristic of his *fu* are found there in an undeveloped form.

[3] *Han Shu*, *T'ien Wen Chih*, completed by his sister, Pan Chao, after Pan Ku's death.

writing a résumé of the findings of the great scholars' conference in the White Tiger Hall.

Pan Ku then set to work on his "*Fu* on the Two Capitals." In what year he finished and presented them to the throne is doubtful, but the immediate background to his meditations must have been that of Emperor Chang's court.[4] Again there was universal admiration, but still no higher post was given to him. Since the record of his character has it that he was "amiable and accommodating, not exalting himself above others because of his talents," he can hardly have been comfortable in mind. Finally General Tou, brother to the Emperor's chief consort, went on campaign and took Pan Ku as a member of his staff. Again fortune was cruel. On Tou's return the animosity against him at court came to a head. He was impeached, and Pan Ku was accused along with him. Before that blow came, an unruly slave of Pan Ku's household had offended the Intendant of the Capital. He bided his time, and then, when Pan Ku's name was under a cloud, he dispatched lictors to waylay him and throw him into prison. Before his friends could come to his rescue, he died. The record has it that the Intendant was later "reprimanded" and one of his officers "punished."

Pan Ku's "History of the Former Han Dynasty" (*Han Shu*) in a hundred chapters has made his name a household word among scholars all down the ages; and today, in spite of the uninhibited approaches of modern critical scholarship, his reputation stands as high as it ever did. As an overall view of a period his book is an astonishingly mature exhibi-

---

[4] Li Shan (d. 689), the first great commentator on the two *fu*, and a man whose cautious statements created a general confidence in him, remarks at the outset of his commentary that Pan Ku presented his *fu* "with the intention of remonstrance, and Emperor Ho was greatly pleased." Since Emperor Ho was only thirteen when he succeeded in 89 and his entourage was not one likely to welcome remonstrance, this seems unlikely, particularly as Pan Ku died in 92. In any case, since Emperor Chang died in his thirties, Pan Ku must have written the poems with the intention of presenting them to him.

tion of the science and art of historiography. To conceive of a period history as entailing treatment from four different angles of approach, each shedding a complementary light on what happened, and to do this not in rough outline but in detail on judiciously handled information derived from state documents, may be described as an intellectual achievement which has no counterpart in other ancient cultures.[5] The plan of the book owes much to Ssŭ-ma Ch'ien's "Record of History" (*Shih Chi*) of a century and a half earlier, but Pan Ku greatly improved on the patterns embodied in that work. One question ranges round the extent to which Pan Piao conceived the scheme in its entirety and whether he was the author of parts of it.[6] The question has to be asked, since Pan Ku has from time to time been accused of being unfilial in taking all the glory to himself. It seems unlikely, if Pan Ku had before his eyes the example of filial piety set by Ssŭ-ma Ch'ien, that he would have deliberately omitted all recognition of his father's claim to a substantial share in the final product.

Pan Ku has also a great name among connoisseurs of literary

[5] To enable Western historians to get some idea of this achievement in historiographical method, here is an abstract of the "History of Former Han Dynasty" (*Han Shu*) : *Section I* (12 chapters) : a record year by year of the main acts of the twelve emperors with some account of the circumstances in which the more important decisions were made. *Section II* (8 chapters) : tables containing lists of the royal princes, the ranks of nobles, the officials of each reign, and the great men (graded in 9 classes) of past ages. *Section III* (10 chapters) : substantial monographs on the Principles of the Calendar, Rites and Music, Principles and Applications of the Law, Food and Commodities, Sacrifices in the Suburbs and Outlying Localities, Operations of the Five Forces in Nature, Geography (Irrigation Systems etc.), Catalogue of the Imperial Library. *Section IV* (170 chapters) : biographies or short memoirs of 240 royal princes and all other kinds of eminent men of the dynasty, including the most eminent litterateurs. This section also includes chapters on "the Scholars' Grove" (with details about 27 famous teachers), on Lenient Officers (6), on Tyrannical Officers (12), on the Wealth of Merchants (11), on Wandering Bravoes (7), on Palace Favorites (7), on the surrounding Barbarian Tribes, on the Empresses, on Wang Mang the usurper, on various aspects of the Pan family, developments of scholarship, and the plan of the book as a whole.

[6] See H. H. Dubs, *History of the Former Han Dynasty*, vols. 1 & 2 (Baltimore, 1938, 1944), passim.

style. According to Fan Yeh, "forty-one of [Ku's] pieces were extant in his day." Of these the ones treasured in the *Wen Hsüan*[7] show competency in many of the polished literary modes practised in Later Han, including jesting conversations at feasts. But his outstanding poetic achievement was the "*Fu* on the Two Capitals." There he followed Ssŭ-ma Hsiang-ju's (179-117 B.C.) original lead in transmuting the *fu* genre into a depiction of things instead of emotions, of large-scale objects of attention in contrast with mythological or trifling ones. In sheer length Pan Ku's "*Fu* on the Two Capitals" far surpassed any previous *fu* composition. It is also distinguished by its interplay between two *dramatis personae*—a device used by Hsiang-ju to give point to his irony and wit. Of the Pan Ku compositions preserved in the *Wen Hsüan*, his *Tien Yin* (ch. 48) seems to me the more revealing document, both in its foreword and in the eulogy itself. It brings out most vividly Pan Ku's feeling of dependence on Emperor Ming's personal favor.

Chang Heng (*tzŭ* P'ing-tzŭ), born in 78, died in 139, came of a provincial family in the south of the modern Honan. His grandfather was Governor of the Ch'eng-tu Commandery (Szechuan) during the last two years of Former Han, but apart from him there is no record of the family being distinguished in any way. It must have had means because Chang Heng was sent to the capital for schooling. He graduated in due course, being recommended as a *hsiao lien* (lit. "filial and upright"). Instead of seeking an official career, he went home and devoted his time to learning. He did not find common intercourse easy. Mathematics in relation to the heavens was his forte. In the course of time he was able to produce a new armillary sphere, and to construct a chart of the sky which was both detailed and clear. Philosophically he had a passion for Yang Hsiung's (53 B.C.-A.D. 18) *Hsüan*

[7] Famous anthology of verse and prose compiled by Hsiao T'ung in the 6th century.

Ching which he placed on a level with the "Five Scriptures." His technological ability showed itself in various ways. For instance, he made a flying machine—which apparently could raise itself from the ground but did not stay long in the air. In 132 he produced a seismographic apparatus, able to record the direction of earth tremors which were imperceptible to the ordinary senses.

It was in those years of seclusion that he was stirred to emulate Pan Ku by writing a "*Fu* on the Two Capitals." Ten years had passed before he finished it; it is not known when he presented it to the throne. It is difficult to believe that he did so at a time when an official career in keeping with his talents was opening before him. This was at some unspecified time in Emperor An's reign (A.D. 107-125), presumably when An was twenty or more years old. He sent for Chang Heng and after making him a cadet-in-waiting appointed him Director of Recording in charge of the sub-department engaged in recording astronomical and meteorological events. About the time of young Emperor An's death the appointment apparently lapsed,[8] and it seems likely that it was at this time that Chang Heng completed his "*Fu* on the Two Capitals," presenting it to Emperor Shun (A.D. 126-144).[9] Emperor Shun "again transferred him," and he was reinstated as Director of Recording. Finding himself out of sympathy with the dominant officials, Chang Heng resigned

[8] There is no record of when and why, nor of whether or not he retired to his home.

[9] Chang Heng could hardly have passed for government service until his early twenties. On the basis of the biography's "ten years" spent in composing his "*Fu* on the Two Capitals," this brings the date of its completion down to the middle years of Emperor An's reign, i.e. about A.D. 120. It was about then that a carriage was sent to bring him to the capital. Dowager-Empress Teng died in 121, and it is difficult to believe that certain passages in the Ch'ang-an *fu* were written with the prospect of their meeting her dour, prudish eye. The two poems would seem to have been written mainly, but not completely, in his years of seclusion, after he had stretched the wings of his mind with his scientific studies. Further, his Loyang *fu* reveals an intimate acquaintance with the downward trend in court morale, and that points to his having had some years at court.

and was out of a post for five years. The grossly superstitious tendencies in the *Wei Shu* ("Woof Books")[10] aroused his special scorn, and he expressed this bluntly in a memorial to Emperor Shun. Yet he became a gentleman-in-attendance on the Emperor and even a confidential secretary. The eunuchs were afraid of what accusations he might make against them, and they made opportunities to slander him. This shook his nerve, and he found relief in composing his great *Ssŭ Hsüan Fu.*[11] The Emperor's confidence apparently was not withdrawn.

In 136 Chang Heng was appointed Minister in the princedom of Ho Chien where the prince's disgraceful lawlessness had encouraged the lawless behaviour of a number of rich and powerful families. On his arrival Chang Heng acted with the utmost promptitude and courage, and the leading offenders were imprisoned. The princedom was brought to order, but Chang Heng felt the burden of his years and petitioned for leave to retire. He was brought back to Loyang and appointed a secretary in the Secretariat. Shortly after he died aged sixty-two (western reckoning sixty-one).

The Biography records "thirty-two pieces" of Chang Heng's composition: poems, *fu*, inscriptions—a very miscellaneous list.

---

[10] Apocryphal supplements to the Scriptures, mostly written during the Han dynasty.

[11] The internal evidence of the *Ssŭ Hsüan Fu* raises doubt as to the strict accuracy of this dating as given in the Biography. Rather, the poem would seem to represent the frame of mind which brought Chang to resign and go into retirement. That was earlier in Emperor Shun's reign. The following features of the poem are surely significant: (1) The poem is written on the pattern of Ch'ü Yüan's (third century b.c.) *Li Sao.* (2) Chang Heng, like Ch'ü Yüan, takes an imaginary journey about the earth and in the sky. (3) Whereas Ch'ü Yüan at the "Gate of Heaven" is barred entry, Chang Heng is welcomed and comforted. (4) Whereas Ch'ü Yüan's poem ends in despair, Chang Heng ends by finding peace and inspiration in his studies.

An alternative possibility seems to be that late in Emperor An's reign he was besieged with doubt as to the right course to take and finally made up his mind to retire. This would account for the Biography's mysterious detail of his appointment lapsing. At the same time it would go flatly counter to the Biography's assignment of date.

A considerable part of these have survived, among them scientific works to be found in Yen K'o-chün's *Ch'üan Han Wen*.[12] There was also a commentary on the *Chou Li* which has not survived. Chang Heng had plans for a work on Confucius' theories on the "Changes" Scripture (*I Ching*), and sought permission to complete the unfinished work of the court historiographers on the previous reigns. None of this planning came to anything. Amongst his works the most treasured has been the "*Fu* on the Two Capitals" preserved in almost perfect textual condition in the *Wen Hsüan*—as also has the *Ssŭ Hsüan Fu*. His importance as a writer on scientific subjects has also been known to a few specialists in these matters. It is only in the last thirty years that his outstanding significance has been recognized as one, perhaps the chief, of China's first real scientists.

For the four *fu* on the Two Capitals which are the heart and soul of this study, the text used has been that in the *Ssŭ Pu Ts'ung K'an* edition of the *Wen Hsüan*. For textual variations I have relied on the critical apparatus prepared by Ku Kuang-ch'i (1776-1835) and attached to the Hu K'ê-chia edition (1809) of the *Wen Hsüan*.

---

[12] The *Ch'üan Han Wen* includes 9 *fu*, some over 1000 words long. For the scientific works, on which I am unable to give an opinion, the reader is referred to *Science and Civilisation in China* by Dr. J. Needham and Dr. Wang Ling.

Chapter III

PAN KU'S "*FU* ON THE WESTERN CAPITAL"

◇◇

Preface

One opinion is that the *fu* has come down from the poetry of antiquity.
In the old days [of Chou] . . . when the royal unction was exhausted, *shih* [songs] were not composed.*

In Han times at first no one had leisure for good writing, but in Emperor Wu's time and then Emperor Hsüan's there came a new respect for ritual and music and for the achievement of literary excellence. In this the common people took delight. Famous songs (four specified) were sung at the imperial sacrifices; reign years were named after poetic objects of happy augury.

The result was that those servants of the Emperor of the kind whose powers of language were of assistance to him, Ssŭ-ma Hsiang-ju and . . . [six others specified],

morning and evening debated and took thought, daily and monthly made offerings [of compositions];

whilst great officers of state, Imperial Archivist Ni K'uan and . . . [four others specified] from time to time composed.

There were those who made themselves channels of popular feeling, and so communicated satirical remarks, others who published abroad the emperor's *virtus* and thus perfected their loyalty and filial piety.

* *Note to the Reader*: In Chapters III-VI the indented material is direct translation from the four *fu*; the remainder, set full width, is summary and paraphrase.

[25]

Here was something of like significance for posterity as the songs in the "Odes." Consequently in Emperor Ch'eng's reign these modern compositions "were assessed and entered up, and of those presented to the throne there were over a thousand pieces." The brilliance of Great Han's literature thus became evident, "equal in repute to that of Hsia, Yin and Chou."

> To go further, although both the Way and scholarship have their vicissitudes, yet the principles by which Virtus is established do not vary.

> Explore high antiquity and it was like that, examine the Han House and it was like this.

Unimportant though this matter (of *fu* writing) may be, yet the new Han as well as the old literary models ought not to be lost.

Your servant has observed that with peace on all sides and extensive buildings and embellishments in and around the capital, Loyang, there are still old men in the West who resent these developments. They boast of the ancient institutions of Ch'ang-an, aiming to disparage the city of Loyang. Consequently I have composed these *fu* poems on the Two Capitals in order to expose the errors in these men's minds and to confound them by the beautiful ordinances of the present. The wording of the *fu* is as follows:

1. *Introduction of the Dramatis Personae*

There was a guest from the Western Capital who asked his Eastern Capital host saying: "I have heard that at the beginning of August Han when plans were made, the purpose was to make Loyang the capital:

that then they stopped and went no further, going west and building our Supreme Capital there.

Have you, my host, heard of the ground for this, and have you ever surveyed the state and order of Ch'ang-an?"

The host said: "I have not. I pray you, set forth your store of cherished recollections, disclose your hidden feelings with their thoughts of the past:
enrich me with [knowledge of] the August Way, broaden me with [the glories of] the [former] capital of Han."

2. *The Topography and Geography of the Site*

The guest then describes first the topographical position of Ch'ang-an and its adjacent territory with mountains guarding it to the east and west, girdled by three rivers, the Yellow River, the Ching, and the Wei. Thus the site was fertile beyond all other sites in that northwestern region, and at the same time it was safe from outside assault: "Heaven and Earth's outstanding site." The Chou Sage-Kings elected to rule from here and so emerged like the dragon; and here the Ch'in (tyrant) gloated like a tiger (over its prey). Then, following the founding of the Han dynasty,

Heaven and man being here in responsive harmony, royal intelligence was displayed: . . .

. . . favor was extended to the West, here in very truth the capital was built.

There followed the continuous prosperity of twelve successive reigns. Along with that went lavish government expenditure.

3. *The City and Its Suburbs*

The walls were [as] of iron, a myriad spans in extent; the encircling moat dug deep as an abyss.

Three stretches of highway were laid out, twelve gates of ingress and egress were erected.

Within were the streets and cross-streets, the ward gates numbered a thousand.

Nine market places were opened, the merchandise displayed, kind by kind in ordered rows.

[27]

[The throng was so great] men could not face about, the carriages [so many] they could not make a turn.

The town was so full that it overflowed into the suburbs, with a hundred stores on either side: . . .

The red dust rising everywhere, the smoke [of the fires] linking in clouds.

Thus numerous and thus rich was the populace, its gaiety without limit. . . .

Its knights for hire looked like dukes and marquises, its shopgirls more sumptuous than great ladies.

In the spacious environs of the city were the quarters for the aristocracy, and there silken tassels and (princes') crowns were to be seen, and carriage canopies were as thick as clouds in the sky. More especially was this so near the imperial tombs where high provincial dignitaries and the merchants enriched by the trade of five provincial capitals had their residences. This was a device of imperial policy: "to strengthen the trunk and weaken the branches."

4. *The Imperial Demesne*

Beyond the city's environs lay the imperial demesne of a thousand *li* with its soaring hills, its forests and shady valleys to the south, with Lan T'ien and its beautiful jade. Water was abundant, so there were fruit orchards and plantings of sweet-smelling herbs and fragrant flowers. To the north were the Nine Peaks, partnered by the Dale of Kan Ch'üan ("Sweet Water Spring") with its spirit-inspired palace buildings (*ling kung*). There also were the irrigation canals (engineered) by Cheng and Po, sources of clothing and food (for the people), and fifty thousand marked-out plots of arable land in which were grown the five cereals and mulberry trees and hemp in abundance. To the east were larger canals carrying boats, linking up with the Wei and Yellow rivers, and so threading the mountain ranges and lakes and finally mingling their waters with the waves of the sea. To the west was the imperial hunting park together with enclosed pleasances, with fishponds and stretches of uncultivated low-lying lands, containing in all thirty-six buildings of one sort and another for the entertainment of the court, the whole area being more than four hundred *li* in circumference. Here were to be seen unicorns from Chiu Chen (Annam), horses (of a famous breed) from Ferghana, rhinoceroses from Huang Chih (three thousand *li* away, say the commentators), and birds from T'iao Chih; and strange species from outlandish countries thirty thousand *li* away beyond the K'un Lun Mountains (Northern Himalayas) and the great ocean.

5. *The Emperor's Personal Dwelling-Places*

The buildings of the imperial palace in their formation were made symbols of the heavens and the earth, their cross-lines in keeping with the Yin and the Yang.

They were situated to conform exactly to spirit [emanations] from the earth, patterned after the round and the square of the T'ai Wei and Tzŭ Wei [constellations].

Here were ornate gate-towers reaching up into the sky, here crowning the hill were the vermilion-coloured halls.

Built of rare materials, its rafters were shaped like dragons' pinions, its pillars had bases constructed of jade, the rich interlacing of colors making an impression of luminous splendor.

The palace being on a hill, the approach was by three flights of steps with balustrading at the top. Within, the rooms communicated, having either large or small doors to give access. There were sculptured pillars in the central court and rows of metal statues of men at both sides of the main entrance. Other separate palaces, sleeping apartments, belvederes, etc. were studded here and there on and below the precipitous summit: the Cool Pavilion, the Hall of Proclamation, the Warmth (in winter) Apartments, the Fairy Pavilion. . . . It is impossible to discuss them in detail . . . everywhere places for resting or feasting.

6. *The Rear Palaces*

The Rear Palaces (i.e. the women's apartments) consisted first of two buildings, one for the empress, and one for the first-rank concubines, and then Joy-in-Concord, Crowned Walls . . . (twelve buildings in all mentioned by name); but Blazing Sun built by Emperor Ch'eng was especially fine. Its chambers did not reveal the building materials, the walls did not disclose their shape, the surfaces being covered with embroidered silk hangings. Pearls, gold, jade discs, kingfisher feathers, and precious stones adorned the walls. The hall itself gleamed with precious stones, with coral and precious woods. And there were the ladies, with red silk sleeves fluttering in the breeze, with their flowered silks of various hues . . . they looked like goddesses. There were fourteen degrees of rank housed in these buildings and the numbers of inmates had to be counted by hundreds.

7. *The Administration Offices, the Archives, and Other Buildings*

In the buildings to left and right were the locations for the hundred officers of state:

where Hsiao [Ho], Ts'ao [Ts'an], Wei [Hsiang], Ping [Chi], [famous statesmen] made their polices for the crown.

As they lent strength to the [heaven-given] mandate, so they handed down the sovereign rule, and as they gave wings to the government, so they made civilization [for the people], spreading abroad the magnanimity of Great Han, removing the poisoned stings of derelict Ch'in.

This caused the people here [in the city] to sound forth

the voice of musical accord, to compose the song "Write the Word for One."

Their merit and their *virtus* shone in the founding emperors, the unguent of their favor imbued the masses.

Here also were the T'ien Lu and Shih Ch'ü [buildings], where the archives were kept, where venerable elders patient in instruction, famous Confucians and learned scholars were commanded to expound and discuss in relation to the Scriptures [lit. Six Arts], to scrutinize and collate in relation to the disagreements and agreements.

Here also were the Ch'eng Ming and Chin Ma Chambers where the work of composition went on, where fine poets and men of penetration congregated.

Having gone to the roots of things, and having exhausted [their powers of] seeing and satiated [their powers of] hearing, they unfolded sectioned compositions, compared and regulated abstruse patterns of diction.

Beyond all these buildings there were on all sides other buildings housing functionaries of the court.

Here were gathered the officers of rites and ceremonies, men who had come first in the examinations, the upright and the filial from a hundred prefectures: [also] officers of the guards, keepers of the robes, controllers of eunuchs, guardians of the gates, halberdiers of the throne room—a hundred different offices, each with its prescribed duties.

There were the thousand rows of huts for the garrison of the Palace, whose patrols crossed in all directions; there was the well-planned route of the imperial chariot; and there were the flying galleries which led from the Wei Yang Palace via the Ming Kuang Hall (where memorials were delivered) to the Ch'ang Lo Palace, and from thence crossed the western city wall to the Chien Chang Palace outside.

8. *The Chien Chang Palace and Its Appurtenances*

The description runs along without very discernible para-
graphs although changes in rhyme and the length of the
sentences mark the movement of the narrative.

This palace had been built with close attention both to
artistic workmanship and the creation of auspicious influences.
It had a thousand doors and its ten thousand windows had
shutters which could be opened and shut. In the soaring
interior of its main hall the roof beams went higher and
higher so that it overtopped the Wei Yang Palace, and both
it and the other three halls and the T'ien Liang Palace were
cunningly devised so as to catch the light of the sun. The
adjacent high terrace was such, reaching up into the clouds,
that even though one were light and agile, it would be as
if, with eyes startled out of focus, one could not ascend. So
also with the Ching Kan Tower:

> . . . in ascending it before one is halfway in the ascent
> of the tower, the eyes swing round and the attention is
> astray.

> One loses hold of the railing and thus misses its support,
> is about to fall headlong but yet held back.

> In bewilderment of soul from loss [of sense] of distance
> —round one turns in one's tracks and goes down step by
> step to the bottom.

If, in spite of fears, the top of the tower is reached, the
descent by the dark spiral staircase is equally daunting.

> As for the two lakes in front and behind, they had three
> islands [the names having fairy connotations].

> Here were undying plants which bloomed in winter,
> spirit trees in verdant groves: jagged rocks and beetling
> crags, an imposing spectacle of metal and stone.

> Here [statues of] Immortals placed high overhead on

metal columns stood holding bowls for dew: a reaching out beyond the defilement of [this world's] clogging dust to gain the limpid elixir of pure, transparent *ch'i* [constituent gas or essence of the physico-spiritual universe].

He [the emperor] was carried away by Wen Ch'eng's windy verbiage, transported by the principles that Wu Li laid down: with the intent that he might consort with (Ch'ih) Sung [Tzǔ] and [Wang Tzǔ] Ch'iao [magician-immortals of legend] and their like, and they from time to time keep company with him in this very court.

An abode for immortals—not a place where we mortals can find peace.

9. *The Imperial Hunt*

And then there were the imposing spectacles of the reviews, the martial displays in the hunting park, useful for the intimidation of barbarian tribes. When the imperial order went out, markers were set up and the beaters drove bird and beast in those directions, whilst troops of soldiers encircled those areas. The Emperor and his attendant officers having been driven to prepared lodges, there six bands of hunters started the final drive. They terrified the game with thunderous bangings and lightning-like flashes; hills and pools were obliterated in the process. Then the slaughter began with arrows and spears and swords wielded by the soldiers and their officers, a wind of feathers and a rain of blood covering the ground and darkening the sky. Skilled hunters did prodigies of daring, killing maddened tigers and rhinoceroses with their own hands. Lions and bears and elephants were among the bag. Nothing was left of the grass and the trees, the birds and beasts were all massacred.

10. *After the Hunt*

Then the Emperor went up to the Shu Yü lodge, from there to survey the heaped-up masses of the dead, the trophies of his soldiers' valor. Having enquired as to who had specially distinguished themselves, he awarded prizes to them. The provision and wine carts then arrived and a quaffing from goblets was followed by a barbecue of the freshly-killed game, this by the light of torches. After the feast everyone relaxed, some by the shady trees and fragrant plants at the K'un Ming pool. Rare birds were to be seen there (eight names of species given), like clouds collecting, like mist dispersing.

Meanwhile the palace ladies had arrived in their carriages and begun to disport themselves in decorated dragon-shaped barges floating like the wind and dispersed among the hundreds of adjacent buildings. With provisions there in plenty the festival air continued. Finally offerings were made to the spirits above and below, and the company returned singing various kinds of songs.

11. *The Western Capital Guest Sums Up*

Throughout this period the provincial capitals looked across to each other, the townships were linked one to the other: satrapies relied on the foundations of tens of generations, families carried on the inheritance of a hundred years: scholars gained their living from the repute of their ancestors' [lit. ancient] virtues, peasants served the irrigated acres of long-tilled fields: merchants sold what their families for generations before had sold, craftsmen used the compasses and measuring square of their fathers before them.

Everything fresh and abundant: everyone in his right place!

An insignificant person like myself, looking for remains on an old scrapheap, and listening to the tales of old men does not get one part in ten, indeed cannot present a comprehensive [picture].

Chapter IV

CHANG HENG'S "*FU* ON THE WESTERN CAPITAL"

◇◇◇

1. *The Introduction of Two Interlocutors*

There was a nobleman Stayed-on-Vanity; he had a super-cilious mind and an arrogant carriage.

In a gentlemanly way he liked to be learned about antiquity, [and] was versed in the old historiographers.

Hence, having much information about former generations, he had a conversation with a teacher by the name of Where-did-he-Live [i.e. Anonymous].

He said: If a man be living in a *yang* time [of good fortune], then he is comfortable: if he be living in a *yin* age [of ill fortune], then he is miserable.

This is a matter connected with the class [of facts] called Heaven.

If a man's dwelling-place is on fertile soil, then he is in easy circumstances: if it is on lean land, then he is burdened with toil.

This is a matter connected with the class [of facts] called Earth.

To be miserable is to be short of pleasure, to be burdened with toil is to be straitened in [the] kindness [one can give or receive].

Rarely are there men who are able to go counter to these [conditions].

In small matters this is certainly so: in large matters it is also bound to be so.

Hence emperors accord with Heaven and Earth with a view to perfecting culture, the masses accept instruction from above and thereby fashion custom.

Since [the two] bases of culture and custom have an adjusting effect on each other, how do we verify these [matters]?

The Ch'in line having their base in Yung [a rich soil area] became strong, Chou being in Yü [a poor soiled area] became weak. The first emperor of Earlier Han made his capital in the west, and was [? could be] lavish; the first emperor of Later Han dwelt in the east and was [? had to be] frugal.

As to the rise and fall of governments, it is invariably according to these factors.

You, Sir, may I say, have not looked into Western Capital matters: allow me to present them to you.

2. *The Topography and Geography of Ch'ang-an*

The cultured nobleman first gives a description of the region. There is the moral, that the site of the city is a naturally protected area and the valleys round are fertile, some with fields of the highest grade (*shang shang*). The area constitutes a "hub" of auspicious influences. According to an ancient legend, "Ta Ti" (Supreme Sovereign) invited the ruler of the Ch'in state and having feasted him, and being himself well liquored, very kindly made him a gift of a gold tablet as deed of ownership over this fertile area. This accounts for the amazing fact that Western Ch'in was able to unite all the states (the seven powerful states of Warring States China). Then when Emperor Kao Tsu entered this area the stars gave evidence of this being the right place for the capital,[1] and when Lou Ching, taught by Heaven, urged

---

[1] Chang Heng's actual wording is "five *wei* [planetary orbits] converged so as to lodge in the [constellation] Tung Ching." This precision of language equates this passage to that in the "Acts of the Emperors" under Kao

him to go west, did he not repress his longing for his native place in the east.

3. *The Palace Buildings*

First the city walls were built. Then, inside the Wei Yang Palace was elaborated the Tzŭ Wei Palace with its long ridge-beams all colors of the rainbow and carved pillars on jade pediments. A gently graded road led up to it. "Double doors were reinforced to guard against the treacherous." It was planned to face four-square to the four points of the compass whilst the other buildings clustering around it (eight are designated) were like the stars encircling the North Star.

Within were the ushers in constant attendance, to take orders and do service to the emperor.

Without were the Lan T'ai and Chin Ma [buildings] where [officials] were by rotation on duty for the night.

Next came the T'ien Lu and Shih Ch'ü [buildings], the places where the collation of texts proceeded.

4. *The Rear Apartments*

Among the Rear Palaces were . . . (eight designated) in which were "bevies of modest young women, beautifully bedecked—how one would admire what one saw if one looked." The furnishings there were profuse, richly carved and ornamented, "kingfisher feathers and pearls strung together with fine jades . . . and pearls of different hues like candles in the dark." What with flying galleries communicating and the art of skilled craftsmen carried to perfection, here was the place for unceasing delight. Wherever the Emperor went, there the music stands were ready and a feast prepared. "If

---

Tsu's first year. The student should note Dubs' investigation of the alleged convergence (Dubs, *History of the Former Han Dynasty*, I, 151-153). Apparently the Han records (see "Record of History," 37) were in error astronomically to the extent of one to two years. As far as Chang Heng is concerned in this matter, what he stated was that Kao Tsu assumed imperial authority when he entered the Kuan Chung area and won a victory. That would seem to be true, whatever the actual year of the planetary convergence.

he stayed to the end of his days, forgetting to return to his chamber, [the pleasure] would be inexhaustible."

5. *The Outbreak of Megalomania*

Yet such was [the sense of] the divine beauty appertaining to great monarchs, the fear was lest the difference between high and low should not be marked.

Spacious as the palace area was, their hearts' desires knew no bounds. They yearned to outdo the Ch'in Emperor, so the old lodge in the Kan Ch'üan (Sweet Spring) healthy up-land was rebuilt as a summer residence . . . (three palaces specified). And on the range above was built a tower, Sky-Communicating Tower, calculated to excite awe: so high that birds could not reach the top of it, so thrilling, for as one leant on the balustrade, one heard the thunder reverberating below.

6. *The Chien Chang Palace Area, with Its Spirit-Revealing Tower*

The Po Liang Terrace (built by Emperor Wu in 116 B.C.) having been destroyed by fire (in 104 B.C.), a barbarian shaman advised on magic techniques. So the Chien Chang buildings were erected twice as gorgeous as those of the Wei Yang. The craftsmanship was of a high degree of virtuosity (*kuei wei*), with its achievement of revolving weathervanes "hovering to the breeze."

The Shen Ming [Spirit-Revealing] Tower reared itself aloft and the Ching Kan Tower, in a hundred piled-up storeys,

One storey succeeds another, as you go up and up—you catch sight of the North Star, and are thrilled with delight.

Rising free from the world's dust into the upper air,

You spy out the long back of the curving rainbow: you study the leaning together of the Hyades. If you go on to the flying balcony and look beyond, you observe straight before you Jade-Light and String-of-Jade.

You are about to go on—but before you have gone half-way you are shaking with fear, filled with apprehension.

Without the Tu Lu's [climber's] agility, who can climb high and keep going higher?

7. *The Chien Chang Area* (continued)

Four lofty and spacious halls are specified with rows and rows of roof beams and the eaves elevated so that light could penetrate. Then there was the Sky-Bridging Palace with a portico so huge that with only one leaf of its door open a four-horse carriage with banners flying could drive through with a loose rein. It was such a medley of corridors and pavilions . . . "with a hundred doors and a thousand windows," with such a medley of interlacing paths that "as you gaze, you cannot find your way back." And then there was the Chen T'ai Terrace dipping up and down as it went east to cross the city wall, making a private means of communication, with the watchmen always on guard.

Two spacious lakes were there with islands on which were replicas of the fairy mountains, Ying Chou, Fang Chang, and P'eng Lai, arranged in a pattern with the Hunting Park rising to view beyond. And round about were herbs of mystic potency, and in the lakes hugh fish which sometimes got caught in the shallows.

After this fashion he [Emperor Wu] selected Shao Chün's doctrines and believed in Lüan Ta's dogmatizing.

He held that with such techniques a man's natural life could be extended.

He admired [the immortals] of the past, [Ch'ih] Sung and [Wang] Ch'iao, met Hsien Men in the roads of the sky: he thought of mounting the dragon from the Lake of Tripods [as the Yellow Emperor was said to have done]—how could he care for conventional ambitions? But if it was really possible to live from generation to generation, why such feverish activity in building his mausoleum?

8. *The City and Its Suburbs with Their Inhabitants*

We pass now to view the city with its walls and three gates each admitting twelve carriages and its criss-crossing streets, with its building plots evenly spaced and its raftered dwellings in orderly rows. In the northern quarter were the highest grade houses, stoutly built by the very best crafts-men, "with the timbers adorned like the silk of robes, with the earth [walls] colored in red and purple," and stands of weapons from the imperial armoury. "Unless he were a Shih [Hsien] or a Tung [Hsien] [notorious palace favorites], who could dwell here?"

For the nine markets there were official guards. "Those who sold goods made a double profit, those who sought goods did not [go away] empty-handed." Actually merchants and pedlars of all degrees, (especially) the men and women hawkers, sold inferior goods mixed with those of high qual-ity, "deceiving stupid rustics, and making fools of small-town folk."

The merchant families were "dressed as luxuriously as the scions of the imperial house." As for the families of Weng Po, Cho, Chih, and Chang Li (well-known millionaires of the time), "bells were struck [for meals] and they ate out of *ting* [cauldrons]. . . . The dukes of the Eastern capital [today] cannot better them in appearance." The "wandering braves," men who were reckless of death, made gangs among themselves, and had followers "like clouds . . . quick to quar-rel, roar—of a sudden, like tigers, like wild cats." As for the scholars from the country round, ready to debate any topic, they were in every street and alleyway, "splitting hairs, tearing muscles apart. . . . Those whom they liked grew the fur and feathers [of a career], those whom they hated, grew the boils and bruises [of no career]."

9. *The Hunting Park*

The Imperial Demesne [*chi*] of a thousand *li* was under the control of the Intendant of the Capital.

Within the area were one hundred and forty-five pleasure buildings of various kinds. North, south, east, and west were . . . landmarks. Within this area was a preserve for birds and beasts and fish. Of trees there were . . . (eight named) growing thickly. . . . Of herbs there were . . . (thirteen named), with dwarf bamboos growing luxuriantly in clumps. Endless were the hills and valleys and level pastures. There, also, was the dark pool of K'un Ming, encircled by an embankment which was planted with willows. There were all sorts of strange species of fish in it. With regard to the birds (five species named), "at the beginning of spring they were ready to arrive, at the end of autumn they sought a warm climate: so many different shapes and voices that it is impossible to describe them." In the winter the foresters prepared the terrain for the hunt. They burnt over the woods, cleared away the timber, and cut back the brambles.

10. *The Imperial Hunt*

The Son of Heaven came riding in his six-horse carriage with the appropriate symbolic appurtenances. Accompanying him were a thousand carriages thundering along and ten thousand horsemen galloping like dragons.

It was not only play, for there were books of magic and lively tales, based on Yü Ch'u's nine hundred [chapters]: what was wanted in relaxation, all waiting ready.

Thus it was that Ch'ih Yu grasped his halberd, spread

his shaggy coverlet [a tiger skin], a guard against aught uncanny.

By this means was known the malignant [tricks] of the spirits among the mountain and water demons, not one could cross the emperor's path.

The imperial guards were on parade at two points, the torches lighted, the drums a-thunder. The hunt was on. Birds and beasts were completely panic-stricken and in their terror dashed themselves against the carriage wheels, having nowhere to take cover . . .

No arrow was fruitlessly discharged, no dart flew in vain.

The stiff corpses of the slain, bird and beast, glistened like tide-washed pebbles [on a beach].

And there to view were the strung-together [victims] of the traps, battered to death with staves and poles . . .

Before the sun was down and [the shadows] come, the killing was done, out of ten, seven, or eight.

If the pheasants or crafty hares were so swift as to escape, there remained the swift of wing and the light of foot: they were bound to be struck down into the falconer's glove or be crunched by a dog at the end of a leash.

As for the savage indomitable beasts, with bristles erect and eyes glaring out of the corners of deep sockets, the terrifying *ssŭ* (rhinoceros) and tigers whom no one could withstand—there at work were the professional huntsmen of the kidney of Chung Huang and the stamp of [Hsia] Yü and [Wu] Huo, with red fillets in their bristling hair, bare-armed and spear-handed, advancing and circling, striking and grabbing. They could plunge through bramble-brakes and tear fences apart. High-hearted and nimble, they could dive into caves and snatch a fox from its hole, dash up overhanging hills to catch the wild ass, or swing out to the end of a branch and seize hold of a monkey.

11. *After the Hunt*

At this time would come the ladies of the harem, laughing and chattering, delighted to be there. After gazing their fill at the dead birds and beasts—and turning round for another look—they would repair to the Ch'ang Yang lodge.

> Those who hunted on foot were rested and the horses and chariots were paraded.

> The corpses of the birds and beasts were put in piles, their numbers counted, many or few: the plunder was apportioned out, victor's bounty carefully awarded.

The regiments were drawn up in a thousand rows, and wine and meats were distributed in the light of torches. A steward came on horseback to inspect. Such was the Emperor's bounty "the runners and drivers were pleased, the soldiers forgot their fatigue."

> The carriage-officer ordered the horses to be reharnessed and the carriages to turn and move over to the right.

> They wandered by the Wu Tsa lodge, they circled or stood by the K'un Ming lake.

The Emperor and his entourage would climb the terrace on the island there and proceed to shoot at high-flying wild geese and cranes. Then they would go to the Warden of Boats to provide entertainment. Barges with feathered sides and covers put out into the lake: "the oarswomen breaking into song, one leading, the others coming in with a chorus." Also the Huai Nan and Yang O action-songs were performed, and water demons and snakes frightened away. Then fishing started with hooks and nets, including drag-nets—but since the Warden of Marshes himself broke the regulations, what did it matter? The spawn were exterminated and the water weed dragged up by the roots.

> [This] overweening lust for hunting and fishing, [these] exertions for capturing small fry.

[43]

This ransacking and scouring, this womb-grabbing and egg-snatching [*ch'ü*]:

Snatching [*ch'ü*] at pleasure today, [how] have I leisure to pity what comes after me tomorrow?

In a time of settled peace, how realize it [all] will totter to ruin?

Then the Emperor took his ease in the midst of his priceless coverlets and other appurtenances of extraordinary beauty. Then he favored the arena with his presence. There was staged the "marvelous entertainment called '*chüeh ti*' [horn-butting]." Strong men balanced weights, acrobats and jugglers performed (six kinds of feats noted). Choirs dressed as fairies sang, and men in the skins of leopards and bears danced, and others as white tigers struck great lutes, whilst green dragons played flutes. Some dancers at first would be like the whirlwind and then like falling snow. A colossal beast would appear, eight hundred feet long, and when it turned its back it was a fairy mountain with precipitous sides and bears and tigers pouncing on each other. . . . Conjurors would suddenly change their appearance and split their shapes, swallow swords and belch forth fire . . . smoke growing darker and darker.

[But there was the case of] Old Master Huang [a magician] of the Eastern Ocean who with his sword of gold worked spells,

aiming at pacifying white tigers—in the end he could not save himself.

He hugged his evil, poisoning magic—and thus it was that it did not work.

12. *The Emperor's Undignified Amour*

So then, when the final scene was staged, with masts erected and flags displayed, when boy acrobats flitted up and down between the masts, seeming to fall yet caught by the heels.

Thus, with the completion of these many scenes, the mind [of the Emperor] was intoxicated.

With the round of pleasures carried to the extreme, boredom came ravelling in his breast.

The sentries of the gates being warned, [the Emperor] would creep out incognito.

He descended to the level of the common man, and roamed through the suburbs.

The dragon's ability to transform himself manifests the true imperial majesty.

Thereafter he would seek a pleasure house and a compliant beauty, who would exercise all her languishing and provocative blandishments.

One ogling glance enough to topple down a city's defences! Who, whether a Chan Chi [Liu-hsia Hui, an incorruptible Chou scholar] or a Buddhist monk, could avoid being moved?

With fourteen ranks [of women in the harem] competing in fascination and grasping at the honor, favor and disfavor are never constant; it is personal feeling [*ai*] alone that clinches the matter.

[Emperor Wu's] Consort Wei rose through her luxuriant locks, [Emperor Ch'eng's] Consort Flying Swallow came to favor by the lightness of her body.

13. *Final Conclusions*

So then—his intent full set to exhaust desire, giving himself up to enjoy to the full, he took warning from the Songs of T'ang: "If you do not enjoy your possessions now, another will enjoy them."

The authority was his to create a precedent—where then the restraint of established procedure [*li*]?

[Emperor Ch'eng] added [to the harem] a new rank

above that of *chieh yü*, Tung Hsien [Emperor Ai's fa-
vorite] being already made a duke was yet further ennobled.

[Emperor Ch'eng] promised concubine Chao that there
should be none above her; [Emperor Ai] thought to
exalt Tung Hsien as [Sage-king] Shun was exalted by
[Sage-king] Yao.

[This was when] Wang Hung in attendance at the side
protested that the Han years had been ones of peace not
of revolutionary change.

Emperor Kao Tsu created the heritage, his descendants
built on his foundation.

Labor for a season brought lasting ease, order was maintained without overt action [*wu wei*].

With pleasures all there to be indulged, why should one
worry, why should one take thought?

For so many years was this so, two hundred seasons and
more: merely the soil was fertile, the outlands productive, all commodities in heaped abundance: the high
passes bringing safety on every hand, forming a girdle
easy to protect.

Those who had gained them had the power; those in
possession of them endured in the land.

Where a stream flows far it is hard to stop, where the
roots are deep [the tree] can hardly rot.

The result was the dissolute temper of luxury in excess—
a sweet odor became pungent and more and more rank.

14. *The Nobleman Makes His Bow*

Your unworthy pupil, Sir, was born three hundred years
after [the beginning] of Han, and hearing these things
from those who never heard them [i.e. learning them

only from hearsay] has been uncertain as one in a dream and cannot grasp even one part of them.

Today [our] Imperial Masters share the title of "Sovereign August" with Heaven; they have covered the whole world and made it one family.

Of all rich inheritances, there is none so great as ours.

The pity is that [now] we are not allowed to make lavish elegance the country's glory.

Yet parsimony goes with a mean spirit and forgets what the "*Song of the Cricket*" says.

Is it not true that what we want we cannot get and what we can get we do not want?

I am stupid and in error to be sure—pray let me hear the view by which these matters are [rightly] explicable.

Chapter V

PAN KU'S *"FU* ON THE EASTERN CAPITAL"

◇◇◇

1. *The Eastern Capital Host Jibes at the Western Capital Guest's Opinions*

The Eastern Capital Host drew a deep breath and exclaimed: Alas, the effect that habitat and custom have on people! You, Sir, are indeed a man of Ch'in, boasting proudly of buildings and the protection of boundaries by mountains and rivers.

In truth you know about King Chao-hsiang and have an understanding of the First Emperor. How [then] can you discern the words and deeds of great Han?

Take the First Day of Great Han: it burst forth from a humble commoner ascending the imperial throne, from a few [momentous] years initiating a myriad generations.

This was something the Six Scriptures could not describe, something it was impossible for the former sages to mention.

At this juncture [the rising emperor] attacked the contumacious, thus conforming to [the will of] Heaven, punished the trouble-makers, thus following the desires of the people.[1]

So it came about that Lou Ching, having calculated the situation, offered his theory [that the capital should be at Ch'ang-an]; Hsiao Ho, having weighed what was required, extended the layout of the Capital.

[1] For the problem raised by textual variants at this point see Sun Chih-tsu, *Wen Hsüan K'ao I*, ch. 1, and G. Margouliès, *Le "Fou" dans le Wen-Siuan*, Paris, 1926, pp. 55-56.

Was this because the times were flourishing and [the Emperor] was content with it [the decision and the palace Hsiao Ho had built]? Indeed no; it was perforce the policy.

My dear Sir, you have not discerned [this matter] aright; and being dazzled by the trifling accomplishments of succeeding generations, are you not in a state of darkness?

2. *Wang Mang's Usurpation and the Salvation of the Country*

Now I will speak to you about the government of Chien Wu [Emperor Kuang Wu's opening term of rule] and about the events of Yung P'ing [Emperor Ming's reign], scrutinizing their supreme purity in order that I may correct your erroneous frame of mind.

In the previous period there was Wang Mang's revolt and the Han line was broken midway.

Heaven and man embarked on concerted slaughter; all within the six points of the universe joined in destroying him [Wang Mang]. In the ensuing disorder the living were almost wiped out, the ancestors were cut off, no coffin in the valley was not destroyed, no house in the city's precinct left intact; corpses filled the countryside, rivers ran with blood:

The disasters of the war between Ch'in and Hsiang Yü were not half so frightful: since writing began no such tale has been recorded.

Therefore the common people wailed aloud, made their plaint on high; the Sovereign on High [Shang Ti] in pity looked down, and gave mandate to the Sage Emperor [Kuang Wu].

Thus it was that the Sage Emperor made divinations and found the right prognostications, and then, in his indigna-

[49]

tion, launched thunderous attacks. Having crossed the Great River and strode over North Peak, he named his regime and established his capital at Loyang.

He restored the ravaged [works of] a hundred kings, assisted the cleansing powers of the universe.

Fixing the beginning of a new era, he established his government, in very deed continuing [the act of] Heaven.

He revived the tradition of [Sage-King] Yao, restored the line of Han, bringing food and plenty to the living, restoring the frontier lands of the state, his merits beyond all those in the past, his labors more than the labors of the Three and the Five.[2]

It was not that he merely unified social standards and paraded a pompous show of hierarchy and dealt with that necessity, of the present as of the past, to have one sage man tread the path of bringing order out of anarchy.

He also on that First Day [of the new order], when Heaven and Earth were in revolution, everywhere within the four seas recreated husbands and wives; made a [new] beginning for fathers and sons.

Sovereign and subject were for the first time established, the relations of man with man started.

These were the very means by which Fu Hsi [the first Sage-King] founded the *virtus* of emperors and kings.

So also it was with the efficacy shown by the Yellow Emperor in dividing the provinces and establishing market days, making boats and carriages, implements and weapons: with the glory of royalty shown by T'ang and Wu in enacting Heaven's punishments. In his changing of the capital our Emperor emulated the middle revival of the Yin era, and

---

[2] There are various traditions. A contemporary one identified the "Three" as the Sage-kings Fu Hsi, Shen Nung, and Sui Jen, and the "Five" as the Yellow Emperor, Chuan Hsü, Ti K'u, Yao, and Shun.

that of the Chou. In having at first "no inch of ground or man to command" he was on a par with Emperor Kao Tsu. In his discipline of himself and observance of tradition he was more reverent than Emperor Wen, in searching antiquity and performing the *feng* sacrifice on Mount T'ai he achieved greater glory than Emperor Wu. Thus Emperor Kuang Wu

> . . . schooled himself in the *virtus* according to the Six Scriptures, brought past ages into focus and argued their merits: and his humane sageful works being completed, the *tao* of the emperors and kings was perfected.

3. *The Emperor Ming's Achievements*

Coming to the Yung P'ing (Lasting Peace) period of Emperor Ming, this splendor of perfection was redoubled, showing itself in developing the lofty procedure of the Three Yung (the Ming T'ang, Ling T'ai and Pi Yung),[3] in the ritual robes, in the fostering of literary refinement, in the display of conspicuous beauty, in the solemn gathering in the Kuang Wu fane. The Emperor made a royal progress throughout his dominions, examining everything,

> . . . in his own person seeing what the myriad states had and what they lacked, examining the extent of his influence, diffusing the royal light that it might brighten dark places.

Thereafter he enlarged the ancient city of Loyang,

[3] I have not attempted here or elsewhere to give English equivalents to the terms "*ming t'ang,*" "*ling t'ai*" and "*pi yung.*" All three were sets of functional buildings, and these names give no indication as to the various functions fulfilled. *Ming t'ang,* lit. "bright hall," may signify bright with the brightness of the sun, or of imperial prestige, or of sage-like intelligence, or of widely influential moral excellence. *Ling t'ai,* lit. "spirit terrace," gives a clue to the primitive pseudo-science of astronomical observation dating from the time when signs in the heavens struck an animistic awe into the hearts of the watchers. The title does not do justice to the use of instruments and strict mathematical calculation in Han times. As for *pi yung,* there were alternative forms to the graphs. Pan Ku seems to favor the interpretation which indicates a circular moat of flowing water with square buildings within the circle. Another interpretation was "sovereign concord."

. . . fanning it out on a grand scale, in towering grandeur and resplendent symmetry; [thus] embellishing [his] Han capital in the midst of Chu Hsia [China], making a control for all parts of the world and forming their crowning point.

Here within the royal city the houses were resplendent, revealing a divine artistry, which prodigality could not surpass, which frugality could not call prodigal.

Outside the city he constructed a park where the rich herbage nourished the animals, and a lake where water plants concealed the fish. The size of it was of the modest proportions of the parks of antiquity.

4. *The Imperial Hunting Preserve and the Seasonal Hunts*

In the park on suitable occasions the Emperor conducts the seasonal hunts, reviewing horse and foot and training them in martial exercises. In so doing he is sure to use the "Royal Regulations" and hunting songs in the "Odes" (four mentioned). After certain rites the carriages move off with the Emperor leading in his jade-adorned carriage with horses of the due seasonal color . . . "majestic, debonair." With the nature spirits in attendance the first stage of the hunt has begun "with a thousand chariots thundering along, and a myriad horsemen whirling in flights," lances sweeping the clouds, feathered plumes obliterating the rainbow, banners brushing the sky, "a brilliant scintillating display. . . ." On arrival at the center of the park, the three army corps are drawn up, each detachment taking its allotted station. The signal torches are raised, and the whole force of drivers, horsemen, and bowmen rush to meet the driven game. There is no time for bird or beast to escape.

In the blink of an eye, suddenly the game carts are full, [for] the pleasure of the hunt is not indulged to the full, there is no wholesale slaughter.

The outriders return to the roads, the carriages move off in due order.

5. *All Nations Turn to Loyang*

Thus it is that he [the Emperor] offers the Three Sacrifices [to Heaven, Earth, and the Ancestors], presents the five sacrificial animals, does his duty to the gods above and below, cherishes the hundred dieties.

In his audiences [with the Five Ti] in the Ming T'ang, in his visits to the Pi Yung, displays his glory, diffuses his august influence.

Ascending the Ling T'ai, examining the favorable auspices, as he looks up and looks down to the Ch'ien and the K'un [symbols of heaven and earth] he relates the signs to [his] Sacred Person.

He marks Central Hsia [China] and diffuses his *virtus* there, he scans the four frontiers and uplifts his sublimity there.

West, east, north, and south goes his influence into outlandish regions where the borders of one country are not neighbor to another. In lands where the might of Emperors Wu and Hsüan had not brought submission.

No one on land or water but breathless and trembling comes running to pay homage.

Forthwith peace comes to Ai Lao [in Yunnan] and it becomes the commandery of Yung Ch'ang.

On the first day of the first month at the beginning of the year all meet in the Han capital, and

. . . the Son of Heaven receives maps and reports from the four seas, accepts the tribute treasures from ten-thousand countries.

He tranquilizes the barbarians as well as the *Chu Hsia* (Sinicized states). So in tents in the Cloud-Dragon Court there are officers to assist the *ch'ünhou* (vassal kings) to comply with imperial etiquette. A great feast is held, with a myriad vessels of wine, with goblets of gold and jade, with rare delicacies and fat bullocks. The Music Master and his orchestra and dancers are there and perform traditional measures. The barbarians also present their music from the four quarters, inspired by the Emperor's far-extended *virtus*. So with the Emperor in convivial mood his subjects drink well and the primordial vapor of harmony descends. At the sound of a bell the officers retire.

6. *The Joyful State of Sober Simplicity and Earnest Endeavour, with Schools Everywhere*

Thus it is that the Emperor, surveying the pleasure of joy in ten thousand places, as he bathes them in the unction of his grace, fears lest the spirit of extravagance may arise and there be sloth over the staple occupation of the East [i.e. agriculture].

He revives old regulations, sends down clear fiats: publishes statutes to exalt frugality and moderation, with economy to show complete simplicity.

He discards the beautiful ornaments of the women's apartments, dispenses with the trappings of his carriages; he stops the demoralizing pursuits in which craftsmen and merchants [engage], he exalts the great work of tilling the soil and [planting] mulberry trees.

So then the orders go forth to all within the four seas, unessentials are discarded, and a return made to basic [needs], the meretricious is outlawed and men abide by the true; women weave silks and fabrics, men give themselves to ploughing and weeding; utensils for daily use are of clay or calabash; with clothes, preference is given to plain white and black.

He [the Emperor] counts the prettiness of fine silks a disgrace and will not wear them; he despises the rare and exquisite and attaches no value to them: he leaves gold in the mountains, pearls in the depths of the waters.

Thus it is that the people cleanse themselves of blemishes and cast away impurities, and so can mirror to themselves the height of purity: body and soul untroubled, the senses inactive, the fountain head of concupiscence is extinguished, and the spirit [lit. heart-mind] of modesty and shame is born.

No one but is free and easy and satisfied in himself, [no one but] possesses the sheen of jade and the ring of gold.

This is because within the four seas central schools are as a forest, country schools full to the doors: there is interchange of civilities, the ritual implements in good supply: dancing below, singing above, treading out *virtus* [*tê*], singing over *jên* [man-to-man-ness].

At the feasts when the courtesies of bowing are ended,
All praise the mysterious *virtus* in beautiful and noble terms.

Their mouths are filled with concord, they breathe its essence forth, acclaiming the day of abundance that is here.

7. *The Eastern Host's Final Argument*

Nowadays people who engage in discussion only know how to recite the books of Yü [Shun] and Hsia, to chant the songs of Yin and Chou, to expound Fu Hsi's patterned lines in the *Changes*, to discuss Confucius' *Spring-and-Autumn Annals*.

Few there are who are capable of getting the essence of what is transparent and what is blurred in the past and the present, [capable of] enquiring deeply into the way in which the *virtus* of Han came to be.

You, Sir, are well acquainted with past institutions, but you are also speciously carried away by non-essentials.

To recall the past and [thereby] know the present has become difficult, and those who understand the *virtus* are few indeed.

Also, to live away there on the western frontier guarding the passes, how can this be comparable to living in the center of the realm, to which "ten thousand places converge like the spokes of a wheel"? The western rivers and mountains do not compare with those of Loyang where the Yellow River makes a girdle and the Lo River flows past, the (two) waters of the (Mystic) Diagram and the Script. The buildings of Chien Chang and Kan Ch'üan, with the offerings there made to minor spirits (*hsien*), do not compare with the Spirit Terrace and Bright Hall where the concord between Heaven and man is effectively controlled. . . . How can the Ch'ang-an pleasure ground be equal to the Pi Yung, encircled as it is by water which symbolizes the four seas and brings the riches of the Way and the *virtus?* The lawlessness of your bravos and dissipated townsfolk is not to be compared with the universal observance of right procedure (in Loyang), its rhythmic order and strict behavior (*i i ch'i ch'i*).

Vainly have you studied the O Pang, the Ch'in [Palace] that soared into the heavens; you are ignorant of how Loyang conforms to a plan: you know well the guarded pass at Hsien Ku, but you are ignorant of the fact that true Kingship has no frontiers.

8. *The Guest's Discomfiture*

The host's speech was not concluded when the Western capital guest, his eyes jumping from right to left, being out of countenance, shrank back and round to descend the steps in plain fear; minded to take his leave, he held out his hands in farewell.

The host said, "Go back to your place, I am going to give you five pieces of verse [which I have composed]."

The guest, having finished reading, exclaimed, "How admirable!

"These verses are in their main ideas more right than Yang Hsiung, in relation to their matter more real than Ssŭ-ma Hsiang-ju.

"Not only are you, my host, most erudite, but also you have lighted on this happy age.

"Child that I am, I talk wildly and disrespectfully, I do not know how to discriminate.

"Now that I have heard the True Way, I beg leave to chant these verses all my days."

9. *The Five Odes*

The Odes are as follows:

MING T'ANG

Hail resplendent Ming T'ang! Ming T'ang of [heavenly] radiance!

The Sage Sovereign [Emperor Ming] did sacrifice, reverently, majestically!

[Here] the High Gods are feasted, at five stations in timely order.

Who is *p'ei* [ancillary] to them? Late-Ancestor Kuang Wu.

[Under] universal Heaven from end to end of Earth, each [dignitary] assisting according to his office!

How superb, how continuous, verily bringing many blessing!

PI YUNG

Here flows the Pi Yung with its rippling waters.

The Sage Sovereign arrives, a bridge of boats made there [for him to cross].

The silver-haired veterans of the state, [whom he treats as] fathers and elder brothers!

What strictness of deportment, what brilliance of filial piety and friendliness!

How majestically the All Highest reveals the ways of our Han!

Their transforming power so wide, so god-like! To all time may we see their success!

LING T'AI

And here one traces the Ling T'ai, the Ling T'ai long venerated!

Careful to time the Emperor ascends, here he examines the proofs of blessing.

Sun, moon and stars disclose their essence, the five forces display their sequence.

How gently the auspicious winds, how abundant the sweet rain!

The hundred grains burgeoning forth! The plants all growing in profusion!

Rich harvests again and again! What joy to the Emperor!

PRECIOUS TRIPODS

Ah tributes from the high peaks, treasures from the great rivers! [May be] emitting a metallic sheen, [may be] beclouded with flying vapor!

Precious Tripods appear, their colors mingled in confusion!

Radiant with sparkling light, covered with dragon script! Presented in the ancestral fane, offerings to the sacred spirits!

Giving lustre to [their] spirit *virtus*, for a hundred thousand years!

WHITE PHEASANTS

Open the spirit books, unroll the auspicious drawings!

The capture of white pheasants, the presentation of white crows!

Happy auguries abound, concentrated in the Capital.

Ruffling their glistening wings, with tail feathers erect!

Their appearance so clean, so pure, so exquisite!

How they display the Sovereign's *virtus*, equalling [King] Ch'eng of Chou!

Extending ever further in space and time, fulfilling the blessings of Heaven!

Chapter VI

CHANG HENG'S "*FU* ON THE EASTERN CAPITAL"

◇◇

1. *The Teacher's Reaction*

TEACHER ANONYMOUS at this point was like one who could not speak: he was disconcerted for a moment. Then he regained his composure, smiled and said:

> You, Sir, are one of those called learned in non-essentials who have gained [only] surface impressions and have prized the ear and despised the eye.

> If there be the breast [only] and no mind, then there can be no self-restraint coming from *li* [the code of honor].

> No wonder there is this despising of the present and glorifying of the past.

> Yu Yü, the poor exiled minister among the western barbarians, [could yet] deride Duke Mu [of Ch'in] for [pride in] his buildings.

> How then, with your cherishing the past [and so] knowing the new [present], discriminating the true and the false, could you approach these erroneous [conclusions] of yours?

2. *The Real Lesson of the Dynastic Revolutions (Third Century B.C.)*

Take the last days of the Chou dynasty. "It could not govern" . . . and so fell to "a tiger from the west." At that time the Seven Powers strove for preeminence, rivaling each other in extravagance. . . . Ch'in with its voracious beak struck from afar and won the whole area. He [the First Emperor] thought to monopolize luxury, counting none equal to himself. So he built his palaces and taxed to the limit, for small defaults punishing barbarously. . . . The poor "blackheaded ones" [the common people] went in fear and trembling.

Treated as serfs

the people unable to bear this usage, rested their shoulders against Great Han, were happy to honor Kao Tsu.

Kao Tsu, in obedience to Heaven, issued a "great war cry" and swept away his opponents. He had no time, he said, to build another capital. His western craftsmen, "their eyes playing over O Pang," went beyond all bounds. He cut their plans again and again, although even so they transcended the Chou buildings.

Observers despised them and called them mean; the Emperor ridiculed them as too big and uncomfortable.

3. *The Grossness of the Nobleman's Blindness*

Moreover, Emperor Kao Tsu under heavenly authority established a family and remade our land of China. Emperor Wen, a man of personal frugality, governed by exalting the *virtus* of peace. Emperor Wu enormously expanded our territory and made the sacrifice on Mount T'ai. Emperor Hsüan, by his severity, reconciled the Jung and Ti barbarians, so that they came to pay homage. All the emperors kept their spirit tablets enshrined and served them with due seasonal offerings. Also, the inscribed sacrificial vessels were continuously made more and more splendid. Thus in omitting the Emperor's true excellencies and noting their bad qualities,

. . . no wonder you have not been disgusted by the past, have thrown into the shade the good and displayed the evil; [and] in fact, my dear Sir, have been ignorant of [the forces of] words.

If you must make unbridled luxury reputable, this is to make the Yellow Emperor's [thatched] Ho Kung and

Shun's [thatched] Tsung Ch'i[1] definitely not equal to Chieh's Yao Tower and Chou's Ch'iung House.

Who, then, could have been a [Ch'eng] T'ang and [King] Wu, making revolution by force of arms?

You should also make observation of the conditions in the Eastern Capital and thereby awaken yourself [to the major facts].

4. *The Rightness of Loyang as the Capital for True Sons of Heaven*

Moreover, the true Son of Heaven has the Way, his sphere of protective power goes beyond the [four] seas.

In protecting his throne he uses human-heartedness, he does not depend against injury on the defence of passes.

If there be no good faith in the people, why speak of craggy mountains and a girdle of narrow passes!

The Ch'in regime put its trust in the Two Passes, and it fell through their twice being penetrated. How much wiser to have a site central to a wide circumference! Thus an early king (Ch'eng of Chou) examined all the Nine Regions, and

. . . with a measuring tablet [*t'u kuei*] marked the shadows, neither too short nor too long.

There at the meeting point of the winds, and rains, he thereafter built a royal city.

There with the Yellow River at the back and facing the Lo River . . . with the hill slopes and the valleys encircling it (named details given).

A hot-water spring issues from a red and black rock. . . . The Goddess Fu Fei there has her haunt, and in high antiquity first a dragon and then a turtle emerged from the river, bringing mystic writings.

---

[1] The names by which the Ming T'ang of the Yellow Emperor and that of Shun were known.

Lord Shao examined the localities, only Lo was auspicious: Duke Chou began the foundations, his [? inked] string was straight.

Wide roads and battlemented walls were built, a *ming t'ang* erected, and here was "a city and township in balanced proportions." The beginning of Han broke the succession. Then came Wang Mang and his wicked interregnum.

Throughout thrice six successive years he took his ease as a thief on the heavenly throne: in that time throughout the nation, not one dared have an opinion other than his.

The Father of our Age (Kuang Wu) in his rage at this flew like a dragon into battle.

He gave battle-axes to twenty-eight generals, and the usurper was destroyed.

With his (Wang Mang's) malignant influence extirpated, the elements were again in harmony.

The wise man, with mystic penetration (*hsüan lan*), discerned the Capital, this Loyang.

He said, "Abide here"; he said, "Glory will be continuous here."

So with the Way flourishing in the realm, the ascent was made of Mount T'ai and the sacrifices of peace-returned celebrated, and kinship claimed with the Yellow Emperor.

5. *The New Palaces and Pleasaunces Described and Appraised*

We pass to Emperor Ming's time, with prosperity increasing in every direction: so, a new Towering-*Virtus* [palace], followed by erection of Solar Virtue.

Then was opened the special gate [to the palace enclosure] Southern-Beginning, and the stately structure of the Door-of-Fulfilment.

Benignity and mercy shone on [the gate] Honor-for-the-Worthy, the repute of justice was extolled [in the gate] Winter-Metal.

Cloud-dragons were painted on the gate that led to the Eastern Road; Spirit-Tigers were depicted in the western quarter.

Built were the twin watch-towers Symbol of Majesty, emblems of the time-honored standards in the Six Scriptures.

Within the enclosure came *Virtus*-Embodied, Tower-of-Beauty, [the halls] Celestial-Prosperity, Light-Dispensing,

Reviving-Decrees, Welcome-of-Spring, Enduring-Peace, Lasting-Repose.

Flying galleries through which the Emperor passed like a spirit, unseen by mortal men.

There in a pleasaunce is Glittering-Dragon Pool and Fragrant Grove. . . . There stands the palace Lasting Peace with bamboos in winter leaf, with an underground stream . . . and various kinds of birds (6 species noted).

To the south (of the Palace of Solar Virtue) are a terrace and two other buildings . . . with rare trees and precious fruits "in the charge of the *Kou Tun* officer." West of it is the Shao Hua hill with a kiosk on it. Within the [ancient Chou] Nine Dragon building space is what is [now] called Felicitous-Virtue.

Its west and south doors being without ornament or carving, this absence of it pleased our Sovereign (Emperor Ming), lover of moderation.

(Thirty *li* away) to the east is the Great Lake . . . with its water fowl, its bulrushes, tortoises, and shellfish. On its west side is the Peace-rejoicing campus with its wide views and its metal statues of dragon birds in curling flight, and heavenly horses rearing into the air "cunningly wrought and glittering in the sun."

Costly spending has not run to excess, economy has not resulted in crudity: the [old] kingly standards have been kept, in all the activity of a set goal.

Behold, here is *Li* [the Ritual Mind], the right and fitting in full display: from the beginning no violent haste, "the work completed before the day is out."

As if [the sovereign] had said "The laborers labor, the dwellers are at ease."

So, with recollections of Sage Kings and their "thatched cabins," there was construction of the three sets of buildings, the Ming T'ang, Pi Yung and Ling T'ai, "where doctrine is disseminated and abiding principles are set forth." The Ming T'ang consisted of

duplicated shrines, a series of lodges, with eight windows to each of nine compartments.

[Above] they are circular like the sky, [below] square like the earth, and the seasons are followed at successive sites.

A bridge of boats was constructed across the transparent pool, its waters deep and wide.

To the left the Pi Yung was built, to the right the Ling T'ai established. The good were promoted, the incapable replaced, the worthy recommended, the talented selected. The P'ing Hsiang [official] observes [impending] malignant influences; intercession is made for their removal, prayers offered against calamities.

6. *The Empire and Beyond Doing Homage*

Thus it is, on the first day of the new year the princes of the realm assemble from all parts, and with them a crowd of officials, also by invitation representatives of border and remote countries, "all subjects of the emperor, offering treasure and bringing ceremonial gifts." Below the audience hall is a crowd divided into two companies, in front of them rows of graded dignitaries also divided into two companies (left and right). The bells and drums are there, the guards on the steps, as the imperial carriage comes to the porch, with "banners brushing the rainbow." Torches in the hall are ablaze, and the thunder of the drums shakes the whole neighborhood, crash on crash. . . .

The Emperor dismounts by the eastern robing-room

. . . dons the Heaven-Communicating crown, grasps the jade seal, ties the imperial tassels, girds the *Kan-chiang* sword. With his back to the axe-screen and seated on a bamboo mat with silk edging, with jade tables to left and right, he faces the audience.

As the hundred dignitaries enter the hall they are marshalled according to rank, and their tribute treasures presented.

The Son of Heaven with three grades of formal bows makes ceremonial acknowledgement.

How stately, how majestic!

How correct, how impressive!

Truly the most impressive spectacle in the world!

The emperor then invites some *kung hou* (princes and high nobles) and chief ministers to come up to the throne. There he confers with them on untoward circumstances and government measures.

He pities the people in their sufferings and removes their woes.

Should one man not obtain his place [in life], it was as if he [the Emperor] had pushed him into a dry moat,

Bearing the heavy burden of *T'ien hsia* [All-under-Heaven] having no idle moment for being at rest.

The emperor opens the granaries with their wealth in reserve and distributes largesse to the officials down to the meanest, increases their allowances and gives presents of sacrificial animals to ducal families.

At the feast all drink rich wine and savory meats, "prince and subject intoxicated with good will." Then the great company disperses in elated mood, but the emperor

... labors at repeated investigations, unceasing in energy.

His pure repute unites with the Dark *Virtus* [of the universe], his weighty influence is imbued with the self-soness [of nature].

Patterned on the Early Spirits [i.e. the Sages], following in their tracks, he is sure to think thrice for fear of transgression.

He summons the virtuous from obscurity; is open to reproof in the straightest language.

He invites some village incorruptible, sending him the silk of commission.

High and low communicate in fellow-feeling—behold, there is peace and joy.

7. *The Sacrifice to Heaven*

Turning to the sacrifice to Heaven, the report in the suburb of Earth's achievement [with the crops], [the Son of Heaven] prays to Heaven for prosperity [*fu*], takes thought how to be scrupulously careful [? in all he does], with every prescribed action complete in [its] reverence, every rite perfect in [its] solemnity.

Thereafter the sacrifice is made in unalloyed sincerity, the offerings are presented: as is said, "In very truth a Son of Heaven!"

With robes and sacrificial crown correct in every required respect . . . a special carriage is used with a special banner symbolizing "the undeviating order of the heavenly bodies," and six black horses with special ornamented harness; and bells, attached to the carriage, chime as it moves. . . . Robes and carriage trappings make a harmony of color.

"Nine-times-nine carriages" (three abreast) follow, with their scalloped banners and blue-green canopies; and only when the previous carriages are given the command and are away, do the next first carriages move off: a color scheme of *luan* banners and tiger-skin covered carriages and silken flags. Then come the household cavalry with their standards (specified), a mass of halberds with their horses' manes embellished and the men wearing pheasants' tails.

Flanking blood-horses from the Ch'eng-hua [stable], streaming along with tossing trappings.

Light troops follow . . . and the whole procession moves decorously and smoothly in mass formation, the carriages squeaking and clanging (*su su, hsi hsi, yen yen, ling ling*).

Before the rearguard is out from (under) the city gate-tower, banners are wheeling on to the suburban plot.

[All this] in admiration of Sage-King Yü's supreme beauty of [sacrificial robes], in devout reverence for the discerning gods!

The flutes and zithers with the accompaniment of the drums discourse six numbers, and when that is finished, the ranks of palace dancers perform.

The great Sacrifice is celebrated, the spirits of the hills and rivers all served in due order.

The flames of the massed fire soar up, higher and higher goes the smoke, up to the Supreme One.

The gods enjoy the odors and take note of the virtue [thus displayed], they bless the discerning lord with New Year good fortune.

8. *Other Ritual Duties and Moral Allegorizing on Them*

A. *The Ming T'ang and the Five Shang Ti*

Thereafter honor is paid to the [Five] Shang Ti in the Ming T'ang; Kuang Wu is promoted to be associate.

[Their] directional positions are distinguished aright and the procedure rectified, the Five Essences take the lead [in turn] and come pressing forward.

[Special] honor is paid to the Fiery-colored One, the four [other] spirits are energetic and indeed sympathetic.

Thus it is that spring and autumn follow in due course, the four seasons come and go.

B. *The Ancestral Sacrifices*

[Lo] the fervently filial heart touched by the [seasonal] products, thinking much [of its forebears]!

In person the Emperor sees to it that the utensils and meats for the four seasonal sacrifices are all in order in the several ancestral fanes. The rites are then carried out with "enlightened decorum" and the Wan dance performed. The spirits of the departed emperors descend and feast. Having all been well wined, they "send down good fortune in masses."

C. *The Ploughing of the Field of Heaven*

When the day of good omen for the farmers arrives, and the pulses in the fertile earth begin to stir, the Emperor goes in his *luan* carriage with azure colored horses, riding with a plough by his side. In person he drives three furrows in the "heavenly field," preparing the thousand *mou* (each about one tenth of a Western acre). There the millet for the sacrifices to his ancestors and to Heaven is grown, so there he perfects his thoughtfulness in physical exertion. Thus the mass of his subjects is stirred to "be energetic in weeding and hoeing."

[69]

D. *The Archery Rite and Its*
   Preliminaries

Alike in the spring there is held in the Pi Yung, at sunrise, the ceremony of the contest in archery: a symbol of concord. The preparations are duly made beforehand: the stand for the bells and drums . . . every instrument in place, flags a-flutter, with

> Po I as originator and helper in procedure, Hou K'uei seated and doing his task.

The targets are set up with their five inner and outer demarcations, the tweezers in readiness (for plucking out the arrows from the targets).

The imperial carriage at dawn waits by the eastern steps until the mists clear and "the sun has risen over Fu Sang." Then the Son of Heaven starts the carriage moving and with "Ta Ping to gentle his steeds along and Feng Hou as escort" smoothly approaches the archery building.

E. *The Mystic Arrow: The Significance*
   of the Wine Festival
      and Entertainment of the Veterans

> With the rites duly unfolded, with the musical instruments all there, with the Wang Hsia finished, with the Tsou Yü being played, the thumb-ring fitted, the carved bow stretched.

> It [i.e. the hitting of the target] stimulates the extra grain-shoots in late spring, reveals the heart of integrity in a far-reaching parable.

> He [the Emperor] promotes enlightened virtue [tê] and exalts the imperial heritage; he washes away the fierce appetites of ravening greed.

> The spirit [lit. wind] of humanity overflows and streams abroad; righteousness is stimulated and speeds into distant parts.

[70]

When sun and moon are met in the Tail of the Dragon [tenth month], he pities the pain of labor in his people's tasks.

They all rest from their labors and merriment is increased by the spring wine.

So also he (the Son of Heaven), with his right arm bare, cuts up the meat for entertaining the country's veterans, condescending from his high estate to inculcate the spirit of respect. Thus by his own strict attention to decorum he teaches his people "not to snatch," and the fame of his principles overflows into the heavenly regions.

9. *The Later Han Hunt*

The civil *virtus* having been revealed, restrained martial energy is set forth.

With three quarters of the year devoted to agriculture, [in the fourth quarter] the dazzle of might [is displayed] in China.

In the second month of winter, a great review is held in the Western Park.

Before that the game-keepers get to work, round up the birds and beasts. On completion they report "All ready." Then the light carriages are started with four well-trained horses to each, "with lances and spears like a forest" and banners all flying. The troops arrive and take up their stations, awaiting the signals for staying, advancing, and retreating. Being fully directed, those in charge kill the sacrificial animal as a warning of what will happen to those who disobey, the principles and prohibitions being clearly set forth.

With their torches upheld, the soldiers are like the stars in their dispersion, some in goose-crane [wedges], some like fishes in files, or fanning out like a spread of wings.

The carriages drive with reasonable speed; they shoot in a straightforward way, and the arrows do not tear the fur.

Every kind of bird and beast is caught. . . . Three drives are enough on the principle of propriety, for (the Son of Heaven) "does not exhaust his pleasure, with a view to teaching moderation, does not exterminate the creatures with a view to displaying human-heartedness." He admires (Sage-King) Ch'eng T'ang for leaving one side of the net open and in his sacrificial prayer showing concern for the common man, and takes pattern from King Wen at Wei Yang where he "lost a bear but captured a man."

> The dew of his mercy extends to insects and worms. His majesty overawes the eight directions.

He thus being both "truly refined and truly warlike"

> . . . the [Chou] pursuit of the chase in Ao, what a trifle it was: [King Ch'eng's] spring hunt in Ch'i Yang, how can it be taken as worth reckoning?

10. *The Driving Away of the Demons of Plague*

And then at the end of the year there is the warding off of pestilence, the expulsion of a host of demons.

The Fang Hsiang officer is there, battle-axe in hand, and shamans carrying rush brooms. Also a great crowd of boys and girls in red turbans and black clothes, with peach-wood bows and arrows. These they shoot off aimlessly, like a rain of stars, and "malignant demons are sure to all fall dead."

> Like flames they race away, are like falling stars, Ch'ih I [Red Epidemic] is driven out of the Four Seas.

> Thereafter, the demons having ascended the Milky Way, their flying bridge [with earth] is cut.

> The *li chu*[2] are killed, the *hsü k'uang* [headless goblins] are cut in two, the *wei i* [with head like a wheel] beheaded, the *fang liang* [marsh goblins] brained.

---

[2] It is not always clear whether these are individual or class names. My conclusions are based on the commentary, *Shan Hai Ching*, *Chuang Tzŭ*, ch. 19, and the essay "Defining *Kuei*" in Wang Ch'ung's *Lun Heng*.

Keng Fu is imprisoned in Ch'ing Ling (stream), Nü Pa [drought demon] drowned in Shen Huang [stream], the K'uei [dragon shaped monster in trees and rocks], the *hsü* [drought demon] and Wang Hsiang [tree and rock bogy] destroyed, [the eight brothers] Yeh Chung [roving fire demons] exterminated, and Yu Kuang [a fire demon] wiped out.

Because of this the demons all over the world quake with fear—how much more the baby goblins and [Old Father] Pi Fang [who sets houses on fire].

The Tu Shuo [fairy mountain] is a protection, with Yü Lei on guard, with Shen T'u to aid him—an interlocking device, a roped together fence.[3]

With eyes searching every hole and corner, the officer [and his lictors] arrest the demons left over: the houses in the capital being scrupulously cleansed, nothing is there which is *wei* [contrary to right and to rule].

11. *The Tour of Inspection*

Thus with the Yin and Yang interchanging harmoniously, with all creatures burgeoning in due time, with the oracle having been taken for a felicitous journey, [and] the final reply being truly favorable, he [the Son of Heaven] ascends his carriage and goes in royal progress to Mount T'ai, urging [the people] to the work on the land in the Great Plain.

---

[3] *Shan Hai Ching* ap. *Lun Heng* 65 (the modern text of *Shan Hai Ching* does not contain this passage) says, "In the middle of the Cold Ocean there is the Tu Shuo Mountain, and on it a great peach tree, in size 3000 *li*. The north-east side of its branches is called Demons' Door, where 10,000 demons go in and out. Above are two god-men, one called Shen T'u, the other called Yü Lei. They control the 10,000 demons, and the malignant, injurious demons they bind with cords of rush and feed to tigers. Thus it was that the Yellow Emperor made a rite by which they could be expelled. He made a statue of a man out of peach wood, painted Shen T'u and Yü Lei and the tigers on the door of the house, and hung up ropes of rush with which to keep away the demons."

[As] he unifies weights and measures [everywhere], standardizes the wheel tracks, [so] he metes out equal treatment to the poor and the well-to-do.

He examines the shady and reputable officials for demotion and promotion; then he turns round his banners and goes back.

He observes the old burial grounds of former sovereigns, musing at length, cherishing the past.

He waits for the autumn wind, and then he goes west [to Ch'ang-an], and there makes faithful sacrifice to the High Ancestor [the first Han emperor].

As his journeyings coincide with the rousing of the insects in spring, so he plans abundant harvests and rewards the industry of the field bailiffs. His scope of observation extends "from the valley of the rising of the sun" to the dark region of K'un Lun in the west, and from there he projects his mind to the ends of the heavens and the further days in the future, thereby planning the pattern for future ages to follow. So "he returns home to be free from his labors, bearing in his breast many blessings along with peace."

All felicitous influences are gathered to perfection, the (fabulous) *tsou yü* and *t'eng huang* horses, stabled and "obedient to favor," the (fabulous) *luan* and *feng-huang* birds singing, (fabulous) trees and plants flourishing in the royal orchard.

The repute of the [imperial] grace is a wide-spreading coverlet, the dew of it reaches to obscure deserts: in the north bringing peace to Ting Ling [30° N. 80° E.: Siberia], in the south concord in Yüeh Shang [South Annam], in the west including Ta Ch'in [Roman Empire], in the east going over to Lo Lang [Korea]: to peoples whose languages must pass through nine [different] interpreters, all bowing their heads and doing homage.

12. *The People's Argument with the Throne*

Hence, if there be discussion over removal of the city and changing the capital, then it should be in accordance with the precedent of P'an [Keng's removal to] Yin: [if discussion on] change from luxury to frugality, then it [should be] in agreement with the [simple] beauty [of the buildings] in the *Ssŭ Kan* [*ode*]: [if discussion on] an ascent [of Mount T'ai] for the *feng* [sacrifice] and descent [to Liang Fu] for the *shan* [sacrifice], then the [Han] *virtus* [should be] united with [the *virtus* of] the Yellow Emperor.

With action being non-action and busy-ness not being busy, there is the lasting [allegiance of] the people bringing all-pervading peace.

He [the Emperor] observes moderation and economy; he esteems untrammeled simplicity.

He muses on Confucius' "self-subduing"; he treads in Lao Tzŭ's abiding sufficiency.

Thus he can cause his mind not to be deflected from the right course, his eyes not to see what can arouse desire.

He despises rhinoceros horn and ivory, looks askance at pearls and jade; he lets gold lie buried in the mountain, thrusts aside rare jade in the gorges.

Cock-kingfisher's feathers he does not tear off; tortoise shells he does not collect.

What he honors is solid worth; what he prizes is grain.

[Thus] the people discard the branches [non-essentials] and go back to the root [essentials], cherish loyalty and embrace sincerity.

At this very time all within the [four] seas join in rejoicing, exclaiming, "The *virtus* of the Han emperors, how excellent is its scent!"

The *ming chieh*[4] [a fabulous plant] is difficult to grow, and therefore in a neglectful age it is not to be seen.

Only our sovereign lord can plant it, using supreme harmony and peace, [only he] will be able to count [its leaves] on the palace steps.

That being so, then how can the *Tao* [Way] not cherish, how can the [imperial] transforming power not soothe?

Fame flies along with the winds [of Heaven], mercy follows the movements of the rain-clouds [of Heaven].

[The Emperor says] "It is We on whom all creatures depend—what else is there for them to seek!"

"The *virtus* covers [all], as the heavens cover [all], a flame that blazes, a light that shines.

"[We] count the small house [i.e. institutions] of the Three Kings [the Hsia, Shang, and Chou regimes] too meagre a dwelling, [We] overtake the Five Emperors in their long and urgent course.

"[We] tread in the far-off steps of the Two August Ones [Fu Hsi and Shen Nung]—who says [We] have started too late and cannot overtake them?"

13. *Sundry Reflections on Emperors and Their Way of Life*

I have not finished cataloguing the excellencies of the Eastern Capital. Since I happen to be suffering from a stupid complaint, I am unable to assess such subtle essences.

Hence my reply [Sir] is crude: in rough outline it is as follows.

Suppose a man slipping into dissipation and forgetting to

---

[4] The *ming chieh*'s leaves were supposed to open on the first day month by month. Hence the Emperor had an infallible guide for the longer and shorter months in the year and could keep the calendar right.

turn back; he would be giving rein to his mind without being aware.

[Suppose] him enjoying himself without any restraint, later he would be entangled in misery.

"One word can come near to destroying a country"—it is not I who have learnt it.

[As the proverb has it], the man with expertise in carrying pitchers holds on to it and does not lend his vessels out.

How much less can the inheritor of the imperial patrimony treat his heaven-given station lightly!

Look up to the Two Ancestors [Emperors Kao and Kuang Wu] and their immeasurable tasks; their upward flight was constantly attended by fear of danger, as if a man rode at a gallop and had no bridle.

[Take the story] of the white dragon who assumed the guise of a fish and was roughly handled by Yü Chü.

[So] [the lord of] a myriad chariots, although he has nothing to fear, may yet be intimidated by a common man.

All day he does not leave his protective entourage [baggage wagons][5]—if he makes incognito excursions, where does he go?

Monarchs stop their ears with [voluminous] yellow robes; they do not gaze abroad from within their carriages.

Girdle pendants control their demeanor; carriage bells cause measured [pacing on] the road.

In walking [the chiming] of the jades does not change, in driving [the horses] do not break step.

---

[5] Allusion to *Tao Tê Ching*, 26: "A man of consequence though he travels all day will not let himself be separated from his baggage-waggon." (Waley)

[He] turns back the fleet horses to draw dung-carts, not even begrudging such steeds as Yao Nao and Fei T'u.

14. *Plain Facts of Social Economy*

When he [the Emperor] proceeds to use up the [nation's] wealth and avail himself of its goods, there is the constant fear lest the [different] classes of commodities be all used up: [when] he taxes and uses the *corvée*, there is the constant fear lest men's strength be exhausted.

Let [the goods] be allocated according to principle, [the labor] be used at the proper times.

On the hills let there be no [indiscriminate] felling and lopping, in hunting no killing of [life in] the womb.

Then the plants and trees will flourish, the birds and beasts will multiply.

The people will forget their toil, will be happy to contribute their wealth [to the nation's use].

So the hundred clans will be alike in having abundance; high and low share this peace and amity.

The abundant compassion [of Han rule] has long been stored up, men's hearts [long] been solidly knit together [in loyalty to the Throne].

They hold fast to fair-dealing and pay regard to their Lord, ordinary people cherish integrity and restraint.

15. *The Nobleman Forced to Face Unpleasant Facts*

Enraged by the treacherous violation of Heaven's mandate, resentful at the severance of the imperial line

Whereby Wang Mang, having launched his dark machinations and conducted them in secret, succeeded for eighteen years in his treason,

The Emperor ascended the steps of the throne, and the blessings of Han rule were displayed in due order.

With such a consummation we rightly rejoice in the royal heritage.

You, Noble Sir, are now irresponsible, wanting to exhaust the people in the service of [your] pleasures—you forget that their hatred becomes a mass vendetta.

You would exhaust commodities in inflating your arrogance—suddenly the underdog rebels and creates misery.

It is by water that a boat is borne up, by water also that it is capsized.

Solid ice is forming when frost is on one's shoes; an eight-foot tree springs from planting a sapling.

If [you] rise at dawn [and] become distinguished, [your] descendants may still be lazy: how much more for him who at first cuts [his] robes on a lordly scale is it impossible to change [their] cut [to an economical size].

16. *The Final Word from Teacher*
Anonymous

When Ssŭ-ma Hsiang-ju and Yang Hsiung made their poems on the Ch'ang-an hunts they envisaged, Ssŭ-ma Hsiang-ju the removal of the park walls and surrounding ditches, Yang Hsiung a ban on nets and traps. But even if these measures had been taken,

. . . in the end they would have been unavailing in the existing conditions, they would only have revealed the defects and excesses [of the regime].

Ministers increased their extravagance and overrode their sovereign, forgetting the enduring foundation of ruling a country.

Hence, while at the Han Valley [Pass] in the east, [Wang Mang's troops] were beating their drums, in the west the seat of government was crashing down with no hand raised [to save it].

It is human for the mind to think that what it has learnt is right, for the limbs to be comfortable in habitual postures.

A person in a dried-fish store is not conscious of its smell, he being used to what assailed him when he first went in.

The [Yellow Emperor's and Yao's] *Hsien Ch'ih* music is not in tune with the croaking of frogs [i.e. lascivious music]—but some undiscriminating commoners would have doubts [as to which is better]. Of those who have no doubts, is Tzŭ Yeh [the great Chou music master] the only one?

17. *The Nobleman Repents*

The Nobleman, intoxicated with high doctrine, satiated with civilized principles, stimulated to virtue and scared of rebuke, with pleasure and fear at war [within him]: his wits were astray like a drunkard, day and night jaded and weary, like one robbed of his vital essence [*ch'i*], stripped of his fleshly soul [*p'o*].

He forgot what he had argued about, lost what he had bragged about.

After a lengthy pause he said:

What a vulgar fellow I am, having learnt everything wrong and persisted in error!

Happily I have you, my Master, to point out the true south [of doctrine].

What your servant has heard is specious and not according to fact; what you, Sir, have said is to be believed on the evidence.

Vulgar fellow that I am, and lacking in discernment, from now on I know that the scent of the *virtus* of Great Han is all contained here.

Formerly I often deplored the loss of the *Three Mounds* and *Five Codes* [ancient scriptures].

Looking back into past history, I could not descry the beauty of Yen Ti or Ti K'uei [mythical emperors].

Now that I have heard the overflow [from your] learning, Sir, how could Ta T'ing's [a Taoist worthy, pre-Fu Hsi] [*virtus*] surpass the present one?

Your messenger, although unintelligent, has more or less come to understand this.

Chapter VII

CRITIQUE OF PAN KU'S "*FU* ON THE WESTERN CAPITAL"

◇◇◇

BEFORE coming to a detailed critique of the *fu* it is necessary to diverge for a moment into the field of the literary critic, both generally and in relation to the translations as translations.

Consider first the dramatization effected by Pan Ku's putting his story into the mouths of two imaginary characters, the Western Capital Guest and the Eastern Capital Host; and by Chang Heng's putting his story into the mouths of a nobleman and a *hsien-sheng* (teacher), the one old enough to have amassed considerable historical knowledge but not having the mature wisdom of the other. The question is: why this dramatization? In Pan Ku's case the answer is to be found in the concluding remarks to his preface. Since his purpose—the ostensible one at least—was to stop people grumbling over the change of the capitals, this kind of dramatization was a very effective device by which he could enable the supporters of the Eastern Capital to score a dialectical victory over their opponents. This he does to his own satisfaction, with almost too crushing effect. Amusing as the discomfiture of the Western Capital man is, and as Pan Ku obviously meant it to be, yet as drama it is on a very simple level. But it is not quite as simple as it looks to the modern mind, versed in the achievements of the dramatic poets and philosophers of long ages; for Pan Ku had in mind the poets of the first century B.C., who had originated this device for objectifying their subject matter, and had done so with the intent to sharpen the ironical edge to their tongues. On the other hand, irony and satire are not entirely lacking in simple literature: witness the Chou folk songs in the "Odes." In Pan Ku's case his use of the device is sometimes lacking in subtlety. He makes his point with so bludgeoning an effect, that one is compelled to wonder whether there is something behind it. At once the question springs to mind: was the question of the capital so live an issue at the time when Pan Ku wrote his two poems as he makes it out to be? That time was fifty to sixty years after the event, and it is open to doubt whether any but a few old Western scholars were still grumbling over the change. We may surmise that as a matter of fact the lively presentation of the argument was an excellent means of belauding the existent regime—whether in flattery or from honest convictions must remain to be seen.

With Chang Heng it was a very different matter. His bitingly ironical reference to the upper and wealthy classes demonstrate this beyond a doubt. Consequently his two interlocutors, Nobleman Stayed-on-Vanity and Teacher Anonymous, are much more subtle characterizations, more in the true vein of Ssŭ-ma Hsiang-ju and Yang Hsiung. Chang Heng's objective is clear; and if in one sense he was imitating his predecessor, he did so with the purpose of showing up the dangerous superficiality of Pan Ku's much-acclaimed production. For Chang Heng the really important thing was that "what is sauce for the goose is sauce for the gander," or, for that matter, "people who live in glass houses should not throw stones." If Great Han in its former manifestation was open to dire criticism as being half barbarous, this later Great Han in its present manifestation must be judged by the same yardstick: admitting that the later rulers have shown themselves less barbarous than the former, does it follow that the present regime is really civilized?

Thus by comparing the two authors' use of the literary device of dramatic personalization we not only achieve some measure of insight into their respective standpoints and respective sincerity of mind, we also have a vivid illustration of the way in which literature works inside a culture. It may be a simple reflection but it is a far-reaching one, that Author A having produced a striking work of literary art, Author B, of the same generation or a later one, reads it and is galvanized into following the lead given and striving to go one better on it. Admiration leads to criticism, criticism to emulation in the deepest sense. Only so can cultures remain alive. In the case before us there is also this to be borne in mind: there was in the Later Han period the clearest consciousness among scholars that, as the ancient "Book of Odes" (*Shih Ching*) revealed the ethos of that less developed society, so the poetical writings of every age, and more particularly their own, were a touchstone of its real ethos in all its heights and depths. In a word—and using a Han image of speech—literature, that is imaginative literature, is the mirror of its age.

From this point we turn to the problem which may well be in the mind of the reader after struggling with these four prose poems. Is this kind of writing really poetry? Perhaps not, in the specific modern Western sense. The treatment of the subject is conducted at so many points with such prosaic attention to detail, with such frank and careful attention to argumentative effect, that the works in question can only be regarded as prose—rhetorical prose, of course, but none the less prose. Yet, can such a judgement be right? Compare Euripides' plays, Virgil's *Aeneid*, not to speak of Shakespeare's plays and Milton's *Paradise Lost* and *Paradise Regained*. It is here that the reader must go carefully because of the unavoidable defects of a translation. The translations of actual passages given above have been made with the primary object of achieving accuracy of meaning and clarity of impression. For the sake of this object the brevity of those strictly-ordered sentences in the original has perforce again and again been sacrificed. So also has the rhyme with all that rhyme creates in the way of crispness and pungency of communication. So also has the sensuous alternation of alliterative sounds and the skilful interchange of longer and shorter sentences. The only way in which the non-Chinese reader can get some inkling of these essentially poetic effects in the original is by looking carefully at the more succinctly and successfully rhythmic couplets which yet contain some bracketed words added. Having ascertained the meaning, then read the sentences envisaging those bracketed words left out, and so realize how rigorous an attention the author paid to form, and how this *fu* style entailed the achievement of such ringingly apt language that the scholarly reader of the time could not fail to catch the fine shades of meaning without the pedestrian help of connectives and the like. But—if that was achieved to any substantial degree—then what is produced *is* poetry. There is no need to labor the obvious by emphasizing our two authors' command of poetic imagery.

Finally, on the point of poetry versus prose. A *fu* poem was primarily descriptive of an object (*wu*), either a physical object, as for instance a capital city, or a non-physical object, such as a state of mind. The description of a physical object may take the *fu* writer over into the spiritual realm, as happens in our four *fu*, and equally a description of a non-physical object may entail much detail as to the physical concomitants—as happens in Chang Heng's *fu* on Thought in its transcendent phases, the setting to which is an itemized journey round the world and under and over it to the verge of ultimate space. Being descriptive, these long *fu* poems furnish a large quantity of miscellaneous information, and thus the authors had to deal with the problem of arrangement and orderly presentation. In the later years of the Former Han dynasty, Yang Hsiung showed himself a master hand at this, so the tradition and technique of marking paragraphs was there by Pan Ku's time. But no one had attempted description on so colossal a scale as he did in his account of the Capitals and the distinctive practices that went on there. That he succeeded in the opinion of his generation is evidenced by the applause which these two poems elicited.

To the modern reader both Pan Ku's and Chang Heng's productions constitute a problem, one to which the above combination of direct translation and summarization gives rather haphazard insight. Arrangement clearly there was, but the movement of the authors' minds from one phase of their subject to another is discerned by the use of more than one device. One was rhyme: the final rhyme of the previous section would be changed—but then the rhyme may change every few couplets throughout a section. Another device was change of rhythmic tempo, e.g. from a four-word sentence structure to a six-word one; or the final sentence of one section, or the first sentence of the next, might be irregular in length. Or again there might be an introductory connective phrase such as *yü tz'ü chih shih* ("at such a time") or *erh nai* ("thus it was")—although such phrases can be found in the middle of a paragraph lending emphasis to a particular point. One way and another, even to the stumbling non-Chinese reader, there is a guide to paragraphing. The only criticism that can be made is that these *fu* are lacking in arrangement on the grand architectonic scale, namely with a plain differentiation of major and minor sub-paragraphs. On the whole Pan Ku with his simpler and more superficial objective made a better job of proportionate arrangement. Chang Heng's objective was more complicated, and this is reflected in his craftsmanship.

We are now more prepared to examine what each man wrote, first about Ch'ang-an and then about Loyang. The order of examination is, naturally, to extract the gist of each author's poem, then make critiques, and then compare those critiques, taking the two Ch'ang-an poems first and the two Loyang ones afterwards.

The Preface to Pan Ku's "Fu on the Western Capital"

The practice of writing a preface to a *fu* seems to have begun with the philosophically-minded Yang Hsiung (53 B.C.-A.D. 18). It is a striking feature of the new northern school of *fu* writers, and explains the circumstances in which the poem was written. Thus a preface puts the reader *en rapport* with the author's mood and enables the author to concentrate his attention from the very start on the matter in hand. This preface here is, therefore, to be taken as self-revelatory—at any rate up to a certain point.

The words "*huo yüeh*" ("one opinion is") are redolent of the contemporary controversial style. On the evidence of the *Po Hu T'ung* and the *Lun Heng*, the use of this phrase implies that there are one or more other opinions on the subject in question. Pan Ku does not mention any, but his vivid account of the mid-Han literary excitement affords a clue. To the bright young court litterateurs of Pan Ku's day it might easily seem that the new style which had surged into existence in the previous century was a new creation by Ssŭ-ma Hsiang-ju and those others mentioned in this preface. Pan Ku, the historian *par excellence*, knew better than that, as is demonstrated by the postscript to the four classes of *fu* itemized in Liu Hsin's Catalogue (see *Han Shu*, ch. 30), which draws special attention to the innovations made by Ch'ü Yüan, the mid-Yangtze Valley poet and by Hsün Ch'ing, the northern scholar who had taken refuge in the south before the Ch'in regime emerged.

Concerned though he was for the understanding of history, Pan Ku's main interest here is that literary new birth of the previous century. To do full justice to his statements it would be necessary to take each of the writers he mentions—Ssŭ-ma Hsiang-ju, Yü-ch'iu Shou-wang, Tung-fang Shuo, Mei Kao (interesting that, for he seems to have been a quite frivolous kind of writer), Wang Pao, and Liu Hsiang—and mark the wide range of new subjects which attracted their interest and the new powers of language which they exercised. Most of these men have writings extant today, as also have the high court officials Ni K'uan, K'ung Tsang, Tung Chung-shu, Liu Tê, and Hsiao Wang-Chih, mentioned as occasional composers. But such a study would carry this book too far afield.

It must suffice to elucidate the special more general features of Pan Ku's account.

It must be noted here that the *"huo yüeh"* opinion cited by Pan Ku is found in Mao Ch'ang's "Preface to the Odes," as also the fact that Mao Ch'ang (second century B.C.) and his treatment of the "Odes" was, both in the first century B.C. and in Pan Ku's day, not popular with the dominant schools of Scripture exegesis. Was Pan Ku standing up for him by citing his opinion?

A second feature is Pan Ku's use of the term *"yen yü shih ts'ung chih ch'en,"* servants of the emperor whose service consisted in exercising their powers of language. That jabs one's mind. Since when had there been men of this kind holding salaried posts at court? In one sense the Ju of the old Chou feudal courts had been such, but they were mostly scribes, technicians of the pen, in what was a much less literate age. There had been, of course, the Chi Hsia and other groups of philosophizers, living on the charity of ambitious princes. Pan Ku was not forgetting them, for he pays tribute to the glories of the literature of the "Three Dynasties" (Hsia, Yin, and Chou). It is difficult to imagine Pan Ku having any other meaning in his mind than that from the time of Emperor Wu on there was a new and unprecedented phenomenon, a set of salaried men at court whose real business and main-time job was creative writing. The study of the biography of Ssŭ-ma Hsiang-ju and that of Yang Hsiung in the "History of the Former Han Dynasty" reveals this clearly enough. They were not expected to be administrators but to be poets.

A third feature is the striking emphasis laid on there having been two kinds of creative writing. One, to be sure, was singing the praises of the imperial *virtus*; and one would like to know what Pan Ku meant by his "and thus they perfected their loyalty and filial piety." It looks suspiciously like a reference to a sense of high duty driving a man to soft-pedal the shortcomings of the throne. However, the other kind of composer—and Pan Ku mentions them first—interpreted popular feeling on current affairs "and so communicated satirical remarks." Ssŭ-ma Hsiang-ju's *fu* poems in the *Wen Hsüan* are admirable examples of this class, and one delicious illustration comes in Yang Hsiung's *Kan Ch'üan Fu* where he describes, in the preface, how he was ordered to write up the special sacrifice at the Kan Ch'üan palace, and how a "wind of irony" caught him as he did so.

A fourth feature is Pan Ku's comparison of the new literary creations with the old as found in the sacred Scriptures. In point of value the former are to him just as important as the latter. Thus in that Scripture-worshipping age of Later Han, here is one writer frankly comparing antiquity and recent times on an equal footing. His language of comparison is a masterpiece of neat aptness, clarity, and conciseness. The old literature was *ju pi*, "like that," the new is *ju tz'ŭ*, "like this." The contrast of a "that" out there in the distance with a "this" intimately known in one's self, is a feature of the Taoist philosopher Chuang Tzŭ's terminology, and in the *Tao Tê Ching* (ch. 12) stand the words "discard the that and lay hold of the this."

In conclusion, it is only in his last words that Pan Ku reveals his motive—or at any rate his ostensible motive—in contrasting the two regimes. Since he gives this as the confounding of certain Ch'ang-an grumblers, why then all the detail about the creative writers? There are two questions which naturally arise. One is whether after fifty years of success in Loyang there could have been any serious agitation for return to Ch'ang-an. The other is whether the markedly controversial and theological temper of the scholarly world was not tending to dry up the fountain of creative writing. My conjecture is that by the double emphasis in this preface Pan Ku wished to commend his composition to Emperor Chang and his advisers as thoroughly loyal in temper, and at the same time urge the importance of fostering poetic talent. I can find no evidence of recognized buildings in the Loyang court where the budding masters of language were encouraged to congregate.

1. *Introduction of the Dramatis Personae*

As the reader gets further and further into each of the four *fu*, he will find himself questioning at certain points whether the sentiment expressed is really representative of Interlocutor A or B speaking *in propria persona*, or whether Pan Ku or Chang Heng have more or less forgotten that they were not speaking in the first person. The question that thus arises in the field of literary criticism does not concern us here, but, assuming that the disguise does in places wear very thin, the quality of self-revelation thus made does concern us. Certain contrasts between the personality of the two poets may thus emerge to view.

2. *The Topography and Geography of the Site*

The case for Ch'ang-an starts off with the argument for it as the premier site for the seat of government, possessing as it does unique natural advantages. The ordered recital of the mountains and rivers is impressive, for it is a completely naturalistic statement—one seems almost warranted in saying, a severely scientific approach to the subject. Mountains with fortifiable passes for protection, an abundant water supply, fertile soil, these are the factors stated as influencing the royal decision. Add to this the details given in Section 4: the "five grains" (presumably including rice) with the help of irrigation producing abundant crops and a canal (or series of canals) linking the Wei River with the Yellow River and so establishing boat communication with the sea. Pan Ku's purview stretches from the China Sea to the upper reaches of the Yellow River in the west (about meridian 95°). That is the scale on which he views the setting to the Ch'ang-an site, and if his mundane naturalism seems to be lessened by his reference to the Chou regime as ruling by the *virtus* of the dragon, it is noteworthy that in the next clause the more recent regime of Ch'in is symbolized by the realistic emblem of a tiger. We descry here, therefore, a highly naturalistic mind at work, one with quite acute appreciation of geographical features. The section is a masterpiece of orderly summarizing.

3. *The City and Its Suburbs*

Quite clearly Ch'ang-an was what we call a metropolis: a small one (according to modern ideas) but none the less a metropolis. The description of the walls and moats and the crowded streets may strike us as exaggerated, but there is no mistaking the verisimilitude attaching to the picture as a whole. It is a very striking picture, and to the historian a very valuable one, for, although Pan Ku may never have been to Ch'ang-an himself, his father had—and possibly choked over the dust clouds in the streets. The glimpse we get of well-to-do bourgeois shopkeepers introduces us to a social phenomenon of Han times, namely flourishing retail trade with its concomitants, trade in luxury goods, large scale manufacturing, in some lines at any rate, and the power of trade-produced money. The question arises: how far is this mercantile Ch'ang-an comparable to the Rome of the Caesars or Paris of the late Middle Ages, or even of Louis Le Grand's time? Chang Heng's picture will add to our knowledge, but for the moment the relevant document for consultation is Pan Ku's "History of the Former Han Dynasty" (ch. 24), the "Monograph on Food and Money" of which Dr. Nancy Lee Swann has made so copious a study.[1] There we find ample confirmation of the picture drawn here, and this from the point of view not merely of the capital but also of the provinces. Particularly clear is the continued plebeian status of the great Han capitalists. They had influence in all sorts of ways, within the law and without, but the Han social order remained essentially a patrician-plebeian one. This is patent also in the Western man's description of the further suburbs

---

[1] Nancy Lee Swann, *Food and Money in Ancient China*, Princeton University Press, 1950.

where the aristocrats and captains of industry had their homes. They did not live in the crowded streets of the city. The information given is particularly useful because Pan Ku stresses the fact that it was imperial policy to have them there. Through much of Former Han times the struggle went on on the part of the provincial magnates, the scions of the imperial house and the great families plotting in the hope of partial or complete independence. Hence the skilful device of calling on potential trouble-makers to honor themselves by guarding the High Ancestor's tomb.

The final emphasis must lie on the fact that never before had the country had such a metropolis. Clearly, the story of it captured Pan Ku's imagination.

4. *The Imperial Demesne*

The area under scrutiny is given under the term used in Chou feudal times, the "imperial demesne." In some sense the idea of a privileged area where the royal beneficence could most make itself active was still a real thing; a contented peasantry in localities so near to the imperial residence was plainly of importance. The nature of the crops is noteworthy, not only cereals but mulberry trees for silk manufacture and hemp for the ordinary people's clothing. The narrative does not overtly indicate that the high productive power of the region was by no means the work of unaided Nature. For that we have to go to Pan Ku's historical work "History of the Former Han Dynasty" (ch. 29). There we see how the establishment of a great capital constituted a problem of food supply, one with which the Ch'in Emperor had tried to deal. It was not, however, till Emperor Wu's reign that the problem was adequately tackled. There was an enormous expenditure of forced labor on large scale irrigation, for the work was of an experimental kind, and where one experiment failed, alternative measures were tried. The construction of canals, useful for transport as well as for irrigation, is an indication of the ultimate success attained. In this way came a considerable advance in the techniques of water engineering. May we not say, with all due respect to the legends of Sage-Emperor Yü, that here for the first time in China's history a powerful and vigorous central government had had the resources and the engineering intelligence sufficient for accomplishing a large-scale agricultural miracle?

With regard to the exotic birds and beasts native to such very distant countries, the rational imagination boggles over the problem of transportation. For example, for so bulky an animal as a rhinoceros to be brought from the Malay Peninsula must have required months of sea passage and a successful solution of the problem of feeding en route. Is, then, Pan Ku by any chance exaggerating wildly? On the other hand, he is so very precise in his details of location, and the existence of a zoological enclosure in the West Suburb is well-enough attested. (See Section 9 on the Imperial Hunt).

5. The Emperor's Personal Dwelling-Places

Pan Ku has been so good thus far with his precise, if somewhat impressionistic, descriptions that, now that he reaches the palace buildings, it is disappointing to find how sketchy he is. We get no conception of the size of the main building, nor how it stood in relation to the subsidiary buildings round it. There is ground for the surmise that Pan Ku got tired of his prolonged task with the "History of the Former Han Dynasty," involving as it did endless attention to detail, and that the writing of this *fu* and the one on Loyang was a relief. That being so, we can understand his being a littly sketchy here. But there may have been a lack of detailed information in the imperial archives at Loyang: most of Ch'ang-an went up in flames when the Wang Mang regime collapsed.

One thing is noticeable. There is no mention here or in Chang Heng of any building for the service of religion. Apparently there were no specifically religious rites carried out in the palace enclosure. All that was relegated to places outside the capital, and the question is whether some old, old taboo was not operative behind this arrangement. On the other hand, there is a categorical affirmation of what appears in various passages in the Canonical Scriptures, namely that the ordering of life at the imperial level should conform to, and thus symbolize, the order of Heaven and Earth (viewed as two correlated and correlating mystic entities). The statements on this matter with regard to Chou institutions are necessarily subject to some suspicion as denoting an ideal rather than an actual state of affairs. In the light of Pan Ku's statement, however, we clearly have to take into account the probability that the earlier Han, and yet more the later Han dynasty, made serious attempts to carry the symbolism into effect. That would seem to bring religion right into the palace.

With regard to those cross-beams and pillars, etc., etc., they belonged to the building that the first Han emperor's chief minister erected for him (end of the third century B.C.). As all educated people knew in Pan Ku's age, the Emperor had been annoyed at the extravagant expenditure entailed, but abated his anger when the minister explained to him that as a matter of royal prestige it was necessary for him to impress his subjects with the pomp and magnificence of his court. The Western Guest has nothing to say on that point, but his creator clearly wanted to bring home that the building had been constructed regardless of expense. With regard to the whole set-up he makes his point. In true *fu* style, he specifies nine of the buildings by name and says there were more which "it is impossible to discuss in detail," and then goes on to a shower of descriptive expressions, "with solid foundations, soaring into the air, above and below a blaze of color: a medley of shapes cunningly contrived, to the eye each different from the other. . . ." We stumble on the question which must occupy our attention later: did those dragons' pinions on the cross-beams only have reference to old animistic beliefs, or were the royal craftsmen spurred on to new flights of imaginative workmanship, seeking to make beauty for beauty's sake?

6. *The Rear Palaces*

The information we get here is of the kind which does not appear in the same way in the sober works of the period; and yet the influence of the harem is discernible on most pages of Han history. The large number of buildings is, as Pan Ku points out, indicative of the numbers employed there. These ranged from expert ladies' maids to the meanest scrub woman, and in that connection Pan Ku notes one characteristic of life there: the fortunes of the inmates were constantly changing. There was no bar to a beautiful girl of humble parentage being employed and finding favor with her mistress, becoming a lady-in-waiting and so maybe catching the imperial fancy. Europe had the same experience in much the same form. So also this picture of "Corinthian luxury" is familiar to the historian of the west as well as the East.

7. *The Administration Offices, the Archives, and Other Buildings*

Having devoted about 80 lines to his rococo description of the housing of the emperor's personal ménage, Pan Ku disposes of the rest of the palace hill in 26 lines. It is a marvel of compression, disappointingly so when we think of the information we should like on the office structure of the various ministries. However, what detail we do get in the whole passage is of exceptional value.

The first part is in quite conventional language after the pattern of eulogies. Yet even there we find a nugget of gold, the reference to the popular song made in the capital. It strengthens the impression which H. H. Dubs' *History of the Former Han Dynasty* fosters, namely that a rule of law and the rudiments of a constitution began to emerge. Pan Ku would have us believe that this was appreciated wholeheartedly by the citizens of Ch'ang-an. The emergence of a constitution, tentative and uncoded though it was, is a fact of major importance in the history of the Han era.

Coming to the four specified buildings (which were to the north of the Wei Yang Palace), we are introduced first to that epoch-making innovation of the last decades of Former Han, a state library, in which a collection of manuscripts of all kinds was reduced to order, classified and catalogued (see "History of the Former Han Dynasty," ch. 30). To what extent the governmental records were stored in the T'ien Lu and Shih Ch'ü buildings does not appear, but the reference to specially-commissioned officials setting forth the teachings of precedent points in the direction of the more important documents being stored there under lock and key. Pan Ku's picture is that of a repository to which only a select few were given access. Among these, it is natural to assume, the Erudites, should be numbered, they being the chief official exegetes. Actually *"po shih"* ("Erudites") does not occur in Pan Ku's phrasing here, and in any case the Erudites did their teaching at the Ta Hsüeh, the university which Emperor Wu inaugurated, the buildings of which were two miles from the city. However, since the conference of Erudites and other famous scholars in 51 B.C. held its sessions in the Shih Ch'ü Pavilion, it is clear that Pan Ku had this conference in mind as he wrote. That being so, the student can refresh his memory of the proceedings by reading over Tjan Tjoe-som's admirable *Po Hu T'ung* (I, 89-94 and passim; Leiden, 1949). Pan Ku's summary throws no new light on it, unless the use of *"Liu I"* ("Six Arts") can be proved to be a term affected by opponents of the Kung Yang dogmatic school.

We now come to the other two buildings, the Ch'eng Ming and Chin Ma chambers, where the writers congregated. Here Pan Ku's interest is deeply engaged. It is a writers' club which he depicts, where, as the Preface informed us, they met morning and evening and from day to day discussed and took thought. The Ch'ang-an Guest takes us further still in language which surely must represent Pan Ku's own mind. These masters of language "went to the roots of things." Not only so: they were keenly alive to all that their eyes and ears could tell them. Although so many of the *fu* of that time have not survived—yet arguing from those which have, and from the titles itemized in the fourth of the *fu* sections in Liu Hsin's Catalogue—there can be no question but that the writers' seeing and hearing was in relation to what they saw with their own eyes about them. The description is most impressive and throws an arresting sidelight on that court which after Emperor Hsüan went down hill in such disastrous fashion. Recognizing this, we have also to recognize that it was in the days of the decline of Athens that Plato and the Academy flourished; the one series of events was no bar, indeed was in some ways the very stimulating force behind the other series. Although, therefore, we should not idealize the members of this Ch'ang-an literary coterie—there undoubtedly were sycophants and place-hunters among them—yet they must be taken as upholding the banner of free enquiry. They gave themselves to exploring the possibilities of language in the interpreting and ordering of personal experience. The interesting thing is that although they worked apart from the more soberminded scholars and administrators, they at the same time had their influence on them, for these latter also "from time to time composed," as can be seen from the entries in the *fu* sections of Liu Hsin's Catalogue where the names of various statesmen appear as authors. The writers, for their part, although free from burdensome administrative duties, were there on the spot to be used in drafting decrees or preparing memorials (cf. Wang Ch'ung, *Lun Heng*, XXIII, 3 and XXVIII, 2).

For the rest of the palace area the picture is even more in outline. Yet it is instructive as far as it goes. Thus, the glorifier of Ch'ang-an can only speak of a medley of buildings where the interior officers of the imperial household carried on their duties. Also, the only mention of living quarters, apart from those of the emperor and the harem, is in relation here to the guards. We can infer from other passages that officials did find places to sleep when their duties required them to be on the spot, but the only possible inference is that the arrangements must have been sketchy. Well-salaried officials had their town houses elsewhere, and the young princes, once they were free of their nurses, had their establishments outside the palace gates.

With regard to the officers mentioned as ranking first class in the examinations, it was in this period that there began the practice of examining candidates for state service. Emperor Wu inaugurated the practice along with the establishment of his Erudites as a group of teachers officially charged with preparing candidates, striplings in the capital of proved intelligence and men selected by the heads of the different kingdoms, provinces, and commanderies.[2] The term *"lien hsiao"* (the "upright and filial" men) occurs again and again in the "Acts of the Emperors" (*Pen Chi*)[3] in the first century B.C. It was the technical term for suitable candidates, and there is no need to infer a very exceptional standard of morals in these men. What is important is that there was no bar to prevent a man of plebeian origin being recommended. As for the nature of the examination, there is good evidence that it was in writing and consisted in answering questions on the political needs of the moment. The call to the country was not made regularly, but came from time to time as need emerged for getting fresh blood, or as an emperor thought it advisable to restore his credit among the scholars of the empire. The phrasing of the passage here conveys the strong impression that the people specified were junior officers being tried out. Of these the top grade of successful examinees went to the Ministry of Rites. For all of them, as the biog-

---

[2] The development of education is treated in more detail in Ch. XI, section 7.

[3] Title of the section in the *Han Shu* and other dynastic histories devoted to court annals.

raphies in the "History of the Former Han Dynasty" show, there was the hope of advancement, and this for the most part meant a settled office in some provincial administration.

As for the "flying galleries" (*fei ko*), they were a private, closed-in means of communication with the harem and the various buildings mentioned. They must have been elevated on struts for them to be called "flying." Doubtless the hugger-mugger of buildings here described and the coming and going of lesser folk made them a great convenience. Galleries of this kind are mentioned in the "History of the Former Han Dynasty" (Dubs, I, 113).

8. *The Chien Chang Palace and Its Appurtenances*

From the "History of the Former Han Dynasty" and from Chang Heng we learn that in 104 B.C. there was a fire in the palace grounds, and from another source that in this year Emperor Wu began the Chien Chang Palace. Its construction took a number of years—Pan Ku's description, plainly drawn either from detailed records or very observant eye-witnesses, demonstrates that it was one of the worst extravagances of that megalomaniac period. The reader will notice the reference to artistic workmanship on the one hand and the creation of auspicious influences on the other hand. There is the problem we stumbled on in the critique on Section 5. In the light of the elaborations planned and put into effect in the Chien Chang layout, we cannot but suspect that something in the nature of real scientific accuracy was necessary, not merely the accuracy of skilled workmanship, but even more the accuracy of mind which could plan and draw diagrams. We know from a number of earlier books that there had been drawing-compasses and T-squares and the like in use for at least four hundred years before 104 B.C., and the evidence of fine tools for especially delicate work is accumulating. Not only so: there is evidence to the effect that what the craftsman could achieve by accurate measurement and calculation had for a considerable time been regarded by scholars as an indication of how the mind should be trained to work in the field of ideas (cf. *Mencius*, I A, 7). That being so, what of the obscurantist aspect of the picture as drawn, not merely the construction of centers of auspicious influence, but also the attempt by pseudo-scientific techniques to conquer death?

This last aspect is brought home to us with all the force of pungent wit in the description of the terrace, with the tower above it and the lakes below. The whole *mise-en-scène* of the Chien Chang site sprang from the fantastic determination of one man, Emperor Wu. Spurred on by the magicians to whom he gave his confidence, he set about building this vast conglomeration with precise attention to every pregnant detail, so that in the midst of its luxury he might in addition find the way to become an immortal. It was a case of viewing Nature as having its laws of cause and effect, and of these laws being discernible. Emperor Wu was a man of proved powers of statesmanship, able to conceive far-reaching plans and entrust their execution to the ablest of deputies. This is clear from the "Acts of the Emperors." But alongside that story we have to place the revealing story in Pan Ku's *Chiao Ssŭ Chih* ("Treatise on Sacrifices," *Han Shu*, ch. 25 A and B), where the Emperor is represented as being year after year cheated by a set of glib-tongued charlatans. Pan Ku's attitude is unmistakeable there, for from time to time he makes the caustic comment that no evidence was forthcoming. So here in this passage he is completely outspoken in his condemnation. On the one hand there was the unconscionable extravagance of the whole proceeding. That he makes clear in the first part of his description. In the second part in a monotonous succession of six-word couplets he creates an atmosphere which is as mentally dizzying as the experience he depicts of ascending the terrace and the Ching Kan Tower. May we not assume that he was conscious of this, deliberately adding one mystic, romantic detail after another in order to excite his readers' amazement—and then exploding the fantastic illusion with his "An abode for immortals—not a place where we mortals can find peace!" Yang Hsiung had done much the same thing in his *Kan Ch'üan Fu* on Emperor Ch'eng's special sacrifice to the T'ai I (Supreme One). After a dizzying description of the Kan Ch'üan Palace and the superstitious procedure in the sacrifice, he winds up with

> The chosen magicians were all there, yelling at God's gate, opening Heaven's audience hall and importuning a host of [little] gods: . . .

> . . . a medley of helpers, bringing down on the altar masses of good fortune, heaped up like a mountain.

> Thus it was that with the business finished and the merit colossal, we all went back to the carriages and returned home . . .

> . . . flying clouds spread in the sky, rain descended everywhere—and all this was to go on for ten thousand generations!

Here then emerges to view one of the main foci to the historian's problem of Han mentality, the mentality which was grounded in animism, went on to naturalism, and then did—what? In our search for clues we now descry, within the circumscribed area of a poet's picture, one side to a really great emperor's mentality around 100 B.C. We also descry the poet's reaction some hundred and eighty years later. The Western reader will, of course, bear in mind what the pages of ancient Western history reveal, namely the attraction the mystery religions had for educated people in imperial Rome, and then, in mediaeval and modern times, the long tale of bogus scientists and their dupes in high places.

9. *The Imperial Hunt*

This section with the last and the succeeding one are the longest in the poem: surface evidence of the importance these two aspects of Ch'ang-an life had for Pan Ku, as he planned and wrote. The first point to note is his emphasis on the political aspect of these periodic hunts. They served to keep the troops in training and to warn the barbarian tribes, in particular the obstreperous Hsiung Nu in the north and west, that the Emperor had a mailed fist. But, having dealt with that in a word, the author's pen swings out into the description of what he really wanted to bring home. If we are tempted when we come to Chang Heng's poems, to re-gard Pan Ku as a little superficial, we must do justice to the fact that he revolted against the blood bath which he here portrays with all the dramatic zest that his Western Capital Guest can lend to the account.

The poetic gift of objectification of the mind, the power of putting into the mouth of an imaginary person the words which are burning on the poet's lips but which do not ex-press his own point of view, was quite clearly not absent in the culture of Han times. This fact is of importance in the light of what is so well-known among historians of lit-erature, namely, that whereas the Greek genius produced a Homeric style and the Athenian dramatists, the Chinese genius seems to have done neither. This apparent fact about China of the classical era needs to be restudied, taking into consideration not only these poems but a number of other highly trenchant and dramatic poems by the great *fu* writers of the first century B.C.

Another prevalent notion is that the Chinese people, under the inspiration of a Confucius and a Lao Tzŭ, early evolved a highly pacifically-minded culture. There is something to be said for this notion, but here is the other side of the pic-ture, the side that is made familiar to us at the present day by the discovery of the *id* and other unpleasant phenomena in the cultural history of blood sports. There is also the dis-covery from certain recent world-shaking events that civi-lized man is not so firmly and unalterably civilized as he assumes he is. This then is the noteworthy fact here: that huntsmen and soldiers are depicted as unashamedly excited by blood-lust, and that the imperial court of the Earlier Han is depicted as unashamedly enjoying the sanguinary spectacle.

The carrying out of the hunt on the scale described cannot but have entailed a considerable amount of staff work, that is to say, consultation between the forest officials and the military, and last but not least the personal secretaries to the Emperor. There was an array of beaters, but they would have been ineffective unless there were also planners with an intimate knowledge of the terrain and the organizing power required for concentrating the game at strategic points. There is no marked emphasis on this aspect, but two or three touches in the account show that it was not absent from Pan Ku's mind. It is also well to add that the sport of kings and the subsequent revelry was not shared by the peasants, and that the strict protection of the imperial forests and the savage penalties inflicted for poaching were a direct cause of peasant discontent. It is not clear whether the beaters got a share of the game, but in any case it would be impossible to prevent the professional huntsmen from gossiping to their families and friends. It is easy to imagine the effect on them of those "heaped-up masses" of dead birds and beasts.

10. *After the Hunt*

The account of the hunt feast rings true to fact. East and West would seem to be much alike, and artists will recall the Rajput paintings in which rajahs hunt and wassail with such verve before our eyes. In the Ch'ang-an picture there is a like air of full-blooded jollity about the proceedings, with the wine from the wine carts flowing freely. There has been no mention of the Emperor or his immediate circle taking actual part in the hunt, but we know that princes of the blood engaged in the chase, as the Chou feudal lords had done in their day, so the tradition was there of a strenuous day in the open air followed by heavy eating and drinking. Plainly the stiffness of court etiquette was relaxed for the night and the following day. We can imagine the tired huntsmen and officers rolling off into a corner to sleep, but for the aristocratic part of the company the occasion was of the nature of a picnic with everyone free to wander at will among the "hundred odd" pavilions, the shady groves and sweet-smelling plants and flocks of gaily-colored birds. Again the Western Guest naïvely gives away the fact that the pleasuance in the hunting park had been constructed at very considerable expense: a fact emphasized in the *Shang Lin Fu* (Ssŭ-ma Hsiang-ju).

The share that the ladies of the Rear Palaces had in the picnic is particularly interesting. Not only did they have these two days out in the country, with elaborate arrangements made for their enjoyment, but some of them at any rate took their pleasure in quite strenuous fashion by shooting with the bow and later climbing to a number of view points. These young women were by no means the languorous houris of Western imagination in relation to oriental harems. Also, since appreciation of rugged mountain scenery was so late in appearing in the West, here is a very early instance of that aesthetic sensitivity. As is well-known, in post-Han times it developed continuously, in particular under Buddhist influence; here, however, we find it in evidence just before Buddhist missionaries arrived in China.

A third point of interest is the apparent lack of chaperonage to these ladies. The narrative has not a word on the subject. That, to be sure, affords no ground for assuming that it was not there. On the other hand, the whole atmosphere of this post-hunt picnic is so impregnated with relaxation and carefree gaiety that the historian who knows something of the seamy side to the sex life of the Han aristocracy is bound to pause here and scrutinize the text and commentaries with special care. There is the more need for this since the *fu* writers were master hands at conveying subterranean hints on matters of scandal. As far as I can see, there is nothing to suggest that during the night or the day following there were any clandestine rendezvous. I take it that there was no mention of such in Pan Ku's sources of information, for if it were otherwise, it would have suited Pan Ku's book to introduce into a fair-seeming narrative a hint of a less reputable side. As the narrative stands, the men played in one part of the park, and the women played in another part.

11. *The Western Capital Guest Sums Up*

Pan Ku's historiographic ability is here plain to see. The details he gives in ordered sequence are masterpieces of clear summarization. The picture painted here by this author of the "History of the Former Han Dynasty" is that of a great state and nation triumphantly solving the problems of government over a wide continental area, so that life continues from generation to generation without economic disaster, political disturbances, or invasion from without. The intriguing thing is that the section contains no reference to all this prosperity being due to the imperial grace. As the reader who studies the poem in the original finds, there is no lack of flattering reference to that power of grace in the first of the Han emperors. Yet in the final picture not a word! Now an argument from silence is rightly regarded as a dubious one; but it cannot be avoided altogether, for some silences are glaring. Where such a one occurs in a document produced by a writer with immense descriptive talent who used a poetic genre which entailed unremitting attention to nuances of meaning, it is out of the question to pretend that this gap of silence is not there. Moreover, part of the success of a *fu* in the Ssŭ-ma Hsiang-ju and Yang Hsiung tradition would depend on the author making his point clear without crossing his t's and dotting his i's.

First, what are the unassailable facts? The most outstanding one is that after Emperor Hsüan's reign (73-49 B.C.) this *tê* (mana-*virtus*) of the Han regime declined, and towards the end declined with portentous speed. Alongside of that lies the fact that although the Former Han regime had achieved government over an unprecedented extent of territory and by its unprecedented machinery of administration had brought about an unprecedented prosperity, there had been plots and insurrections against the central authority, and during and after Emperor Wu's reign impossible burdens had been laid on the peasant producer. There had also been scholar families of repute cut off or brought to poverty through court intrigue or owing to malpractice in office. Pan Ku knew all this—none better, after his days and nights on the palace archives.

Second, it has to be borne in mind that if the Later Han emperors had been lineal descendants of Emperor Wu or the emperors after him, it would have been difficult for Pan Ku or any other writer of his time to slur their memory. For the reigning emperor to tolerate that would be to lay himself open to the grave charge of being unfilial. But Kuang Wu claimed only to be descended from Emperor Ching, a generation above Emperor Wu. That fact would ease the situation for a writer who proposed to omit any conventional praise of the regime as it became in the last hundred years of its tenure.

Third, the expressed meanings under scrutiny come from the lips of the Western Capital Guest, and he has been presented in character throughout as a man overwhelmingly impressed by the material achievements of the regime. The new wealth that came into existence, the splendor of the new palaces, these are the features of the regime that captured his imagination. Pan Ku's intention seems to be clear: it was to make the Guest the type of the superficial observer.

The only conclusion that seems certain is that the omission should not be taken as one through sheer inadvertence. On the other hand, it surely might well have happened that Pan Ku, having arrived at the summing-up stage, decided that there was no great need to go into the unhappy story of the final dereliction of the court. Everyone knew it—why then talk about it? In any case, it did not fit the text of the Guest's sermon. If Pan Ku came to that conclusion, one showing a sense of dramatic artistry, the only honest and artistic course was to omit any reference to the *virtus* which had been so dissipated. As the Guest says in his last sentence, his picture "does not give one part in ten."

Chapter VIII

CRITIQUE OF CHANG HENG'S
"*FU* ON THE WESTERN CAPITAL"

◇◇◇

1. *The Introduction of Two Interlocutors*

WITHOUT a foreword of any sort Chang Heng went straight to his self-appointed task. Pan Ku's poems had needed a preface, for he was trying out an adaptation of the *fu* genre to a wider and more patently dialectical purpose than any of the earlier *fu* writers had attempted. For Chang Heng, with Pan Ku's achievement still in men's minds, the situation was different. There was no need to explain any circumstances. The very fact that his composition would bear the title *Liang Ching Fu* ("*Fu* on the Two Capitals") would demonstrate what he was about; and if any of his readers should suspect him of merely imitating his famous predecessor, the opening sentences, with their characterization of two completely new interlocutors, would effectively demonstrate the contrary.

This introductory section is highly dramatic. First, there is the *kung-tzŭ*, the nobleman, with the character appellation "Stayed-on-Vacuity," and along with him the *hsien-sheng*, the teacher of a ripe age, by name "Where-did-he-live." These two interlocutors are not represented as protagonists, the one for a Western and the other for an Eastern capital. Thus the center of interest is moved onto a more subtle psychological level than in Pan Ku's poem, a level on which differences of temperament and moral outlook create the dialectic of drama. For the moment Chang Heng is content to give a thumb-nail sketch of the nobleman; it is only in the "*Fu* on the Eastern Capital" that the teacher becomes more than a dim lay figure. There he becomes a person, in many ways representing Chang Heng himself in a fashion that the Honorable Stayed-on-Vacuity does not. Yet who can venture to affirm that Chang Heng did not recognize in himself certain strains which were on a par with the theorizing of his nobleman? The very fact that his "teacher" is characterized as an unlocatable person, as one who may be more up in the air or more with his feet on solid earth, points in this direction. Living when Chang Heng did, under the emperors he served, he would have been a poor poet had it been otherwise.

Second, the nobleman opens the proceedings by laying down the law in arrogant fashion to the teacher, presumably some years older than himself. He sets forth a logical argument by which he proves a proposition which we have good reason for believing Chang Heng profoundly doubted. Thus the argument requires the closest scrutiny, for it represents the poet's power of dramatic imagination. He could put himself inside the nobleman's type of mind and argue solemnly from that point of view.

Third, the argument is based not merely on naturalistic, but also on materialistic pre-suppositions. The nobleman's "Heaven" is not the transcendent Heaven with an operative will for man's good as characterized by traditional religion. The "Heaven" and "Earth" here are the mechanical cause-and-effect forces of the Yin-Yang cosmology. Also, the key to the argument is the soil, in the one case more productive, in the other case less so. In other words, the universe is assumed to be a non-moral one in which the economic factor is decisive. That was perfectly recognizable to Chang Heng's readers, since it was the stark, Legalist position, and that theory had its influence on some of the *Ju*.

Fourth, the argument proceeds on the basis of a strict analogy between small and great nations: an assumption which follows from recognition of Nature's mechanical processes. The dialectic would easily carry Han readers in assent, as it proceeds to *"ti che"* (the class of persons called "emperors"), and to the propositions given under that heading and that of *"chao min"* (the mass of the people).

Fifth, the final stage is an appeal to history in which the fall of the Chou order is accounted for entirely in terms of economic resources. That from a *Ju* standpoint was only half the truth of the matter. Are we not compelled, therefore, to assume that the parallel assertion about Former Han and Later Han were for Chang Heng equally specious? As we probe into the underlying cynicism of the statement, this becomes doubly clear. "Emperor Kao had his capital in the west and was lavish in his expenditure, Emperor Kuang-wu. . . ." In other words, the one regime had the money and so could use it; the other regime had not got the money and so could not. Just that, and no more, with everybody knowing what misery had come about from the Government's prodigal expenditure!

It is assumed, therefore, that here at the outset Chang Heng gives a study in sophistry, the sophistry of a mind which is essentially Legalist. In confirmation of this assumption it is to be noted that the whole passage is in "scripture style," the aphoristic, didactic style so characteristic of the dialectic in the Scriptures, e.g. in the later "Wings" of the "Changes" Scripture. The use of the style here would seem to be deliberate, since the rest of the *fu* is predominantly rhymed. As will appear later again and again, Chang Heng had a genius for irony. So here his poet's pen is barbed.

2. *The Topography and Geography of Ch'ang-an*

The story begins with the topography of Ch'ang-an, just as Pan Ku's does. Chang Heng's description follows the same orderly method, taking the four points of the compass in turn. The points in which they differ as far as I can see are not important; but that is a matter for the geographers to settle. Our point of interest is that both authors, the historian and the scientist, had a trained eye for typographical features.

With regard to Chang Heng's mentality here, he redeems the dullness of his topographical narrative by the lively story of Duke Mu of Ch'in (638-619 B.C.). It is already clear that Pan Ku could let his pen run on a good story, and indeed a good *fu* in those days was expected to amuse as well as instruct. This side of Chang Heng's nature comes out forcibly enough in both his *fu*, so we may well doubt here whether our learned scientist took the story he told to be historic truth. The moral of the supernatural gift to the duke, it should be noted, is in full keeping with the nobleman's theory of economic causes as normally determinative. When, however, the narrative reaches Emperor Kao and his abandonment of Loyang in favor of Ch'ang-an, a supernatural factor is introduced, namely, Heaven's direct inspiration of the unknown exile from frontier duty, Lou Ching. In the "History of the Former Han Dynasty" account of this (ch. 43) there is no mention of heaven-given inspiration, only stressing of the curious means by which Lou Ching managed to see the Emperor and the lightning effect his counsel had. It appears, then, that the stress on inspiration is Chang Heng's own, and we are faced with the question whether he really believed this. Not necessarily so, for it is the nobleman speaking; but all our knowledge of ordinary mid-Han educated mentality leads to the conclusion that emperors were regarded as specially subject to miraculous direction of one sort and another.

3. *The Palace Buildings*

Instead of describing next the city and its throbbing life, as the prototype did, Chang Heng, after just mentioning the city walls, went straight to the palace hill and its buildings, relegating description of the city to be the next center of interest. Both authors would seem to have had good artistic reasons for their respective arrangements, and in Chang Heng's case the narrative goes smoothly from remarks on

Kao Tsu's purpose to what he and his successors did in the way of glorifying their capital.

There are forty-nine couplets devoted to description of the buildings on the palace hill: twenty to the main residence, the Vermilion Palace with its different ramifications, fourteen to a miscellany of other buildings, and eleven to the women's apartments. Chang Heng's account makes it clearer that Emperor Kao's Wei Yang Palace was added to later. His description of its extravagant ornamentation is like Pan Ku's in its piling up of the adjectives, although here again he gets a slightly clearer picture across. His concluding statement dealing with the Audience Hall at the east end and the Jade Tower and K'un Tê building at the west end seem to have a sting in the tail: "with their irregular elevations . . . , any pattern of design was unrecognizable."

The account of the other buildings is not much help, any more than was Pan Ku's description: plenty of names, and they of an animistic-poetic nature, but no indication as to the layout of the departments of state. Hsieh Tsung (d. 243) and the T'ang commentators have no information on this score. However, the information about the Emperor's personal attendants and the departmental officers being on duty at night in shifts is worth having. With this elaborate bureaucracy at work and couriers coming and going, the palace hill must have been a scene of bustling activity, both throughout the day and sometimes in the night. Chang Heng lifts a corner of the curtain, but is a little puzzling, for he makes no mention of Pan Ku's Ch'eng Ming building, but does refer to a Lan T'ai building which Pan Ku omits. Since we know from other sources that the Lan T'ai was used as another storing place for records, the notable feature of Chang Heng's account is that it agrees with Pan Ku's in regard to the places for the collating of records, but has nothing to say on the writers meeting and discussing in the Ch'eng Ming building. That seems very odd until we remember that those writers were salaried officers in some sort of secretarial position. In those circumstances they presumably took turns on night duty, and we can safely assume that the conversation was by no means all on routine business. The only question is why Chang Heng left this side out. Possibly he felt Pan Ku had overstressed this feature.

4. *The Rear Apartments*

Here, as in Pan Ku's poetic effort, there is a luscious description of the harem. Whether both poets regarded these luxuries as rather barbaric will be considered later. It is another aspect which requires stressing: the emphasis laid on the craftsmen and their triumphs. As in imperial Rome so in Chang Heng's Ch'ang-an, the concentration of unprecedented wealth in one man's hands gave an immense stimulus to the decorative arts and unquestionably brought new refinements of aesthetic appreciation.

As for the frivolous remark about looking inside—suitable enough coming from an aristocrat—to the student acquainted with the ritual books of that age it may well cause surprise. Indeed, one would have thought that such a suggestion might easily cause imperial displeasure. Imagine that dour prude Empress Dowager Teng having her attention drawn to this offence against propriety. As a matter of fact, things might be said in relation to a previous regime which might not be said about the present. Also, Han literature is by no means lacking in evidence of male susceptibility to feminine charm. Chang Heng himself is an instance. In his *fu* on thought transcending the normal he uses a delightfully light touch in describing how two goddesses tried to ensnare him, and what a beguiling song they sang.

Then comes something outside Pan Ku's sphere of interest: the psychological effect of these various sense enticements on the emperors themselves. In five tense four-word couplets the picture is painted with trenchant strokes: a constant round of indulgence of one sort and another, every day some new beauty the Emperor had not seen before. There is of course a flourish of poetic hyperbole here. The wheels of government had to be kept moving, even though His Majesty might forget to go back to his own apartments. We are reminded of two people specially in Chang Heng's mind, Emperors Wu and Ch'eng. The former, it is on record, spent continuous nights and days in his harem, and because of this made the innovation of having eunuchs as private secretaries—much to the disgust of the bureaucracy.

5. The Outbreak of Megalomania

Again the psychological interest is to the fore, with this subtle transference from sensuality to the megalomaniac urge. The lurking irony in the last section becomes more visible right from the start. That "divine beauty" (*shen li*) gives the key. The T'ang commentators give no reference to *Hsün Tzŭ*, but there is a striking resemblance to that book's theory that the Son of Heaven should be surrounded at all times by the most aesthetic sights and sounds. So will his *tê* (mana-spirituality) be cultivated to its highest pitch. We see the idea at work here, in very realistic fashion, from the point of view of a Later Han satirist. Again it is Emperor Wu in the first place who is in his mind, although some of the later emperors were tarred with much the same brush. Emperor Wu not only built with reckless expenditure; he also compared himself to the Ch'in First Emperor. That monarch was the mightiest phenomenon in real history. Hence it behooved his Han compeer to demonstrate that his *shen li* was on a grander as also a more refined level. Was not his empire within the four seas much wider? As a side-light on the Former Han attitude to the Ch'in regime, and, yet more, as a side-light on the emperor who brought current Confucianism to the fore, here is a useful directive for the historian.

The Kan Ch'üan Palaces, also initiated by Emperor Wu, are merely touched on. Chang Heng's readers would be familiar with Yang Hsiung's famous description in his ironical *Kan Ch'üan Fu*, where he described the effect on him of the "great palace buildings, a fantasy of clouds and billows spread to view . . . my eyes fluttered back and forth, forth and back, my two souls made small and brought to stupe-faction." This was a reference to Emperor Ch'eng's time, when several emperors had added their respective contribu-tions. Kan Ch'üan with its amenities became a rival to Ch'ang-an, and thereby created a number of problems of secular and religious administration. According to Yang Hsiung it had a site with extraordinary demon-defeating powers. In this the great tower above the valley played its part; so novel and striking a feature as it was in the landscape, and so reli-giously reassuring with its cleaving of the sky. There is no doubt of Chang Heng's appreciation of the constructional problem it entailed. He emphasized two points, one that its planning went beyond "all ordinary computation," the other that it was tapered with precision.

6. *The Chien Chang Palace Area, with Its Spirit-Revealing Tower*

The plot thickens as Chang Heng in his ironical vein takes us to the constructional operations outside the western city wall. Pan Ku had done full justice to this theme, both in his general account and in his witty description of a man fight-ing giddiness as he stumbled up and down those interminable stairs. Chang Heng does not compete with his prototype there. As the man who invented a seismograph, Chang Heng appreciated the problems which Emperor Wu's master-builder had to face. His description is a masterpiece in its succinct-ness and inclusion of essential detail.

What we were only able to suspect in the critique of Pan Ku's "*Fu* on the Western Capital," Section 8, takes shape now as more than a mere conjecture. As we put the language here alongside his statement that the Heaven-Communicating Tower (at Kan Ch'üan) "surpassed all ordinary computa-tion," the demand on the master-builder's ingenuity in experi-ment becomes clear to view. The two towers were built at the same time, the Kan Ch'üan one 30 *chang* high, the Chien Chang one 50 *chang* (in terms of English measurement about 225 feet and 375 feet respectively), the one a solid structure, the other built on the *ching kan* ("well-head") principle. That is to say, the master-builder decided from experience with the Heaven-Communicating Tower that to go up another 20 *chang* with a solid structure was out of the question. The only way was to have an erection of wood and that after the pattern of the protective criss-cross wooden structures used in relation to well-heads. The danger to a solid structure from a high wind was too great: as Yang Hsiung wrote, "a gust of wind with startling force . . . leveled the boughs of the willows." Therefore an open-work structure was necessary, either four- or eight-sided. Then came the problem of weight of timber. Heavy pillars would make the upper stories too heavy, the whole thing would come crashing down. Therefore light pillars must be used. On the other hand, as the Greek and Roman builders discovered with the support needed for heavy superstructures, the ninety-degree angle of a pillar did not afford the necessary rigidity of support. In Ch'ang-an this problem was solved by using pairs of brackets[1] clamped to a regular open succession of beams and their supporting pillars. Thus the principle of counter-acting pressures was brought into action. There is still the question whether an open-work, light-timbered structure could have achieved the amazing height of a hundred stories. The problem is one for engineers to decide. The interesting thing is that the Pharos of Alexandria, built by Sostratus of Cnidus in the third century B.C., was believed in classical times to be six hundred feet in height. Whether that was entirely a solid structure is, I gather, doubtful, but in any case it was built to last. Emperor Wu was not so much concerned about that.

Masters of the works and master-builders are, unfortu-

[1] Wood bent and stiffened by being soaked in water, a practice employed for making certain parts of the crossbow.

nately, seldom mentioned by name in the literature of the time, nor are the artist craftsmen. Section 4, however, has the intriguing statement (omitted in the translation): "orders were given to [? a] Pan and [? an] Erh." This was in relation to the construction of the flying galleries (and possibly the Rear Palaces). By Han times one Lu Pan seems to have been well on the way to becoming the patron saint of workers in wood. One legend has it that he was of princely descent and lived at the end of the sixth century B.C., being master-craftsman to the Duke of Lu. There were also a number of stories about him as the inventor of certain wonder-exciting mechanical toys. Wang Erh is more of a mystery figure, but is referred to in *Huai Nan Tzŭ* (second century B.C.) as a master in the use (? the inventor) of a curved wood-carving knife and a rounded gouge or chisel. Yang Hsiung in his *Kan Ch'üan Fu* refers to one Ho as the author of the dumbfounding patterns of rococo decorating there, and adds that "if Lu Pan and Wang Erh were to see them they would throw away their tools." It is evident that Yang Hsiung thought very great advances were being made in the arts and crafts. Couple this with Chang Heng's description of those timbers and the clamps and the invention of a revolving weather vane and draught-producing shutters, and we seem to have quite a little reliable information about mechanical developments in the Han dynasty. Also the *Chung Yung* ("The Mean in Action," ch. 20) comes to life in this connection: "If daily and monthly trials of skill be held, and grants of better rations be given on the merit of the work done, the hundred crafts are thereby encouraged."

The "Shaman from Yüeh" ("*Yüeh wu*") (or, as Dubs maintains, "shamaness") should catch the historian's eye. The great Emperor, so ruthless in his plans to absorb the surrounding peoples, could nonetheless be led by the nose by their barbarian beliefs. Chang Heng as a Later Han man could feel that, and there can be little doubt but that his reference here was meant to have a sarcastic edge. Whether the founding Han emperors had anything like the same sense of superiority is doubtful, and it still remains to be seen whether further critical studies will not reveal that barbarian beliefs and barbarian mythologies penetrated a good deal further into the Sinitic culture than later ages realized. As for barbarians at court generally in Emperor Wu's time, the words "Tu Lu" reveal the presence of members of that tribe in Ch'ang-an. The Tu Lu were a Turkish people occupying territory a thousand miles west of Ch'ang-an, and acrobats from there were a feature in Han court entertainments. One of their stunts was to climb a pole and then fling themselves higher and catch the pole as they fell.[2] Thus Chang Heng's poet mind had an apt image to hand to clothe his ironical intent.

The final reaction to Emperor Wu's carefully mobilized attack on the problem of transcending the mortal sphere is half one of sympathy. The poet knew by his own experience what it was to long for the Beyond. In his *Ssŭ Hsüan Fu* he described how eventually he was transported beyond the sun and stars and the Milky Way, until he looked out on chaos, on elemental material forces whirling and colliding in the Ultimate Beyond. Thus the tenor of his "before you have gone half-way, you are shaking with fear . . ." is exactly *en rapport* with the tenor of that poem. The Honorable Stayed-on-Vacuity is portrayed as jeering at Emperor Wu for believing that commensurable, mechanically-acting means could be used for prolonging his natural span in life. Yet in the opening sentences of the poem the determination of man's lot by material, mechanically-acting forces was the very theory that the nobleman proved—at any rate to his own satisfaction.

Perhaps the main point of interest here lies in the amazement, expressed with uncompromising bluntness, that an educated, intelligent person could be so led astray by the obvious absurdities handed out by charlatans like Shao Chün

---

[2] See *Han Shu*, ch. 96 (*Hsi Yü Lieh Chuan*) and the *Cheng Tu Fu* of Fu Hsüan (A.D. 217-278), ap. *I Wen Lei Chü* (ch. 61).

and Lüan Ta.[3] We have here the evidence of a Later Han rational reaction against the more glaring superstitions of the earlier age. The historian's question is whether that age was definitely more sunk in superstition. It appears that it was. Apart from Emperor Wu's aberrations from common sense—and he, it must be remembered, was a fully literate man of great executive ability—the high spot of naturalistic speculation in his age was Tung Chung-Shu's semi-rational *Yin-Yang* theories, and those theories not only captivated the scholar intellect during the succeeding century but also had a potent influence in the first century A.D. The *Kung Yang Chuan*, with its intense preoccupation with prodigies and portents, had overwhelming support in the White Tiger Conference in A.D. 79, as it had previously had in the Shih Ch'ü Conference in 53-51 B.C.; and the production of the apocryphal "Woof Books" went on all the time. Yet the Later Han era produced not only a Chang Heng but also that notable iconoclast, Wang Ch'ung, whose *Lun Heng* pilloried the current affronts to commonsense and reason. Add to that Chang Heng's expectation that his court readers would appreciate his slashing sarcasm. There was a new leaven at work, traceable in the works of Yang Hsiung (53 B.C.-A.D. 18) and Liu Hsin (d. A.D. 23); and by the end of that century the new wine poured into old bottles was bursting the more decrepit ones. So much by way of an interim decision on this intricate problem.

7. *The Chien Chang Area* (continued)

The two accounts confirm each other in outline. Chang Heng reveals again his powers of orderly observation, the evidence here for this being very striking. The narrative proceeds as if it were from a bird's eye view: first the two towers with their geomantic layout, then the great huddle of build-

---

[3] Pan Ku satirizes them in his *Chiao Ssŭ Chih* ("Treatise on Sacrifices," *Han Shu*, ch. 25). Shao Chün had an astoundingly long run for his money and died in good favour with his master. Lüan Ta, an even more spectacular success, was caught in the end and executed.

ings which constituted the main palace, then the interlacing paths in all directions and the covered passage running east to the city wall. Then in the distance come the lakes and their fairy hills; and so we reach the hills of the hunting park on the horizon. Poetic power of imagination is there, but that genius so much more often than some theories allow is rooted and grounded in precise information, impressed, it may be, on the poet in his early youth. Thus Chang Heng, born in A.D. 78, was not so far removed from the Ch'ang-an period that he could not have heard from some old man, e.g. his grandfather, his impressions of Chien Chang before it went to rack and ruin. In any case the picture is vividly before the poet's eye: "as you gaze you cannot find the way back." This phrase should be compared with Pan Ku's "gaze out of focus." Both remarks entail a cultivated level of consciousness in relation to the optic sense, a particular lucidity of mind for which the two men's linguistic medium afforded an adequate channel of communication.

8. *The City and Its Suburbs with Their Inhabitants*

May we assume that Pan Ku's vivid picture of the shopping center throng pleased him and his readers as much as it pleases us? It was the first time there had been such a city with so many stores and buyers. He exaggerated, more or less, and since one poet's hyperbole may easily leave another poet cold, Chang Heng got the same effect home by other means. He first drew attention to the occupants of those magnificent houses in the exclusive quarter at the north end. Shih Hsien and Tung Hsien were the outstanding examples of the parvenu in the earlier court, and while they lasted, they had money to spend in the luxury stores. (No mention is made of other families there, but they must have been few, for most of the nobles and great officials had their houses by the imperial tombs.) The account then proceeds to the rich merchants produced by the trade boom and, as it proceeds, we learn in a sentence that everything the heart could wish was there on sale—and profits ran to a hundred per cent. Another sentence gives us the hawkers, and the cheating of "small-town folk."

With regard to the parvenus, Shih Hsien started his career as an office-trained junior, fell foul of the law and was castrated, attracted the attention of that simple-minded monarch, Emperor Yüan, and so became his eunuch in the Rear Palace. His influence was unbounded, and extremely injurious to the state. Tung Hsien was not a eunuch, but a handsome young man with whom Emperor Ai fell in love. As to the extravagant houses these two men built—one of them was known by the same name as an imperial palace—Chang Heng's language is very reminiscent of what Pan Ku's story had recorded, so that we know the source of his information. The stands of arms at the entrance were of course a necessary precaution. Shih Hsien incurred enmity in many quarters by compassing the death of men whom he feared; and, as the story here shows, there were plenty of gangsters about ready to be hired.

With regard to the wealthy merchants, considerable detail on this class is to be found in the *Shih Huo Chih* monograph in the "History of the Former Han Dynasty" and Dr. Nancy Lee Swann's careful translation and annotation of it. Chang Heng names four members of this class: one who made his money in fats, one in selling cooked tripe, one in opening up iron mines in Szechuan, and the fourth by horse doctoring. Since there were valuable horses from Ferghana in the imperial stables and those of the aristocracy, a skilful veterinary would be in continual demand. The odd thing is that luxury goods do not appear in this list, whilst a vendor of cooked tripe does. Presumably there is some satirical meaning behind this. The sense of class distinction between the court and the city was a marked one, and a relatively poor scholar gentleman like Chang Heng would hardly be immune from it, the less so because many of the forty dealers we know of were operators in the money market in direct contravention of the law.

Where Pan Ku makes a brief and colorless reference to the desperadoes, congregated in the capital from all parts of the country, Chang Heng goes into significant detail. He gives the names of four men who not only "formed gangs" but also "joined forces and united their intentions without jealousy." His summing up of them is dramatic enough: "spite-fire eyes over a trifling affront—a dead body in an angle of the road." Add to that the sobriquet "Yang of the Mou Tombs and Chu of the Yang Tombs, quick to quarrel, roaring in a flash." Such is the glimpse we get of the gangster underworld of Ch'ang-an.

Chang Heng's lighter, ironical vein reappears in the treatment of the argumentative, out-of-work scholars. It reminds one of Plato's criticism of the sophists, as also of Helen Waddell's description of the students in Abelard's Paris. We know that in the century after Emperor Wu's inauguration of empire-wide recommendations and tests in the capital for government service, the numbers of candidates went up by leaps and bounds, the total running finally to tens of thousands. Of these Chang Heng refers here only to those of the five home counties—whether prospective candidates or successful ones is not clear. The latter, although given the status of *lang*, did not necessarily get posts right away. They went into a waiting list, and they might have to wait a very long time. Men in that situation doubtless would congregate at the capital, so as to be able to approach what influential persons they knew. Meanwhile they argued at street corners.

That this was a highly argumentative age in the scholarly world has already become clear in the last chapter. But what actual topics caused the fury of discussion depicted here is not clear at all. Chang Heng's "splitting of hairs and tearing of muscles apart," illuminating as it is as to the temper of the rank and file, and his slightly contemptuous attitude to that temper, helps us only very little. In view of the contents of the three chapters on the famous scholars in the two Han Histories, coupled with the contents of the Liu Hsin catalogue, the center of interest was the various texts of the Scriptures, each with its own ardent band of supporters. That being so, the splitting of hairs and tearing apart of muscles presumably was over the variant readings in those texts. Questions of single words and the proper punctuation were enough to produce violent disagreement.

Taking these three phenomena together, merchant millionaires, criminals and gangsters, and out-of-work scholars, we get a side-light on the social order of the time. It is not enough to realize that however rich a business man became, he could not buy his way into the ranks of the nobility. There was, however, a way open to him to raise the social status of his family. He could have his sons trained for government service, and his commercial dealings with aristocrats and officials would give him the opportunity for urging their recommendation for posts. Once a man was started on an official career there was no bar to his reaching the status of enfiefed nobility. So with regard to the underworld, these bands of lawless desperadoes and swashbucklers, some of whom took service in noble families: where did they and their skill in arms come from? When we remember that training in the use of arms was part of the education of a nobleman, that plotting for power by the royal princes and their friends again and again brought not only death to the ringleaders but reduction of their descendants to plebeian rank, we begin to see one source from which the desperado class was fed. And how about the princely families that the First Emperor demobilized and whose memory of happier days may be connected with the Han surname *Kung-sheng*? Did some of their descendants cherish memories of their aristocratic past and inherit some of their ancestors' arms? And how about the descendants of the imperial Lu clan who after five generations had no claim to kinship with the reigning emperor? So with the tens of thousands of candidates for office in the last years of Former Han; for those with the ability and luck to get and hold appointments, they and their children would go up in the social scale. The rest, if from official families, might easily go down. There is, therefore, no substantial ground for taking such pronouncements as those in the *Wang Chih* of the "Record of Rites" (dateable for the main part of it as the product of Emperor Wen's reign, 179-157 B.C.) or those of the *Chou Li* (less easily dateable), as representing a fixed order of society, the members of which could not move up or down in the social and economic scale.

9. *The Hunting Park*

In Pan Ku's poem there is no description of the hunting park itself, no itemization of what was in it. Chang Heng, on the contrary, gave his readers an elaborate picture. First the main landmarks by which they could estimate the huge size of the park, then a very detailed account of the contents, the flora and fauna in their natural setting, with a glimpse of the surrounding wall and the monstrous number of pleasure buildings. He noted the migration of birds in due season and wound up with the care the foresters used in attending to the welfare of the animals in winter. This painter's eye for landscape had appeared in both Ssŭ-ma Hsiang-ju's and Yang Hsiung's hunting *fu*: Ssŭ-ma Hsiang-ju splashing on his colors enthusiastically; Yang Hsiung equally intoxicated with language but careful to give a historical setting. Chang Heng's picture in comparison is more methodical than theirs. What was it in that mid-Han period which aroused this passion for detailed description, for what Lu Chi in A.D. 302 was to call "*t'i wu*"—"embodying an object of observation"? The same epoch produced the first draft of what became the *Pen Ts'ao Ching* ("Classic of Fundamental Herbs") with its 365 plants, as also the *Shan Hai Ching* ("Classic of Mountains and Seas") with its thirteen main divisions in which were plotted out the mountains and watercourses of the empire. There is also the "*Tribute of Yü*"—was that too the fruit of this new talent of the mind, the talent which in Rome first emerged in the writings of Julius Caesar and Virgil?

This section is more than a plain picture: it has a strong satirical vein running through it, starting from the opening words. To speak of a hunting park as an enclosed, interdicted *chi* was a contradiction in terms, a contradiction reinforced by the second clause in the couplet, "under the control of the Intendant of the Capital," i.e. not of the Son of Heaven himself. The words which rang in Chang Heng's and his readers' heads were *"pang chi ch'ien li, wei min so chih,"* "the national demesne of a thousand *li* [300 odd miles] is where the people are at rest." So went the ringing lines in the Shang sacrificial ode ("Odes," *Shang Sung*). What is even more significant here, the tale was told of Confucius that in teaching his disciples he enlarged on these lines with reflections on the *huang* bird twittering happily on its resting place, and then asked whether man should be less intelligent than a bird. So we can almost see our poet-satirist with brush in hand, cogitating on the Ch'ang-an *chi* which was not a *chi*. He would recall Yang Hsiung's *Yü Lieh Fu* Foreword which pillories Emperor Wu for enlarging the interdicted enclosure, and his pungent comparison of that act with the Sage-Kings whose rule "did *not* rob the people of rich crop land, of mulberry and *ch'e* trees [so that] women had ample cloth and men had ample grain." Then down came the brush on the tablet, and he wrote *"feng chi"* not *"pang chi,"* and in the place of a people at rest under the Emperor's beneficent care gave the image of the controller of the park, the man whose business was to punish ruthlessly infringements of the interdict.

10. *The Imperial Hunt*

Considerations of space forbid a detailed comparison of the two accounts, and all the more any consideration of the dependence of our two authors on Ssŭ-ma Hsiang-ju and Yang Hsiung. In general, Pan Ku's story gives a better sense of the organized stages of the hunt. At the same time the old timer of Ch'ang-an rather revels in the details of carnage and destruction. That is not to say that Pan Ku's intention was merely to paint the sensational picture in all its gory detail. That would be wrong, for in the opening section of his "*Fu* on the Eastern Capital" the Loyang host jeers at his guest for being a true son of barbarian Ch'in. Turning to Chang Heng's nobleman, he also is in character, but as his story proceeds, paragraph by paragraph, the Later Han age's contempt for the earlier ethos is more openly displayed. Also the nobleman's creator comes right out into the open as a man of feeling.

We now see why in Section 9 he described so carefully the birds and beasts in their comfortable habitat; the time was at hand when these same birds and beasts would be fleeing in blind panic and be overtaken by an untimely death. And if a stray one should be lucky and escape to the suburbs, it would fall a prey to a falconer or a dog on a leash. We see here, then, not only the literary artist in command of the vivid phrase for depicting the scene in all its picturesque and disgusting phases, but also the humanitarian spirit, quick in its appreciation of the torture that goes with panic, subtle in its delineation of ferocious beasts brought to bay.

It is poetry of a high order here. In the first place the sentence structure ranges jaggedly from four-word couplets to seven, from seven to three, and vice versa, giving the feel of the hubbub and confusion. In the second place, the narrative progresses from point to point with certain subtle contrasts of theme: from the work on Yü Ch'u's magic techniques to the imperial guards on parade, from the poor harmless pheasant and hare to the terrifying *ssŭ* (? rhinoceros) and tigers, and from them to the berserk feats of the professional huntsmen. In the third place, there is the unforgettable imagery at key points: "the stiff corpses of the slain, bird and beast, glistening like tide-washed pebbles"; "before the sun is down and [the shadows] change, the killing is done—out of ten, seven, or eight."

With regard to the books of magic and the "lively tales," the passage is highly revealing in more ways than one. There is, for example, what Li Chou-han noted in his comment as "covert opposition" to these books. That is putting it rather mildly. From the first word "It was not only play" through "what was wanted in relaxation" down to Ch'ih Yu, the resuscitated magician of legend and the demons, not one of which could now cross the Emperor's path, the scorn is completely overt. The picture here is almost too compact, oscillating as it does between the serious business of preparing charms and the lively tales for idle moments. However, with the help of Liu Hsin's Catalogue the passage becomes perfectly clear. The catalogue lists fifteen collections of "lively tales," the last and by far the largest of which is "*Yü Ch'u Chou Shuo* in 943 sections,"[4] and Liu Hsin's comment contains these words: "market-place gossip, alley-way talk, what is concocted by listeners on the roads and talkers on the streets."

As for Ch'ih Yu with his axe and shaggy coverlet, clearly it was through his agency that the imperial party came to know the "malignant tricks of the spirits" (*shen chien*) and could take due precautions.

11. *After the Hunt*

It may well be that this enormous section (as I make it) should be divided into three or more sections. There are, however, prosodic difficulties to doing so. Also Chang Heng's intention is clear, namely to pile Pelion on Ossa with regard to these festivities, and so be able the more effectively to play the critic. In this respect his account strikes a challenging note which is not found in Pan Ku's version, and the dramatic interest is intensified with greater subtlety. Thus, for instance, the center of interest shifts from the general to the particular: first the ladies of the harem, then the rank and file at their feasting, the ordering of the carriages, the court

---

[4] See Wang Hsien-ch'ien, *Han Shu Pu-chu*, ch. 30.

circles and their shooting and fishing. Finally the reader's attention is concentrated on the Emperor himself, in his luxurious lodge by the arena, as a spectator of the grand entertainment—and as a human being surfeited with pleasure and riddled with ennui.

With regard to the ladies of the harem, they fade out of the picture almost immediately, whereas in Pan Ku's version they seem to pervade the scene right down to the end. Probably the divergence is more apparent than real, since both authors were so economical in their use of definitive subjects to their sentences. As for the holiday mood of these ladies, Chang Heng only just touches on it, and then goes straight to a more serious matter: they go and view the heaps of the slain and, as they return, turn back to take yet another look. It is hard to believe that the creator of the poor escaping pheasant and hare did not mean here to suggest a touch of sadism in these light-hearted young women. His sensitiveness to unconscious cruelty comes out again in relation to the fishing with a dragnet and its "womb-grabbing and egg-snatching." And to this must be added an item in the final acrobatic scene in the entertainment: the sensational appeal he notes in the boys seeming to fall headlong and then being caught by their heels. We are brought face to face with that avid desire for violent sensation which characterized the gladiatorial shows in imperial Rome, and which is so near to brutal blood-lust.

Each thumbnail sketch has extraordinary precision of delineation. As part of this should be noted Chang Heng's emphasis on the underlying staff work to these large-scale festivities. There is the steward on a horse going round and supervizing the catering arrangements, there is—of all unexpected figures—the "traffic cop" (*chin ch'ê*) marshalling the carriages in convenient parking places. Then there is the steward in charge of boats, with his oarswomen ready to break into a chanty. And then we are introduced to the inspector

of marshes and fishing—reproved for breaking the very regulations he was commissioned to enforce.

On the other hand, along with this precision of detail goes
a marked vagueness as to time. This was observable in Pan
Ku's account, and it is clear that both authors aimed at depicting a continuous round of pleasure-seeking in which night
was turned into day. There is no need to assume that the
Emperor and his circle engaged in all the diversions available, and Chang Heng's story shows His Majesty taking
his ease, in the daytime presumably, under his priceless *chia i*
coverlets in the P'ing Lo lodge. If the entertainment and
all were crowded into one day, the Emperor's rest must
have been a very short one. One question arises in connection
with the shooting. Did Chang Heng know that wild geese
flew by night or at crack of dawn? From references to these
birds in old poems we may assume that he did know. But
then presumably the shooting party went straight from feasting to their sport, and the historian wonders whether their
marksmanship was really as accurate as it is represented as
being.

What are we to make of Chang Heng's sudden outburst
of indignation against the fishing party? It is a twofold outburst, on account of the breaking of the law by the very
people who should have known better, and on account of
the thoughtless frivolity which brought about such wanton
destruction of life. The historian's question here is whether
there is not on both counts a distinction to be marked here
between the ethos of the Former and Later Han dynasties.
The Chou feudal society had realized the economic importance of repressing the poverty-stricken peasants' lust for meat
and fish, and there seems no reason for doubting that the
former Han law code contained equally repressive measures.
That, however, is a different matter from what emerges to
view here. Chang Heng's indictment is of the court circle
for assuming that they were above the law and for having
no conscience about exterminating the spawn, etc. Since in

that last century of Later Han the moral implications of
high doctrine were only just beginning to win their way in
the higher ranks of society, the strong inference is that Chang
Heng's attitude represents one of the marked differences between Former and Later Han.

Coming to the great entertainment, we find Chang Heng
giving it a name, *"Chüeh Ti"* ("Horn-Butting") and launching straightway into a detailed description from which horn-
butting is singularly absent. That fact plus the strikingly
entertaining characteristics of the show lead us to see what
a radical change came to these old-time contests and mimetic
dances. What originally were tribal rites, functioning as stim-
ulants of tribal unity and *joie de vivre*, now appear in new
and elaborate forms as variety shows aimed at exciting the
interest of a blasé emperor and his court. The actual *chüeh ti*
contests clearly originated in Western Ch'in, as certain dances
came from the Yü River in Szechuan (cf. Dubs' *History of
the Former Han Dynasty*, vol. II, pp. 129-31). To these
Emperor Wu's impresario and his successors added a number of other items from all over the empire and its adjacent
tribes. "Impresario" is the only term that does justice to the
high managerial ability which could not only devise the more
complicated tableaux but also bring them to the point of
successful presentation. The significance of this lies in the
fact that these impresarios took the place of the tribal shamans, and what originally had been shot through and through
with the presuppositions of animistic religion were now
adapted to a completely non-religious end. The process of
change doubtless had begun before the Han era, but it was
the wide expansion of the empire which brought matters to
a head. To the Chinese conquerors the outlandish dances and
mystery stunts they saw were not awe-inspiring but interesting, exciting, even amusing, in a word, of purely secular
interest.

Chang Heng himself is evidence of this secular temper.
His account is solely concerned with reproducing the spec-

tacular effect. For him here was an elaborate specimen of the art of showmanship; and the interesting thing is that he saw it as so elaborate that it defeated its own end. The Emperor in the last resort was not amused: he was bored. That, of course, is the force of the reference to the magician of the Eastern Ocean (the coastal area of the newly-settled dependency of Yüeh in the far south). Just as Old Master Huang's magic powers proved powerless and he was eaten up by the very ravening beasts he claimed to control, so the marvelous succession of exciting shows failed to entertain: "they did not work." The translation hardly does justice to the homely force of the actual expression "*pu shou*," literally "not saleable." If we may assume—and it is but an assumption—that we see here a slang expression current in the shopping quarter of Loyang in Chang Heng's day, the poet's dramatic irony becomes yet more devastating.

12. *The Emperor's Undignified Amour*

The final item in the entertainment would seem naturally to belong to the general account of it. Psychologically it is closely connected with the next phase of Chang Heng's story. In spite of the thrilling nature of this acrobatic display and the patriotic tenor of its finale, the Emperor's mounting feeling of ennui explodes into action. He cannot bear any more. He orders his carriage; and the court follows suit. The stately procession back to the palace proceeds. In the poem so far there is no indication of the emperor's frame of mind beyond the cryptic hint conveyed in the words "*ju shih pu shou*" ("thus it was it did not work"). Then with lightning speed comes the dénouement. In one pregnant triplet the Emperor's boredom is depicted, and in one couplet more he is found creeping out of the palace incognito.

The Son of Heaven, who throughout the major part of the poem has been chiefly a shadowy figure in the background, now comes right down stage and is subject to the full glare of the spotlight. Actually Chang Heng's language is impersonal as usual: only the sense indicates without question that he had an emperor in the forefront of his mind. Thus the first straight view we get of His Majesty is as a very human being subject to petulant longings for freedom of action. Since "the divinity that doth hedge a king" has so marked an emphasis in Han literature, Chang Heng's emphasis on the other side is remarkably worth having. It is the more so because this author of ours, this poet-cum-scientist who belonged to a generation notable for its conventional prudery, gives a most unprudish description of a courtesan and her seductive tricks. He even says—not necessarily in a cynical but certainly in an ironic vein—that even a Buddhist monk could not but succumb to such charms. Approaching this matter from the historian's angle, it is to be noted that Emperor Wu and, four reigns later, Emperor Ch'eng are on record as having made incognito expeditions, mention being made of viewing cock-fights and the like, to which items Chang Heng makes no reference.

13. *Final Conclusions*

So then, human nature being what it is, what follows? The poet outlines the resultant situation, stating the premises in blunt four-word couplets following on with six-word couplets embodying historical evidence, and so moving to trenchantly stated conclusions. His premises are two. The first is that a monarch may be expected to give rein to his carnal desires and pursue a course of "*carpe diem.*" That is the force of the quotation from the "Odes" (see James Legge, tr., *The Chinese Classics*, IV, 176): "if you do not enjoy what you can now, other men will enjoy the possessions you discount." The second is that, given that temper and a man endowed with the authority to establish precedents, you cannot expect him to submit to conventional procedure (*li*).

Thus abruptly does our second-century court official, Chang Heng, bring us face to face with what is perhaps the most crucial problem of all monarchical forms of government.

Certainly it was so for the Han statesmen, engaged as they were in the first Chinese experiment in monarchy on the grand scale. From day to day, from year to year, and reign to reign, it was under the emperor's seal that precedent was created. That fact alone is enough to demonstrate that the issue of a constitution was up for consideration. And the fact that Chang Heng went straight to the issue of "*tso ku*" ("the making of precedent") demonstrates his awareness of the problem. We have already approached this question. Now we can observe it from the angle of what Chang Heng had to say about the last generations of Former Han. He makes an indictment, citing two episodes, one in Emperor Ch'eng's reign, the other in Emperor Ai's. Emperor Ch'eng overrode all opposition and made a slave girl empress, creating a new rank in the harem in order to do so, and then gave way to a passion for her sister, ending by promising her that "none should rise above her," a pledge he kept by murdering two sons of his body by other women who might have risen to be mother of the heir-apparent. (For the whole unsavoury story see Dubs, II, 369-372.) Emperor Ai raised his male paramour Tung Hsien to the most exalted status among his subjects, making him rich beyond any other noble. Not only so: according to the record (see *Han Shu*, ch. 93) at a feast Emperor Ai once said with a laugh to Tung Hsien that he might follow Sage-King Yao's example and make him co-ruler and successor, as Yao did with the saintly Shun.

This flagrant levity brought an instant protest and that, as Chang Heng notes, from a humble attendant. The record gives as his words: "The empire is the Founding Emperor's possession, not your Majesty's. It is of the highest importance that the Son of Heaven should not speak about his great heritage in jest." What Chang Heng does is to take the gist of that statement and use it as a springboard for his denunciation of the regime.

With regard to Chang Heng's final count against Former Han, we are forcibly recalled to the deep-lying materialistic vein of the supercilious nobleman. In profoundly cynical fashion he here enunciates the damning outcome of Han prosperity. True, Emperor Kao Tsu by his labors inaugurated a mighty kingdom. True, his immediate descendants built on his foundation and confirmed and extended his great heritage. But what followed? A temper of overweening arrogance, unbounded extravagance, and irresponsible pleasure-seeking in the capital and the court. The fertile soil was theirs, the capital was safe from attack, why should anyone worry? So runs the poem—up to a point—then it changes. The farther a stream flows, the harder it is to dam; the deeper a tree is rooted, the more difficult its uprooting. But these things do happen. "A fragrance which becomes more and more pungent ends in being nauseating." That is the poetic image, a superbly realistic one, not savagely satirical but imbued with tragic irony. The idea conveyed is of an inevitable doom, brought about not by gods or demons, but by the inner compulsion of events.

Chang Heng's reaction to the situation is the more significant because of what he saw with his own eyes in Later Han, for example, in Emperor An's reign (A.D. 107-125). The boy-emperor was put through the rigors of a strict moralistic education. As a young man he was thwarted by his all-powerful regent, Empress-Dowager Teng. After her death he was theoretically free to direct and rule. By then, however, the damage to his character was done, and this by the indulgence of the same kind of illicit impulses that Chang Heng describes here. Can it be doubted that the poet was here not thinking only of dead and gone emperors of the last regime?

14. *The Nobleman Makes His Bow*

The inexperienced reader may be led astray into thinking that the nobleman's disparaging words about himself either are not in keeping with his character, or are grossly hypocritical. Neither is true. His apparent self-abasement is noth-

ing more than the use of the current coin of polite intercourse. But these stilted phrases should be read carefully.
They show that in the interchange of debate formal homage
was paid to the majesty of truth; and that in this sense, that
a personal point of view was recognized as only too liable
to be prejudiced, one-sided, and so misleading. A debater
might, therefore, be supercilious and dogmatic, but he would,
if he remembered his manners, have to make some such formal apology as this here.

The illuminating remark is, of course, the one about hearsay, carrying as it does the implication that hearsay, compared with direct observation, is liable to be untrustworthy.
There is ample evidence that Chang Heng was not the only
scholar of his generation to be thus awake. Pan Piao had
come very near to raising the problem, if he had not actually
done so, by questioning the reliability of Ssŭ-ma Ch'ien's
"Record of History." Wang Ch'ung was writing his *Lun
Heng* and deriding the cock-and-bull stories that were so
widely believed. And the Ancient-Script scholars were protesting against the fabrications in the "Woof Books." The
interesting thing is that this attitude of doubt is in relation
to a period not more than three to one centuries back. We
have to face the related fact that when it came to the far-
back ages of antiquity both Chang Heng and Pan Ku, on
the evidence of their *fu*, had a considerable bump of credulity.
To all appearance they accepted the Sage-Kings as far back
as Fu Hsi, shrouded though he was in the mists of antiquity.
That being so, we must accept both states of consciousness
as having carried on alongside each other. In some ways we
should expect a critical mind to develop first with regard
to more recent hearsay. There were much more complicated
sets of information to be appraised, and they were not
shrouded to the same degree in the nimbus of traditional
religious belief. The historian bears in mind that in this age
the claims of the central government to settle problems of
belief were accepted in theory but not in practice. The thinkers

wanted to synthesize traditional and contemporary knowledge, old hearsay with new, but they could not agree on what *was* knowledge, what *was* proved fact. This kind of intellectual situation is familiar to historians of Greece and Rome, not to speak of mediaeval Christianity and the age in which Descartes subscribed his belief in the basic dogmas of the Church. The ability to think critically and empirically would seem to have been an uncertain growth, but that is no reason for minimizing the importance of its earlier phases.

To come back to the nobleman and his last words, the emotional links in his mind are delineated with a fine sense of logic that brings his far-back past very near to our modernity. First, there is his exclamation over the country's unparalleled wealth. Then, dyed-in-the-wool aristocrat that he is, he makes aristocracy's unconscious assumption that the main part of such wealth should be at its disposal. Finally, he bewails the fact that nowadays luxury, informed with elegance, is disallowed as not part of "the country's glory" among the nations. Then, with the inevitable gibe at these modern high-faluting principles of frugality, he winds up with a neat confession that naturally he would like to have the palmy days of the old regime back.

Surely one has to acclaim the brilliance of Chang Heng's power of characterization. To go beyond literary criticism to the sterner call of history, that remark about wanting what one cannot get and not wanting, not being satisfied with, what one has, is highly reminiscent of Hsün Ch'ing, the third-century B.C. philosopher who upheld ethical principles, but was deeply tinged with Legalism. He regarded human nature as insatiable in its desires: a man having reached his desired goal this year, next year pines for something more, and so on without end. Thus, he argued, the essence of government consisted in keeping people as far as possible contented in that state of society in which their lot was cast. This entailed not only an iron hand in the government but also education of the people to habits of thought and action which embodied for them at their level the ideals of artistry and perfection. From that he went on to the Son of Heaven at the top of the human scale, set apart from all lesser mortals, but also ennobled by an environment in which beauty and order are displayed at every turn. As a theory emphasizing the basic connection of art with ethics, this doctrine of Hsün Ch'ing's has its very great interest, and his influence can be traced through the Han era. Here, then, Chang Heng introduces the idea, not as a piece of philosophic theorizing but as a natural sentiment in the mouth of the nobleman. And the same lordly individual can cite the authority of the "Cricket's Song" to prove the laudability of his desire for luxury. But the "Cricket's Song," one of the *T'ang* Cycle of the "Odes," was a simple peasant ditty calling for one night's jollification in the midst of months of toil. Thus in one neat stroke Chang Heng pillories the cynicism that lurks behind the lordly viewpoint.

Chapter IX

CRITIQUE OF PAN KU'S
"*FU* ON THE EASTERN CAPITAL"

◇◇◇

1. *The Eastern Capital Host Jibes at the Western Capital Guest's Opinions*

FROM this point on, the author of the two *fu* is not making out a fictitious case but using the *persona* of the man from Loyang to state his own point of view. It would appear that the critic has a simple psychological situation to examine: in a word, the stooge having had his say, we now get the truth—at least the truth as Pan Ku saw it. As we proceed, however, we shall find that the situation is not quite so simple as it looks.

The statement about the effect of habitat and custom on a man's outlook has quite a modern dialectical ring to it. Nevertheless our first-century poet-historian was capable of it, and we know him well enough now not to be surprised at this. We may do well to remind ourselves that his family had for many generations been domiciled in the North-West, in the days before its leading members had obtained high office in the late Ch'ang-an court. Whether this increased the subtle range of Pan Ku's self-consciousness must remain doubtful, but in any case, here is a Loyang man twitting a Ch'ang-an man for being so provincially hidebound. The jibe is highly significant, for it is on the ground that the typical Ch'ang-an mentality has all along been tainted with the virus of the barbaric tyranny of Ch'in. That being so, the real *virtus* of "Great Han," the emergent significance of its words and deeds, is incomprehensible to a Ch'ang-an man. Now, if this sentiment had come from a second-rate, ill-informed mind, we might be warranted in discounting its significance. But it comes from Pan Ku, who had spent long years on the Loyang archives. We have the evidence of his

"History of the Former Han Dynasty" that he not only had very detailed knowledge of those two centuries but was well able to exercise his judgement in the matter.

Assuming the high evidential value of his statements, we find them remarkably illuminating. First, there is the opinion that only a Later Han man, free from Ch'ang-an obsessions, is enlightened enough to appreciate the true worth of "Great Han." That, as subsequent sections will show, means that the high moral significance of the Han Dynasty only came to full expression with Han Redivivus under Emperors Kuang Wu and Ming (i.e. A.D. 25-75). What the full importance of this is will emerge later; but at this point this much is clear, that any attempt to run the two epochs together, or even to equate the mentality of Former Han with that of Later Han, would have brought a protest from our author.

Second, having in his Ch'ang-an *fu* surreptitiously pilloried Former Han from Emperor Wu down, Pan Ku here shows a different attitude to the founder of the line, Kao Tsu. He has a profound respect for him, so much so that he sees him as having broken the mould of history, as having initiated a regime which was unparalleled in previous ages. At the same time he maintains that the Ch'in virus was predominant in Kao Tsu's situation. Hence "the policy perforce" to establish the capital in the Kuan Chung area, where it would be strategically safe, and to overawe contumacious elements by the magnificence of his headquarters. In other words, the founding Emperor, for all he had a commission from Heaven and fulfilled the wishes of the people, yet had no option but to set up a military autocracy. Lou Ching knew, he, the unknown exile who came out of the blue and so unaccountably was able to persuade the Emperor that Loyang would not do; and Chancellor Hsiao Ho, he also knew, and braved his master's anger for building the great Wei Yang Palace on the scale more or less of the Ch'in Emperor's barbarous O Pang. And Pan Ku's point is that having started as a legalist autoc-

racy, the Ch'ang-an government, for all its dazzling achievements, was never able to rid itself of the Ch'in virus. The
real answer can only be given in the light of Chang Heng's
Loyang *fu*.

Third, Kao Tsu's uniqueness consisted in part in the fact
that he was a plebeian. According to Pan Ku there never
had been before such a phenomenon as a plebeian ascending
the throne. An odd statement this for two reasons. One is
that in the versified eulogy of Emperor Kao Tsu in the "History of the Former Han Dynasty" his family is represented
(more or less convincingly) as tracing its descent back to the
Sage-King Yao and having in Ch'u times become "Lord
[*kung*] of Feng."[1] The other is that according to the *Yao Tien*
of the "History" Scripture (*Shu Ching*) and *Mencius*, Sage-
King Shun started life as a plebeian. Since it is impossible
to assume that Pan Ku was ignorant of that eulogy, the high
probability is that here in the poem he states the plain un-
varnished truth (cf. Dubs, *History of the Former Han Dynasty*, I, 13-15). Likewise, it is impossible to assume that Pan
Ku was unacquainted with the *Yao Tien* and *Mencius*. On
the other hand, in the "Record of History" (*Shih Chi*, ch. 13,
init.) Shun appears as a descendant of the Yellow Emperor
and so as a distant relative of Yao; so that Pan Ku may have
had that version of the story in mind and, since Shun was a
sage-king, have accepted it. On the two counts what emerges

---

[1] This is apparently a reference to Emperor Kao's father, but no state-
ment is made as to who raised him to this rank. In the *Ti Chi* (see Dubs,
History of the Former Dynasty, I, 40) the emperor-to-be becomes *kung* of
P'ei by fiat of the more or less bogus King of Ch'u. Pan Ku's eulogy on
Emperor Kao Tsu, on the other hand, is very studied in relation to the
Emperor's ancestors, conveying the impression that the author, presumably
Pan Piao, was not prepared to vouch for the truth of Fan Hsien-tzŭ's
assertion about the family's aristocratic lineage (Dubs, *op.cit.*, I, 147). In
the "Record of History" (ch. 8, fin.) a meeting of ministers refers to the
just-dead Emperor Kao as being of "humble origin." As to the story of
his miraculous conception either under the physical or psychological influence of a dragon (*Han Shu*, ch. I, init.), may we not say that there
the official propaganda was in the records, and Pan Ku's business was to
transcribe it, whether he believed it or not? I come more and more to suspect that he did not really credit such stories.

to view is that in that highly class-conscious society of Han, both sage-kings and founding emperors had by hook or by crook to achieve noble lineage: a familiar phenomenon, of course, in other parts of the world. Further, Pan Ku's age was quite conversant with the spectacle of descendants of kings falling after five generations into the plebeian class. Emperor Kuang Wu was a notable example.

Fourth, what are we to make of that remark about the Scriptures and sages? As an opinion it stands to reason, as any modern can see at once: if Kao Tsu inaugurated an un-precedented kind of era, then what he did was outside the cognizance of the Scriptures and sages. On the other hand, Pan Ku belonged to the first century, not the twentieth, and, in terms of what the prevalent school of thought in his day maintained, all dynastic history, past, present, and to come, followed an ineluctable pattern. Along that line of reasoning Han was just one link in the chain of causation which the Scriptures expounded and the sages foreshadowed. So then, as Pan Ku's mind formed this statement, it was functioning outside the bounds of current belief, and he was not afraid to show this. On both counts we get a side-light on that age, one in which new ideas had come to vigorous birth, and the Former Han type of teacher had to fight hard to retain his prestige at court. Pan Ku, unsure as he was of his future, could yet afford to write in this bold way—although, when Emperor Chang called on him to summarize those conserva-tive conclusions of the White Tiger Hall Conference, he could not afford to refuse.

2. *Wang Mang's Usurpation and the Salvation of the Country*

The prosody in this section is irregular, the sentences not always running in strict pairs, and rhyme very noticeably absent at certain points. The argument is perfectly clear and moves forward by three main stages in well-marked para-graphs. The paragraphs deal with (1) the Wang Mang usur-

pation and the reaction to it of *Shang Ti* (the Supreme Lord);
(2) Kuang Wu to the rescue; and (3) the moral beauty of
the regime which he established.

There is, on the surface at any rate, no cool appraisal in
Pan Ku's attitude to Wang Mang. He condemns him utterly.
In fact the sheer hyperbole of his indictment stirs the suspicion that his words represent no more than the conventional
court attitude of his day. This may disappoint those who are
familiar with Dr. Hu Shih's and Dr. H.O.H. Stange's efforts to interpret Wang Mang favorably, their contention
being that he made a serious attempt to put Confucius' teaching into effect and was defeated by the upper classes' violent
opposition to the infringement of their privileges.[2] A detailed
examination of the Wang Mang regime is beyond the scope
of this critique, but, assuming some measure of truth in this
contention, Pan Ku's evidence is worth consideration. He in-
dicted Wang Mang on the ground that his rule produced
the most ghastly consequences throughout society. In effect
the non-privileged classes suffered disaster equally with the
privileged classes. As Pan Ku's appraisal of Wang Mang's
life puts it (see *Han Shu*, ch. 99C), "within the four seas
there was the din of wailing, men lost the heart to rejoice
in being alive." In justice to Pan Ku it must be recognized
that to upset the equilibrium between the classes was just
as opposed to Confucius' ways of thinking as neglect of the
common man's welfare. There can be little doubt but that
Wang Mang's economic policy was reckless in this as in certain other respects.

Moreover, Pan Ku's indictment contains the word "usurpation," that is infraction of the principle of monarchic legitimacy. It is very difficult for us to estimate the exact force
of this word on a mid-Han man's lips. We are so familiar
with the cycle of the sage-king dynasties as also with the fact

[2] Hu Shih, "Wang Mang, the Socialist Emperor of Nineteen Centuries
Ago," *Journal of the North China Branch of the Royal Asiatic Society*, LIX
(1928), 218-230, and Hans O. H. Stange, *Die Monographie über Wang
Mang*, Abhandlungen für die Kunde des Morgenlandes, Leipzig, 1938.

that "Great Han" eventually did go down, irrevocably, to be followed by other dynasties, each claiming a mandate from Heaven. We tend, therefore, to forget that for Pan Ku, being ignorant of later history, Han *was* unique, with its incomparable *virtus* destined to exist "for a myriad generations." Nor can the historian afford to ignore the possibility—or should I say probability?—that the theologizing imagination of courtier scholars dealt freely with the old myths and legends of far-back heroes with the very intent of substantiating the legitimacy of the Han throne. Compare, for example, Emperor Wu's faithful servants Ssŭ-ma T'an and Ssŭ-ma Ch'ien in the earlier chapters of their "Record of History." There is this also to be borne in mind: a semi-tribal feudal order, as the Chou was, inevitably entailed divided loyalties; its history demonstrated this by a grim logic of events. But the Han monarchy, for all its semi-feudal structure, called with ever increasing force for a supra-regional loyalty to "the One Man." Thus an unprecedented importance came to be attached to the principle of legitimate succession—as Kuang Wu's propaganda shows without a shadow of doubt and, the great tradition of ancestor worship being there to be utilized, usurpation became an unconscionably wicked crime, a dire offence against gods and men.

The third paragraph is as hyperbolic in its encomium of the Kuang Wu regime as the second paragraph is in its denunciation of Wang Mang. The picture is significant for the very reason that it is so whole-heartedly tendentious. The facts are that Kuang Wu had first to give way to a more influential candidate, the Prince of Huai-yang, and after his death had for long years to fight hard for the throne he claimed on that "First Day" (A.D. 25). The situation necessitated not only hard fighting but equally vigorous propaganda, and one of Kuang Wu's first acts was to appoint a group of fourteen Erudites. On grounds of local support his headquarters needed to be south of the Yellow River in a central location, so that Loyang was a natural choice; and, that being fixed, the Erudites could boost its *virtus* as the true capital. Loyang was associated with Duke Chou, the saintly sage of Confucius' adoration, so the propaganda had a rich field in which to spread itself. By what stages those Erudites developed the required mythological halo to their master's person is not clear from the records; and, since Pan Ku was writing twenty to thirty years after Kuang Wu's death and canonization, we cannot assume that the paean of praise here reflects the early propaganda.

Certain ascriptions in this paean stand out as highly significant. First in importance is the repeated emphasis on Kuang Wu as the embodiment of consummate sageness. Claims are made here which surpass in magnitude anything ever claimed for the emperors of the Former Han dynasty. Thus Kuang Wu's merits and labors are represented as going beyond those of anyone of the sage-kings, and this view is clinched by examining various features of his career and personality in the light of recent as well as ancient history. Thus Kao Tsu and his son, Emperor Wen, and the megalomaniac Emperor Wu come into the picture on the same footing as the three sage-kings mentioned. To the modern reader familiar with the nimbus of semi-divinity attached in the Scriptures to the sage-kings, this freedom of comparison may appear extraordinary; but it is on a par with what is said about Kao Tsu and the Scriptures in Section 1. One thing is clear: if the Former Han dynasty started moving in a theocratic direction, then the Later Han dynasty showed a definitely more marked tendency in that direction. As for comparison with contemporary Rome and its emperor worship, it is clear that Kuang Wu's formal apotheosis did not take place till after his death.

Second, there is the striking phrase "Heaven and Earth were in revolution" (*kê ming*): striking because of its apparent re-emphasis on theistic action. Again a theologically minded reader needs to beware of pitfalls. *Kê ming* occurs in the "Changes" Scripture, the scripture which in its appended "wings" embodies a strongly naturalistic attitude to events. The passage comes in the *Tuan* ("Definitive Judgements") under the 49th Hexagram, the name of which was *Kê*. Of the six illustrative definitions given there one reads as follows: "Heaven and Earth *kê* [produce great changes] and the four seasons are completed." It is followed by T'ang and Wu *kê ming* [wrought revolution] obeying Heaven and fulfilling [the wishes of] men." Pan Ku in his argument also refers to T'ang and Wu, but as enacting Heaven's punishments. Clearly the "Changes" passage was running in his head as he wrote, and he felt free to adapt the ideological formulae to suit the rhythm of his thought.

Third, this paragraph on consummate kingliness has another link with the "Changes," namely the remarks about the Yellow Emperor as inventor of regional divisions, market days, boats and carriages, implements and weapons. We turn at once to the famous passage in the *Hsi Tz'ŭ* ("Appended Judgements") of the "Changes." Comparison with that passage reveals that there is no mention there of any sage inventing "regional divisions," that Shen Nung is the inventor of market days, and that Yao and Shun are associated with the Yellow Emperor as responsible for the other inventions. What happened to Pan Ku, then, in this connection? Was his recollection of the passage inaccurate (there are numerous instances of such inaccuracy in later classical and postclassical literature), or did he in summarizing the passage feel free to treat the Scripture passage in this fashion? On the evidence of these two sections of his *fu*, the latter alternative is more likely, and we have another straw in the wind showing that he set a little light to sacred myth and legend. After all, he was a litterateur and not an erudite, and evidence has yet to appear that he belonged to any contemporary school of dogmatic thought.

The next stage in the argument is couched in terms of a profound moral renovation, all the basic relationships except that of friendship) re-created on a higher level of efficacy.

In fact the language about the relation of sovereign and subject seems to indicate that Kuang Wu had built it up for the first time in history. This, however, cannot be Pan Ku's strict view-point, since he claims Fu Hsi as the originator of the idea of basic human ties.

3. *The Emperor Ming's Achievements*

The narrative is extraordinarily condensed, passing quickly from a few couplets on Emperor Ming's initial procedure to his first royal progress, and from that to the enlarging and beautifying of the new capital. Every word, therefore, is significant. Take, for example, the six words *"sheng San Yung chih shang i"* ("developing the lofty procedure of the San Yung," i.e. the Ming T'ang, Ling T'ai, and Pi Yung): they refer to most spectacular innovations of the new regime (see Critique of Section 9 and Chang Heng's detailed treatment). So also with the royal progress, the term "the myriad states" shows that Pan Ku had the remoter districts of the empire in mind as well as the old central states. So also with the building of Loyang, a vast and complicated undertaking: in contrast to the description of the building of Ch'ang-an it occupies only six couplets. Yet in that space Pan Ku strikes a new note in constructional art: the extravagant, the rococo are superseded by symmetry and restraint. So also with the laying out of the park: only three couplets are devoted to it, but stress is laid on its moderate size and the comfort and safety of its denizens.

When all this is added up, checked over with the "History of the Later Han Dynasty," and viewed in the light of the claim that Emperor Ming's reign doubled the splendour of Kuang Wu's achievement, Pan Ku's aim becomes clear. The material glories of the old capital to which he had devoted pages and pages of vivid description in his Ch'ang-an *fu* should be taken as "trifling accomplishments." The new capital in contrast, dignified though it was in appearance, represented a fundamentally different achievement, a spiritual one which brings man at last into right relations with man. This, achieved in the first instance by Kuang Wu on the scale of the central states, is now accomplished by his filial son on the wider scale of world empire. Admitting that the earlier regime brought an amazing development of material civilization, this is nothing in comparison with the moral civilization which the new regime now offers to all mankind.

The temptation is to regard all this as mere court flattery, rather ominous flattery in view of the later terrible decline in governmental morale. Some presage of that decline appears in Chang Heng's *fu* written some twenty to thirty years later. Yet it is well to reiterate that in Pan Ku's day no one could know that that was to come, whilst, on the other hand, peace and prosperity were there on a very wide scale. The real point is, then, whether Pan Ku had good ground for honest enthusiasm over the court he knew. To this angle of enquiry there can be only one answer, namely, that he had adequate ground, and the more so since he saw with such clarity of vision how in the Han era his China had moved on to an unprecedented level of civilized living. To judge by his biography he wrote his *fu* in Emperor Chang's reign, at a time when the principle of the new era had not yet become tarnished. It was still the springtime of Han Redivivus, comparable to what Gilbert Murray has envisaged as happening in the history of ancient Greece, after the Armada and York Town: "exhilaration in the air, a sense of walking in new paths, of dawning hopes and untried possibilities."[3]

4. *The Imperial Hunting Preserve and the Seasonal Hunts*

In his "*Fu* on the Western Capital" Pan Ku used thirty-four couplets in describing the Ch'ang-an imperial preserve, and even more in describing the hunt itself. Here the account of the park and the hunt is complete in thirty-odd

---

[3] *The Legacy of Greece*, Oxford, 1921, p. 13.

couplets. The same poetic power is found at work, producing a vivid picture, sensational in some respects, but completely nonsensational in regard to the actual killing. This can only be taken as deliberate on Pan Ku's part, as also his emphasis on the hunt as a military pageant with large detachments of horse and foot moving to station according to schedule. So with the driving of the game and the marksmanship; it was so expert that not a bird or beast had a chance to escape, yet beyond a certain quota they were allowed to live. In a word, what we are given is a picture of drastic reform, of the blood-lust controlled through the Emperor's direct teaching.

As we digest this section, Pan Ku's objective becomes clear. It is to portray a court that has effectively broken with its semi-barbarous past, which is now truly civilized: in its recognition of fundamental human relations, its conduct of solemn sacrifice, its refinement of the arts, its stately but restrained architecture, even in its hunts which so easily could become brutal orgies. And the guiding principle of it all is *li*, ritual, propriety, courtesy, the right observance, the right action done in the right spirit in the right way: *li* with its characteristic virtues of *ching* (reverence), *chieh* (moderation, restraint), and *jang* (magnanimous concession of other people's rights).

This is not to suggest that before this age religious and social ritual were not much in everybody's mind. That, of course, would be absurd. From the days of the "Odes" down to the last generations of the Former Han dynasty when the ritual experts began to study the philosophy underlying *li*, the evidence is as bulky as it is incontestable. What is meant is that if we take Pan Ku at his face value, the Loyang court envisaged the principle of *li* more clearly than any previous court had done. Kuang Wu's Heaven-given mandate was held to be based not only on his Han descent, but also on his fidelity to all the moral implications of *li*. These went further than strict observance of time-honored rites. *Li* was taken to be a passion-subduing, soul-releasing way of life. It was directly associated with the Heaven-ordained "Five Ties," and being so it was held to operate on the plebeian as on the patrician level. As our study of this *fu,* and comparison of it with Chang Heng's proceeds, these and other aspects of the Later Han *"li chiao"* (the principle and dogma of *li*) will come into clearer relief.

It may seem to some readers that this emphasis on *li* is in direct contradiction to what has been said about an exhilaration in the air, a walking in new paths. But there is no real ground for the idea so often met with in quite learned circles, that under the influence of Confucius the Chinese people gave themselves to the worship of the great god Propriety, so much so that they became ultra-conservative and incidentally acquired abnormal powers of hypocritical pretence. As comparative sociologists know so well, all societies, whether retarded or otherwise cannot continue to flourish without a hard core of religiously sanctioned observance penetrating into every department of their life. Not only so: as public opinion reacts to the pressure of events, custom changes; but the chances are that it does so under the façade of propriety. Thus the term *"li"* in these *fu* conceals the introduction of innovations as well as the maintenance of traditions.

Two references in this section call for comment. One is the citation of the *Wang Chih* ("Royal Regulations," a chapter in the "Book of Rites") and the "Odes." The four hunting songs specified disclose no more than a far-sighted attitude to the preservation of game. The same attitude appears in the "Royal Regulations," but a new note is struck, that of humane consideration for birds and beasts.

The other reference is that to "a thousand chariots and ten-thousand horsemen." In the constant fighting with Huns and other nomads, the Han statesmen had to learn the lesson that trained bodies of mounted archers could by their speed and mobility of manoeuvre break up solid phalanxes of foot-soldiers reinforced by groups of war chariots. The lesson was learnt, and here we see large bodies of cavalry being trained in precision of attack.

5. *All Nations Turn to Loyang*

The speed with which in terse three-word sentences Pan Ku races through these all-important state functions is at first immensely surprising. Had he nothing more to say on the Ming T'ang, Pi Yung and Ling T'ai? In fact he had, but he put it into lyrical poems at the end of this *fu*, so the questions arising in this connection will be dealt with there. The purpose of this omission of all but the barest essentials is clear. The poet-author would have nothing to distract attention from his central object of contemplation, the *virtus*, the Sacred Person, the Son of Heaven exercising his sublime influence impartially throughout China and the whole world.

The high enthusiasm of the passage is unmistakable. Pan Ku might well feel enthusiastic. In A.D. 59 there had been a small-scale durbar; in A.D. 69 Ai Lao, in the far South-West had voluntarily submitted and been made a commandery. The empire, so sadly diminished during the interregnum, was steadily being restored, by punitive, it must be confessed, as well as peaceful, measures. Hence the almost mystical fervor of the phrasing, with the climax "no one on land or water but breathless and trembling comes running to pay homage." As a matter of cold fact Emperor Ming despatched several punitive expeditions during his reign.

Two problems of general history call for notice. One is "Chinese universalism," a bemusing term in its very various contexts. It comes to view in the opening couplets, for they throw into clearer relief the sacrificial function of the throne. It is a function operating not only for the Chinese nation but for all peoples: the Son of Heaven is in principle high priest for all nations, for Heaven is one and the earth is one, and Heaven's regent activates this oneness by his mediatory sacrifices and his calculations in his observatory. The question is, whether this is not in fact the first time in the Chinese history of ideas for this universalist principle to be found clearly superimposed on traditional beliefs. This question is much too big and complicated for any sort of answer to be attempted here, but two sets of evidence may be adduced by way of clarifying the issue.

(1) The Yin-Yang theorists were at work all through Former Han times, and their cosmological rationalizing had its effect on scholars of the main tradition. One result was in the field of the "Changes" scholarship, and there was the production of that section of the "Appended Judgements" in which Fu Hsi, first of the sage-kings and reputed as the inventor of the Eight Trigrams, was represented as discovering the essential relations of all phenomena above and below. By his discovery he was able to give true direction to human affairs. It was to this passage that Pan Ku's mind turned as he thought of his emperor's unique position in the world. He made the tremendous claim that the Son of Heaven here and now, not only is able to do the same, but actually is doing so. Ideologically speaking, this was a movement of the mind going well beyond any such claim for a mysterious sage-emperor shrouded in the mists of antiquity. As we saw in Sections 1 and 2, Pan Ku claimed complete sageness, more than any one sage-king had achieved, for Emperors Kuang Wu and Ming.

(2) The recorded acts of Emperor Wu show that he travelled widely, going out to the frontiers of his empire, and that he sacrificed there to the local gods and gave orders for these sacrifices to be continued. He claimed that the gods concerned responded to his offerings. This would seem to be a first stage, leading to a syncretizing period in which foreign deities might be adopted into the Chinese pantheon. Modern scholarship tends to substantiate such a movement in Han times and evidence pointing in this direction is to be found in Yang Hsiung's *Kan Ch'üan Fu* and Chang Heng's *Ssǔ Hsüan Fu*. Also Pan Ku's special reference in this sec-

tion to the hundred *ling* (deities) points to his having had foreign gods in mind. But his enthusiastic idealism here carries him well beyond the mere recognition of such practices, and that dictated by political expediency. He envisages a world society brought into existence by a world savior, acting as priest at the hub of the universe. Again we are reminded of Virgil and his Caesar Augustus—to the myth-making impulse (if it may rightly so be called) which comes to poets stirred by the opening of new horizons.

The other general problem is that in connection with the dividing line between religion and politics. Quite clearly in Pan Ku's mind there was no dividing line: religion and politics were one. And yet they were not so in the crass unconscious way that they are to the tribesman in a "closed society," as Bergson put it. On the contrary Pan Ku was vitally aware of an "open society" of the world.

With regard to the durbar, Pan Ku's phrasing recalls the Chou feudal procedure, in which attendance of the feudatories at court was required on the first day of a new king's opening year—actually Emperor Ming's durbar was held at the beginning of his second year. We find the world outlook again emphasized in striking fashion, for not only tribute but also statistical tables and reports are represented as forthcoming from "all within the four seas." As the five chapters on the barbarians show in the "History of the Later Han Dynasty," there was in the mid-Han centuries an increasing practice of sending such reports prepared by resident officers in the outlying regions. Once a barbarian kingdom became a commandery, statistical tables were prepared with a view to taxation.

The official record of the durbar in 59 is not lacking in detail, for example, that the barbarian kings assisted in the sacrifice to Heaven and Earth, a detail which Pan Ku omits. We are, however, indebted to him for the information in the vivid picture painted here: the formal reception of the Emperor's guests, the tents prepared for them in one of the palace-enclosure courts, the rows of court-officers in attendance, the coaching of the strangers in court etiquette. The account reads like that of an eye-witness, and, as we know, Pan Ku was attached to the court at that time. As to the feast held in the courtyard, emphasis is laid on it being on a grand scale, but there is no actual statement that Emperor Ming himself was present. The reference to his "conviviality" (*huan chieh*) points to him having graced the occasion. But then why is it that "at the sound of a bell the officers retire" and no reference is made to the Emperor retiring? Perhaps he was not actually present, and his conviviality comes into the picture as part of that mystic influence that is so stressed in this section. In any case here in the feast is an instance of that eudaemonistic strain which in Chinese classical thought goes hand in hand with high political mysticism. As to why arrangements should have been made for the officers to retire, Pan Ku is silent. Presumably, since some of the tribes were known to be heavy drinkers, it was to show that there was no further need for the feasters to stand on ceremony.

The picture is consistent right down to the music and dancing at the feast: barbarian musicians and actors providing their part of the entertainment as well as the court professionals. That the imperial *virtus* inspired the strangers' performance may be regarded as dubious historically; it would seem to be a mere poet's conceit. As a matter of fact, it is exactly in harmony with Pan Ku's line of idealization in this section: it puts a logical crown to it. The interesting thing, however, is that the same idea occurs in the *Po Hu T'ung* (see Tjan, *op.cit.*, p. 396) and with the use of the same terms *tê* (*virtus*) and *kuang* (wide-extending). So, unless Pan Ku, chief author of the *Po Hu T'ung*, is to be accused of slipping his own ideas into that report, the "poet's conceit" was what the majority of the A.D. 79 conference thought about the matter. One of the alternative titles to the book is *Po Hu T'ung Tê Lun* ("White Tiger Discussion on Widely-circulating *Virtus*").

It is worth comparing two outlooks, Pan Ku's here and that of the "Music Record" (*Yüeh Chi*) of the "Record of Rites." In the latter the purview is of one state and nation *vis-à-vis* Heaven and Earth. In our poem here music and dancing are something common to all peoples, a potential force for creating concord among nations, not merely between discordant elements in one community. As Paul Hindemith has said, "People who make music together cannot be enemies, at least not while the music lasts."[4]

6. *The Joyful State of Sober Simplicity and Earnest Endeavour, with Schools Everywhere*

Noticing that reiterated emphasis on "sageness" (or should it be "sanctity") in the man on the throne, and the universal feeling of delight which accompanies its untrammeled exercise, we are prepared for the idealistic picture the author's imagination created. What he presents is a utopian society with its officials all under clear direction from above and themselves models of public and private frugality, with the Emperor and his court turning their backs on luxury. He seems a little naïve here, for his purview is "within the four seas": as he knew well enough, great areas of the western and north-western empire were not suited to agriculture. However, that was not so in vast stretches of the southern empire.

The picture is by no means wholly idealized. Thus, although the "Acts of the Emperors" (*Pen Chi*) do not record any very spectacular series of edicts on frugality, yet various items crop up there and elsewhere which show that Emperors Kuang Wu and Ming had the matter well in hand. For instance, with regard to extravagance over funerals, in Kuang Wu's 7th and 10th year he forbade excessive expenditure in this way, and Ming in his 12th year reiterated the command. Going further afield, we find at the end of the two chapters on Carriages and Robes in the "History of the

---

[4] *A Composer's World*, Harvard University Press, 1952, p. 218.

Later Han Dynasty" a reference to prohibition of extravagance. In the introduction to the lives of the emperors, Kuang Wu is stated to have "cut out elaboration and studied simplicity." In contrast to the "three thousand occupants and fourteen grades" in the harem after Emperor Yüan's time, he had only three grades, the Empress and two ranks of concubines of good character. Emperor Ming is stated to have followed his father's example. In Emperor Chang's time, however, came a gradual decline in the morale of the harem. As for sumptuary regulations, the biographies of Kuang Wu's eleven sons (*Hou Han Shu*, ch. 72) clearly indicate that state officials could and did take action against princely offenders, whilst Prince Ts'ang did notable work as a watchdog, even remonstrating with his half-brother, Emperor Ming, for entertaining the princes too lavishly.

As for the lower orders and the officials whose standard of honor and efficiency made so much difference to their lives, the general impression, gained from the Acts of the two emperors and the introduction of the "Biographies of Upright Officials," is that with the establishment of peace the country quickly recovered; also that the duties of the various types of officials were pretty clearly marked, and they themselves had every inducement to work for popular confidence. In a word, the new broom swept cleanly enough. Adding all these corroborations together, the safe conclusion may be drawn that Pan Ku had some solid basis of fact to his lyrical outburst. To this may be added the quite likely assumption that, writing as he did in Emperor Chang's reign, he had seen signs of an increase in luxurious living and aimed at probing the imperial conscience. This could most forcibly and adroitly be done by painting a picture of the ideal.

What then about these moral ideals with the tale of which a Loyang man could override the upholder of old Ch'ang-an? The first thing to be noticed is that they are generally not so much Confucian as Taoist, and in the first instance not so much Taoist as Mohist. The devotees of the

Tao never advocated hard work as the scholars and the Mohists did, and, for that matter, the Legalists; whilst the main bulk of the scholars had no cult of austerity even for the common people. The surprising thing is that Pan Ku's mind went straight from Mohistic emphasis to the extreme Taoistic "*hsing shen chi mo*" ("body and soul untrammeled": Margouliès, "*concentrés en eux mêmes*"), and from that to the aristocratic scholar's metaphor of "sheen of jade and ring of gold." The passage as a whole is a perfect amalgam of the three schools, as such deserving the closest study; and this the more because later more dogma-entrenched ages took Mohism to have been dead by this time and Taoism basically incompatible with Confucianism.

The obvious conclusion is that what may be true of later ages is not necessarily true of the '90's in Later-Han China. Rather, in that lively and optimistic age active minds were definitely stimulated by all these heterogeneous, doctrinal influences. As with the vast stretches of empire, both actual and possible now revealed, so with Chuang Chou's playing with a space-time infinity and his exquisite correlation of the individual with that infinity, these reflections were exciting intellectual experiences. Pan Ku shows us this here, and Chang Heng shows it in his *Ssŭ Hsüan Fu* when, having made his imaginary flight round the world and beyond into infinite space, he alighted in his ancestral village and found he could compose the quarrels of orthodoxy and Taoism and Mohism. Compare also the critique to the Mohist section of Liu Hsin's "Catalogue." The entertainment of veterans is there directly attributed to Mohist influence.

The importance of the philosophy of education presented in this section lies in two directions. One is that although we hear nothing of Hsün Tzŭ during the early Han reigns, when we come to the exaltation of the scholar official by Emperor Wu and his successors, Hsün Tzŭ's teachings on ritual appear suddenly to have been found full of significance. In the "Record of Rites" his writings are to be found quoted at length (although always anonymously). The natural inference is that serious-minded provincial officials found that here was a potent force for "renovating the people" in their charge. The other direction is in relation to Pan Ku's generation and his own marked adhesion to Hsün Tzŭ's principles. The *Po Hu T'ung* (see Tjan, *op.cit.*, pp. 48-68) delivers judgement on schools in the provinces in the same vein. So the old guard of the Modern-Script party were in agreement on this score. As for Pan Ku, he saw this as the main lever for bringing the whole world of the barbarian peoples into civilized unity of life. Now let us examine what he actually says.

Having explored the effect of imperial example on character, Pan Ku's mind turned naturally enough to formal education. Here again his sentiments are surprising. First, he has nothing to say on the fruits of high scholastic training, nothing on the benefits of scripture knowledge: that is left to the next section of the poem, and there he is highly critical of the results. Here his admiration is confined to the fruits of village education. Second, his "forest of schools" as applied to all "within the four seas" is a gross exaggeration, though not without some substance. Wherever settled government came to prevail, there schools were set up by the regional officials without delay. It paid them to do so.

There is a striking correspondence between the spirit of this passage and the teachings of Hsün Tzŭ—that intelligent psychologist of the third century B.C. about whom later ages have had such doubts as to whether he may be counted a true Confucianist. Hsün Tzŭ, having discerned in human nature an unslakable appetite for grabbing, urged the necessity for not only a stern government penalizing offenders against the common weal, but also the building up of an acquired self, one in which habits of mutual consideration came into effective action. The means to this end were family and community rituals including songs and dances.[5] The sociologist has but to contemplate the daily, monthly, yearly repetition of such emotive, indeed poetic, formulas of speech and action to realize at once their tremendous social potentialities.

School buildings are the setting to the picture, buildings devoted to education, in the government centres and also in the subsidiary village centres. In these buildings gatherings took place not only of teachers and scholars as such but also of plain folk, high and low, rich and poor, young and old, and this anywhere in the empire. The occasion is not specified, but the reference to ritual implements suggests some traditional fertility rites to be performed; and the implements "being in full supply" might well indicate the help of Chinese officials directed to making the rite more impressive, more orderly, and incidentally more Chinese. While the dancing still embodied the old animistic mana, Pan Ku's "singing the songs of *jen*" tells a different tale. A communal feast follows at which mutual deference is the ruling spirit. This is portrayed by a masterly image, "*teng chiang yao yen chih li*," literally, "the feast formalities of [backs] going up and down." One wonders whether Pan Ku and his courtly readers smiled as they envisaged the peasants and their clumsy bows, their mouths full of concord—and their gusty sighs. The *virtus* would be the theme of high converse, the *virtus* which inspires hard work and courteous cooperation, and so brings peace and plenty.

It all sounds like a rhapsodical dream, unrelated to real life. Yet in this greater Han era something happened in that vast area east of the Himalayas. When Han collapsed and the *virtus* myth seemed exploded for all time, that something proved tenacious of life through long centuries of upheaval and barbarian invasion, and eventually the empire came together again. The foundations of Sinicization had been well

---

[5] Cf. Fung Yu-lan, *A History of Chinese Philosophy*, tr. D. Bodde, Princeton University Press, 1952-53, I, 12, especially par. 7.

and truly laid at peasant level, old mores impregnated with a more civilized ethos. In Section 5 the critic has urged that the term "Han Confucianism" is a kaleidoscopic term, and opaque at that. However true that is, the "something" we descry at work was linked with that mysterious figure of the sixth century B.C., Confucius of Lu, over whose message the mid-Han scholars quarreled so violently. In the *Analects*, in that highly hagiographical section, the Tenth Book,[6] there is this revealed: "When the villagers drank wine, the Master withdrew only after the aged withdrew, and when the villagers did their rite against pestilence, he put on his court robes and stood to attention."

7. *The Eastern Host's Final Argument*

Here is the final demolition of the Western Guest's case. The prosody gives a hammering effect to the subject matter, most of the clauses being of four-word length. Of the eight indictments made, most are summarizations of what has been argued earlier in the *fu*, and the critique need not restress them here. This, however, does not apply to the first indictment to which this section gives a very intriguing, indeed surprising, setting. There is also a curious quirk to the statement about the River Chart and Script, whilst Pan Ku's theory of knowledge, here stated with additional precision, requires scrutiny.

As the host at the beginning of the *fu* accused his guest of superficiality of knowledge, so here also; but this time he couples him with those "who nowadays engage in discussion." It is difficult at first to see why Pan Ku drags them in, for his Ch'ang-an *fu* consisted throughout of an appeal to facts. However, the connection in Pan Ku's mind is clear from his remark about the guests being "vainly carried away by non-essentials." The fault in both cases is that they have their heads buried in books, so that they have no eye for

---

[6] Assumed by some critics to be a later strain in the traditions about Confucius.

essential facts, cannot make vital comparisons between the past and the present, cannot trace the real reason why the Han *virtus* has come to be what it now is. The accusation is not that knowledge of the Scriptures is a bad thing, but that absorption in that one kind of knowledge leads to the mind being bemused with trifles—an accusation to which certain remarks in the Christian Gospels about "tithing mint and cummin" lends point in the Western mind. Fortunately we have right-to-hand a document which highlights this accusation. It is the *Po Hu T'ung*. Of the three hundred and twelve subjects dealt with there a very large proportion reveals the meticulous mind at work on trifles, whilst at every point proof is advanced in the shape of scripture citation. We may surmise that the making of this digest of the Conference's conclusions left Pan Ku with a feeling of irritation, so that when he wrote this passage in the *fu* his temper got the better of him.

However we may explain this blunt attack on the scripture-mongers of the age, it is highly revealing in more ways than one. In the first place, the net result of Sinological studies on Han is that once the Scholars got into the saddle, they showed a markedly authoritarian temper of mind: everyone had to subscribe to belief in the sacred Scriptures. Although Pan Ku's outbreak substantiates the idea to a considerable extent, yet the intellectual situation was far from being monolithic. As we have already seen, it was a vastly contentious age with innumerable different recensions to the texts of the Scriptures, and every famous teacher fighting for recognition of his particular brand of orthodoxy. True, the Emperor was the "Defender of the Faith," and the faith was the defender of him, and this naturally induced a dogma-loving frame of mind; but it did not follow that the palace and the Pi Yung (where the Erudites were) saw eye to eye over the question of what dogmas should prevail.

It is here that Pan Ku's outbreak stimulates the right questions. Consider his personal situation. With his "History of the Former Han Dynasty" practically finished he was anxious to get an administrative post, to get his foot on the first rung and so qualify for a high position in the official hierarchy. Is it likely that he would wreck his chances by saying things which he knew would cause odium in high places? Moreover, we know that his two *fu* poems received enthusiastic acclamation at court. That being so, we look for light on Emperor Chang and his intimates. The historians are agreed that he was not a notably masterful person, but that he was intelligent, with an enlightened interest in the more liberal views about the Scriptures. Why he felt compelled to give way to the conservative forces in the White Tiger Conference is not clear. What is clear is that he had a great affection and respect for his gentleman-in-waiting, Chia K'uei. Now, as his biography shows, Chia K'uei had worked with Pan Ku in the archives at the palace, and was a staunch, although not extreme, member of the Ancient-Script party. Also this party, weak as it was in Scholar circles and hated by the Erudites as a body, yet from Kuang Wu's reign on had influence in the palace (see *Hou Han Shu*, ch. 66, in which is given the biographies of the party's outstanding members). We find one Ch'eng Yüan in a memorial to Kuang Wu expressing much the same sentiments about myopic scholarship as Pan Ku does. Since there can be no doubt but that Emperor Chang's sympathies lay with this party, we have a clue to the problem which the poem's blunt denunciation constitutes. We are also encouraged in the belief that the Later Han court was not so hide-bound as has generally been supposed.

Turning to the River Diagram (*Ho T'u*) and Lo River Script (*Lo Shu*), we find this enlightened author of ours stressing not only the natural advantages of the Loyang site but also its cabalistic virtues. That his words come through the lips of a poetically conceived Loyang host is not evidence that his creator either had or had not any doubts about the historicity of the two legends. The Chart was supposed to have been on the back of a dragon which in ancient times came to the surface of the Yellow River and to have contained Fu Hsi's original Eight Trigrams. The Script was supposed to have been on the back of a turtle, which emerged from the Lo River in Sage-King Yü's time, and to have consisted of a mystic pattern of numbers from one to nine connected with the science of government. Now the peculiarity about the reference to them here lies in their having also been used in the Ch'ang-an *fu* to demonstrate that the Western Capital was the Heaven-ordained spot. The fact that such legends could be attached to two very different parts of the Yellow River will not surprise the comparative student of legend and myth, but it seems odd that Pan Ku should have allowed the two statements to stand in mutual contradiction. Again we face the possibility, both with Pan Ku and Chang Heng, that although they believed the old traditions which were universally held to be historically true, they accepted them with a grain of salt. In any case, Pan Ku was not sufficiently interested to clear up the confusion between the two stories.

In sharp distinction to this nonchalant attitude stands his contrasting the worship of very minor deities (*hsien*) at the Chien Chang and Kan Ch'üan palaces with the enlightened procedures in the Ming T'ang, Ling T'ai, and Pi Yung. How, he asks, can they be compared in basic efficacy, in the uniting of Heaven and man? His underlying motif, both here and in the preceding sentence, and most clearly of all in the final two couplets, is that old Han in comparison with new Han was ignorant, benighted. Even though the Scripture obscurantists do not realize it, a new day has dawned with the light of a new knowledge, a knowledge based on reason and giving full weight to spiritual values, in particular the world-uniting *virtus*.

Pan Ku believed that the founders of the new order, Emperors Kuang Wu and Ming, had reviewed whatever was evil and whatever was latently good in the old order and had eradicated the one and brought the other into full play.

At the same time Pan Ku believed that the various principles of this revolution had been envisaged by one sage-king and another. He did not therefore hold that Later Han wrote on a clean slate, but he did maintain that by the implementation of those principles their full ethical grandeur had for the first time emerged to view. That he idealized can hardly be doubted. That there was some truth in his stated belief also can hardly be doubted.

8. *The Guest's Discomfiture*

Here is another example of Pan Ku's sense of humor at work. As was seen in relation to those endless stairs of the Well-Head Tower, he was a master hand at envisaging and depicting the ludicrous aspects of a trying physical situation. It did not occur to him, as it occurred to Chang Heng, that the man who had the tower built was acting in absurd fashion, trying to pull himself up to Heaven by his bootstraps. What appealed to Pan Ku was the stumbler on the stairs in a sweat of nervous apprehension. So here the humor is more of the slapstick kind, not in the vein of polished wit. The poor discomfited provincial is ruthlessly depicted in all the confusion of a man who has made a fool of himself. As a side-light on those much vaunted manners at the Loyang court, the passage is revealing enough. And we can well imagine Chang Heng, with his mordant vein of sarcasm, reading it over and feeling it a little simple and heavy-handed, particularly as the new regime was not quite so perfect as the poem presented it to be.

9. *The Five Odes*

No literary critic, whether Chinese or foreigner, will question Pan Ku's good dramatic judgement in relegating these lyrical outbursts to an addendum. They will also appreciate the skill with which he works them into the final dénouement of the guest's repentance. On the other hand, the odes themselves are so conventional, in phrasing as in thought, that the modern reader finds difficulty in seeing why they should have been regarded as having such a soul-searching effect. To that query the only answer is that since the *fu* received great acclamation, Pan Ku's sense of his public must have been right. His court readers felt that he had said the right thing in the right distinguished lyrical way.

There is one underlying theme to the five odes, namely, the transcendental evidence which is forthcoming to prove that the new regime had divine approval. In the case of the Precious Tripods and White Pheasants these confirmations come right out of the blue. No specific action could bring their presence. Either true kingship was there, and they came, or it was not there, and they did not come. The Ming T'ang, Pi Yung, and Ling T'ai plainly are in a different category. In their case edifices were erected, and carefully planned rites and learned procedures carried out, these elaborate means being adopted to achieve one great end—symbolization of true kingship and proof thereby to gods and men that the occupants of the throne had both a legitimate and moral claim to be Sons of Heaven. That being so, the main question of this book, the difference between Former and Later Han, confronts us in relation to these three institutions. In what ways precisely were these rites and procedures innovations?

The "Treatise on Sacrifice" (*Hou Han Shu, Chi Ssŭ Chih*) states that Kuang Wu in the last two years of his reign began to build a *ming t'ang*, a *ling t'ai*, and a *pi yung*, and that Emperor Ming in his second year in the first month sacrificed in this *ming t'ang* to the Five Shang Ti, proceeded thereafter to his *ling t'ai*, in the third month carried out a rite of archery in his *pi yung*, and in the tenth month entertained the veterans of the state service there. As far as official evidence of specific Han institutions takes us, this is the first occasion on which such a combination of rites was performed in a Han capital, the first occasion on which all three centres were placed near to each other, each being furnished with a surrounding moat of running water. So much is clear to start with. It is also clear from the "History of the Later

Han Dynasty" (*Hou Han Shu*, ch. 18) that there was another *ming t'ang* at Wen Shang near to Mount T'ai, and in that area another *ling t'ai* associated with Sage-King Yao's reputed grave. No other *pi yung* site is mentioned.

With regard to various *ming t'ang* in the past, the "History of the Former Han Dynasty" is highly instructive, particularly in relation to Emperor Wu. At his accession there were certain influential scholars who urged him to construct a *ming t'ang*, presumably in Ch'ang-an; but there is no information as to what function it should perform. The suggestion was quashed by the Empress Dowager, and there is no record of Emperor Wu having thought of it again. But in 110 B.C. on his first visit to Mount T'ai he discovered a ruined building at Wen Shang in that neighborhood and learnt on enquiry that it had been used by the Chou kings when on a royal progress. The Emperor turned to the scholars to tell him what form it had. They could not tell him, but a South-Ch'i shaman produced a plan dating, he averred, from the Yellow Emperor's time. (See *Han Shu*, ch. 25, where in considerable detail is described the cabalistic plan on which Emperor Wu built at Wen Shang a *ming t'ang* in 109 B.C.) This plan with its circular moat of running water, its square structural features et cetera, was at least on much the same plan as that which Emperors Kuang Wu and Ming used later in constructing their *ming t'ang*. This was particularly so in relation to the Five Ti (High Gods), for both *ming t'ang* contained five altars, one to each Ti, ranged north, south, east, west, and centre. 109 B.C. is the first recorded occasion on which the Five Ti were worshipped in a *ming t'ang*. It would seem doubtful, to say the least, whether the scholars of the old Lu State (in the vicinity of Mount T'ai) had any tradition which corresponded to what Emperor Wu had in mind on this occasion, and the same would seem to apply to the scholars concerned in the 140 B.C. move in Ch'ang-an. As to Emperor Wu's purpose in the matter, it is plain enough from his pronouncements at the time: he wanted everybody in China and out to know that he had the special favor of all the regional deities.

Pan Ku's ode refers not only to the Five Ti, but also to "under universal heaven, from end to end of earth, each [dignitary assisting] according to his office" ("*ko i ch'i chih*"). In the "Filial Piety Scripture" (ch. 9) we find this statement: "In times past Duke Chou did a *chiao* [suburban] sacrifice to Hou Chi, making him *p'ei* ["associate, ancillary deity"] to Heaven, and an ancestral sacrifice to King Wen in the *ming t'ang*, making him *p'ei* to *Shang Ti* [one or more High Gods], and herewith every prince and dignitary within the four seas, according to his office came and [helped in] the sacrifice." A very remarkable passage. The point here is that Pan Ku clearly had this form of words running in his head, and that the obvious meaning of *ming t'ang* in such a context is "ancestral fane." According to Ts'ai Yung's (132-172) theory in his "Discussion on Ming T'ang" (cited by Liu Chao in his comment on *Hou Han Shu*, ch. 18), "*ming t'ang*" was the name given by the Chou royal house to their ancestral fane; and in Six Dynasties' and T'ang times this seems to have been generally assumed. Thus it appears that there was another kind of *ming t'ang* embodied in tradition, one associated with ancestor worship and filial piety.

Yet another functional kind of *ming t'ang* appears in the *Wang Chih* and *Ming T'ang Wei* of the "Record of Rites," namely a building erected in Loyang by Duke Chou, in which he lectured the assembled feudatories on their duties, publishing policy and conferring offices. The ruined *ming t'ang* near Mount T'ai would appear to have been an offshoot of this, namely a place of assembly for regional dignitaries when a Chou king was on progress (cf. *Mencius* I B 5). These *ming t'ang* on the face of it had nothing to do with sacrificing to the Five Ti.

On the top of all this come the questions arising out of Pan Ku's "Five Ti." Where did they come from? Fortunately for historians Pan Ku himself supplies the key document in that connection. In his monograph on the sacrifices in the suburbs (*Han Shu*, 25) one of his major concerns is to trace the rise of these several sacrifices in ancient Chou times. As the story goes on step by step, he engages confidence by his warning that he cannot guarantee the truth of the information he gives. Bearing in mind that "*ti*" was a Yin-Chou term, particular as to meaning ("sovereign," "god") yet capable of becoming generic, the story can be outlined as follows. In the great western area where the Chou and Ch'in culture interpenetrated, certain Ch'in princes created over a long term of years a number of high places, at which sacrifices were offered to a White Ti, a Red Ti, a Green Ti, and a Black Ti. Then came the First Ch'in Emperor, and he seems to have rationalized these several worships by relating them to the natural-law symbolism of the Tsou Yen school of thought and the rotation of the four seasons, under the influence of wood, fire, metal, water, and earth. The political aim behind this is clear enough. Emperor Kao went a step further and sacrificed to Five Ti, adding a Yellow Ti, symbolic of earth. These Five Ti were regularly worshipped at one high place, at the juncture of the Rivers Wei and Pa. Then another god appears on the scene, a T'ai I (Supreme One), with sidereal connections, to whom the Five Ti were made ancillary gods (*p'ei*).[7] Emperor Wu, among his other

---

[7] I use the term "ancillary" for two reasons. One is that "p'ei" at this time was commonly in use to denote the functional status of the wife to her husband. She was his mate, devoted to his interests, having a share in his reputation, but always subservient to him, her lord and master. "Mate" would make an excellent translation, but its modern vernacular usage rules it out as having too much an equalitarian connotation. What exactly the status of this relationship was in the list of the "Five Ties" (*lun*) is difficult to say. In some passages it figures high, being placed next to the prime relationship of father and son, in other passages low, although always above "friend and friend."

The other reason is that *p'ei* is the term used in the "King Wen" decade of the "Odes" to denote King Wen's status in Heaven. That takes us back to the largely legendary beginnings of the Chou feudal order. I can find no evidence that *p'ei* was used by the Shang-Yin Kings in similar circumstances, and it seems likely that Duke Chou initiated this usage. Since Loyang was the city whose first building was associated with Duke Chou,

sacrificial innovations, had T'ai I's altar erected at Kan Ch'üan where the new summer palace was. This sacrifice continued throughout the succeeding reigns, as also did those to the Five Ti at the Wei-Pa high place.[8] Gradually the feeling arose at court that all these sacrifices should be concentrated in the capital and a *ming t'ang* be built there. The decision was taken, then reversed, then taken again, then again reversed. There is no record in the "History of the Former Han Dynasty" of a completed *ming t'ang* at Ch'ang-an until Wang Mang was in the saddle. At his orders one was built there, timed to usher in his new dynasty. On what pattern and on what suburban site is not stated in the "History of the Former Han Dynasty" (either in ch. 25 or ch. 99), nor what function it fulfilled. It disappears from the records after Wang Mang's fall.

We come to the *ming t'ang* of A.D. 59 at Loyang. I submit that on the above evidence the Former Han government never sacrificed to the Five Ti in a *ming t'ang* at Ch'ang-an. Since the rites were felt to be vital for seasonal equilibrium, Kuang Wu at the end of his reign decided that he must have them, and have them on the spot. He desired Emperor Wu's numinous power, and the new capital needed to be consecrated, established in men's minds as the main centre of auspicious influences. Kuang Wu died before the buildings were completed and Emperor Ming completed them within some twelve months. Emperor Wu's cabalistic design was followed, but innovations were made in connection with the robes.

With regard to Kuang Wu as "*p'ei*," ancillary to and associate with the Five Ti, the "History of the Later Han Dynasty" (ch. 18) states that there was an altar for him south of that to the Green Ti and facing west. He received his sacrifice of a bull along with each of the Five Ti. In esti-

---

there is a very obvious connection between his making King Wen a *p'ei* to heaven and Emperor Ming making his father a *p'ei* to the Five Ti.

[8] The records are incomplete and we cannot assume that these sacrifices were made yearly.

mating what his precise status and function were, reference naturally should be made to the first poem of the King Wen decade in the "Odes." King Wen is there plainly represented as on the one hand having achieved superhuman status, on the other hand as not only protecting his descendants but also keeping a disciplinary eye on them. Thus the Loyang Ming T'ang rites embodied two of the traditional purposes, the placating of certain Nature-deities and the exaltation of a dead father by his filial son. As for the other function, a holding of audience and a publishing of policy, there is no convincing evidence of such. The nature of the buildings was hardly suitable for such a meeting. It is, however, quite clear that high dignitaries were present at the sacrifices and took part in the procedure as assistants. Visiting vassal kings might be among them, brought in to be impressed by this demonstration of Chinese civilization and heavenly prestige.

The Pi Yung Ode gives no indication that the Pi Yung was the centre of higher education, nor does it refer to the annual archery event, both features a commonplace to Pan Ku's readers. Its concern is confined to the encircling moat and the Emperor's entertainment in person of the state veterans. Quite clearly Pan Ku attached importance to the cabalistic significance of that circle of running water. The question is whether there was such in the imperial college in Ch'ang-an. The evidence is not easy to find, but since archery was part of the old-time education for the nobility, there is ground for the supposition supported by some scholiasts that for purposes of public safety the college campus was surrounded by a moat. As for possible innovations in relation to the Loyang emperors' shooting with the bow and their serving of the veterans, Chang Heng's Loyang *fu* is so much more detailed that the critique will deal with these matters there.

For the Loyang *ling t'ai* it must suffice to emphasize two aspects: (1) Pan Ku is of course correct in his emphatic "long venerated" in description of a royal observatory. There is the "*Ling T'ai*" Ode in the "King Wen" decade of the "Odes,"

and no question but that the Chou kings regarded the possession of an observatory as one of the main royal duties and
prerogatives. (2) To judge by the monograph on "Music
and the Calendar" in the "History of the Later Han Dynasty," Emperor Wu's realignment of the year in 104 B.C.
came up for criticism in Kuang Wu's reign, and there was a
good deal of discussion then and later, the redoubtable Chia
K'uei being one of the disputants. The matters under discussion were highly technical and must be taken as being
beyond the scope of this critique. The *prima facie* assumption
is that where there was so much discussion there were new
ideas brewing in the men's minds.

In conclusion, on this *fu* as a whole, the impression grows
steadily stronger that the change of capital was accompanied
by a number of striking innovations. These changes were
not only in relation to institutions but also to certain more
or less definable movements in the mind of the age. On that
basis of consideration it is worthwhile trying to define these
movements here (this in preparation for more systematic consideration in Chapter XI). On the one hand, the governmental machine in Loyang was more clearly, and even
designedly, constructed on a constitutional basis than the
Ch'ang-an machine ever was—a development marked, for
example, by the establishment and rituals of the "Three
Yung" (Ming T'ang, Ling T'ai, and Pi Yung). On the
other hand, the adaptation of ancient procedures to the newly-
envisaged requirements of government was carried out in a
spirit which was as superstitious as it was intelligent. The
tug of war in Pan Ku's mind between an animistic logic and
a more rational natural-cause-and-effect logic has from time
to time emerged very clearly to view. In the third place,
in regard to "Confucianism" (so called), those enhanced and
rationalized values attached to the worship of the Five Ti
would seem to have little connection with the influence of
Confucius, the sixth-century-B.C. sage of Lu. Yet the sheer

prestige of his name, indefinable yet powerful, becomes increasingly discernible in the last seven reigns of Former Han. Something of immense doctrinal significance was coming through to consciousness, something very much alive but as yet inchoate, something which found clearer expression after the scholars' experience of the Wang Mang episode. One thing is clear. Although the consciousness of world-empire, its glories and duties, brought the advance to a universal ethic, yet neither in its earlier phases nor in its Later Han developments was that ethic the concomitant of a monotheistic religious consciousness.

Chapter X

CRITIQUE OF CHANG HENG'S "*FU* ON THE EASTERN CAPITAL"

◇◇◇

1. *The Teacher's Reaction*

WHEREAS Pan Ku made his Loyang host deal in very supercilious, not to say snobbish and derisive, fashion with his provincial guest, Chang Heng took a strikingly different line. His old teacher is represented as disconcerted by the nobleman's cynical materialism. However, he pulls himself together and is able to start his rejoinder with a smile. Unquestionably, Chang Heng's dramatic psychology is an improvement on Pan Ku's crudity. Also, it shows a better appreciation of good manners, as we would expect from a member of that highly-mannered Loyang court. Here is the man of breeding (*chün-tzŭ*) in action, as the student has come to recognize him in the *Analects*: the gentleman who does not ride roughshod over his opponent's feelings. That being so, we come to see that in that court both dramatizations could be enjoyed, the somewhat vulgar as well as the more polished: in the latter case the teacher's opening words are blunt enough in spite of his smile. There is, for example, the sarcastic comparison with the poor outlawed minister among the barbarians, Yu Yü, of the seventh century B.C. How could it be that he could see things in their right perspective, whilst "you, my dear sir, with all your knowledge of past and present, could be as misguided as you are?"

The nobleman is roundly accused of "prizing the ear," i.e. hearsay, and "despising the eye," i.e. ocular demonstration. In other words, under the urge of masterful desires, he is guilty of wilful self-deception, and able to prove anything to his own satisfaction. Since in his final remarks on the Ch'ang-an period he had wound up with the complaint that an aristocrat's taste for elegant luxury was nowadays stupidly restricted, the charge was true enough. Lord Chesterfield, when taken to court by his pastry-cook for not paying his bill, remarked to the judge that it was a bit hard if a gentleman could not be allowed to enjoy a biscuit with his sherry; and it was this combination of frivolity and class egoism which a generation later brought England to the verge of bloody revolution. In Chang Heng's eyes, for all the virtues of the new regime, this attitude of mind was still alive and a grave danger to the common weal. The couplet dealing with the hypothesis of a breast (*hsiung*) without a mind (*hsin*) deserves by its luminous simplicity to be made a *locus classicus*. The trouble about Han psychology for the modern reader is its confusing complexity, as may be seen in the pages of the *Po Hu T'ung*, notably those on the human frame, including *hsin* in particular. Presumably Chang Heng had very little use for that kind of pseudo-logical synthesizing. It was the last generations of the Chou era which saw the rise of persistent introspective analysis, witness *Mencius*, *Hsün Tzŭ* and the *Lü Shih Ch'un Ch'iu*, not to speak of Chuang Chou's metaphysico-psychological theorizing. It is, therefore, against that complicated background with its wealth of terms, all of them used with varying connotations, that we come to appreciate Chang Heng's blunt extrovert approach with its *hsiung* as the seat of the emotions, passions, appetites, and its *hsin* as that directive intellectual force in man which can control those same unruly emotions.[1] Also, the Western stu-

---

[1] "*Hsin*," one of the comparatively few clearly recognizable pictographs in its pre-Ch'in form, does not appear till a Chou II inscription: so B. Karlgren's *Grammata Serica* states. In the Chou Odes it is found constantly, and, as one might expect in that stage of cultural development, denotes the physical heart as the seat of both feelings and thoughts. *Hsiung* occurs once in *Mencius* (IV A 15) and twice in the *Wen Sang* of the "Record of Rites" and in the *Lü Shih Ch'un Ch'iu*. In the *Mencius* instance it has a vaguely psychological connotation; in the other instances it denotes the physical breast. By Chin times it came to be associated with thoughts as well as feelings. There are no instances that I can find of thoughts being associated with the head, i.e. the brain. *Hsin*, on the other hand, was used right along in relation sometimes to feelings, sometimes to thoughts. Yet by late Chou

dent needs to appreciate Chang Heng's immediate association of this intellectual force with clarity of moral vision. In
this respect, although Taoist speculations threw doubt on
the ultimate cogency of morals, the dominant tendency in
the scholars' thinking was to make that direct association.
They linked reason with a categorical imperative which functioned by means of the accepted code of morals and good
manners. The same tendency prevailed in classical European
thinking from Plato down to the Roman Stoics.

With regard to the consciousness of hearsay as unreliable,
as we have seen, Pan Ku's historical studies had brought him
to the same position. There was Wang Ch'ung also with his
pejorative attitude. It would, however, be a mistake to regard this critical outlook as new to Later Han. As far back
as the last days of the Chou era there was discriminate thinking on this score. Thus in the *Lü Shih Ch'un Ch'iu* we find
(XXII, 6) the following statements under the caption of
"Examine Tradition": "Traditional statements should not
fail to be examined. There are some traditions in which
white becomes black. . . . To hear and examine is happiness:
to hear and not to examine—it were better not to hear."
The author then gives some simple illustrations from traditional history which prove his point. What may well be new
in Chang Heng's outlook here is his association of this unreliability of hearsay with the complexity of past history, his
moral being that the ethical issues are by no means easy to
elucidate. He proceeds immediately to exemplify this.

2. *The Real Lesson of the Dynastic Revolutions*
(*Third Century B.C.*)

As the opening section of Chang Heng's "*Fu* on the Western Capital" shows, the nobleman's approach to history is a

---

times, there is no question, thoughts and feelings were sharply distinguished,
and a further complication arose by the use of *chih*, originally denoting a
concrete aim, coming to be used in the sense in which a faculty psychologist
would use it, namely, denoting the will. At the same time the practice grew
of regarding the *hsin* as the lawful lord of the individual, controlling desire. Obviously, that was Chang Heng's position in his use of *hsin* here.

cynically amoralistic one. Eastern Chou, being centred in a poor-soiled area, was therefore weak and could not stand up against the powerful Ch'in with a rich-soiled area in its possession; and whatever royal line rules, if they are rich, they are sure to live luxuriously—indeed, why should they not? Now comes the Teacher's reply. Chou in the end was incapable of governing and had to die, but each of the Seven Powers was disqualified by its immoral appetite for display. The First Emperor, like a tiger, like a bird of prey, could not be withstood. But when all belonged to him, he wanted all the enjoyment for himself, working his people to death on his megalomaniac projects.

The Teacher's theme, indeed Chang Heng's theme, is the one familiar to Western historians, the Greek sense of a nemesis awaiting the ruler guilty of *hubris*. But here the chain of cause and effect operates on a wider scale. The doom is not the inescapable one operating among the members of a royal family, so that the best of them cannot escape destruction, but the doom of a cruel oppressor of the people. Chang Heng was a central China man, and he conveys with a rugged poetic eloquence the horror the central China people had felt when that half-barbarian tyrant from the west drove them worse than their own deboshed traditional rulers. And in the chain of events there is no sign of this and that god on Olympus pulling the strings. There is just a bare reference to Kao Tsu as "obeying Heaven." The doom of Ch'in came from the people: the "Hundred Surnames" (note the suggestion of family affiliation) "could not endure the usage" they received. And Kao Tsu's power of sovereignty lay not only in mighty deeds of war but in his plain man's revulsion against unnecessary pomp and luxury.

Those "western craftsmen" deserve attention. Emphasis has already been laid on the stimulation of skilled craftsmen resulting from the imperious demands of wealthy courts. Here is another illustration, pinpointing the fact at the earlier date of the third century B.C. Thus the Ch'in First Emperor collected a band of the best artisans, so that what had operated on a small scale in the Chou state courts operated on a considerably increased scale in the Ch'in capital of Hsien-yang. These men became a permanent part of the court establishment, and, since expense was no bar, it paid to stir the more able craftsmen by rewards. Whether Chang Heng had actual information on these Ch'in craftsmen and "their eyes playing over O Pang" we do not know. From the psychological point of view it was the natural thing for them to do, and this was part of Chang Heng's sympathy with workers and their workmanship, to envisage the situation and their disappointment when they found their new master scornful of their efforts.

To take a wider perspective, there is no question about the lasting dint which the Ch'in tyranny made on Chinese consciousness in the Han era. In this connection Pan Ku's emphasis on Kao Tsu being the first plebeian to win a throne proved highly suggestive. Chang Heng for his part had nothing to say on that subject, but the same feeling is discernible in him, viz. that the coming of Han was an event of unprecedented significance. Viewed from the later angle of vision the old ruling families had been hopeless, the new Ch'in a nightmare. Then came this plebeian with his indomitable energy, his resourcefulness in planning, his downright scorn of court flummery: the despairing people could rest their aching shoulders on him. Historians today do well in recognizing his limitations of outlook and in discounting Chia I's (199-168 B.C.) highly-colored account of the peasants everywhere marching to his support, but the question stands whether that typical aristocrat, Hsiang Yü, and any body of traditionally-minded Lu scholars could have created a new will to live, and live under one government. The old regional semi-tribal jealousies were still strong and were to remain so. Yet without the impetus given by the man from P'ei there might so easily have been no united China, indeed no China of the Sages, with its notable cultural achievements. The First Emperor with his forty commanderies had roughed out a framework of imperial dominion, but his regime flouted the needs of the "Hundred Surnames" and was bound to collapse. So Pan Ku and Chang Heng saw it. With Kao Tsu began an unprecedented type of unification, one in which for all its shortcomings the theories of the Chou philosophers slowly took shape in a constitution under which the common people were recognized as having rights.

3. *The Grossness of the Nobleman's Blindness*

The prosody is irregular, with no concern for rhyme. Indeed, the poem here has more the swing of dialectical prose, as the Teacher sets forth the moral perversity of the Nobleman's position. That position is shown to be not merely perverse, but also rationally absurd, since it made nonsense of vital events in the history of the sage-kings. The Nobleman, then, is denounced as "not knowing the force of words" (*pu chih yen*)[2]—a very sharp accusation to bring against a cultured gentleman, and so revealing the strength of Chang Heng's feeling.

With regard to the preservation of the spirit tablets, the main significance of the reference is clear: all the earlier Han emperors down to the end, whatever the vices of the later ones, had faithfully done their duty by their ancestral tablets. The Teacher is not out to whitewash the evils attending those later reigns, but in his eyes the plain fact that the ancestral fanes were kept in repair and the order of sacrificing maintained was proof of effectual filial piety, and such filial piety *per se* was virtue of a high order. There can be no doubt that the Late Chou and the Han eras produced a *hsiao tao* ("way of filial piety") which in its ethical refinements as in its ritual forms went far beyond the original ancestor worship with all its fears of hungry spirits bringing calamity on their descendants. Nevertheless the old fears remained, as is plainly seen in the struggle over the problem

---

[2] An allusion to *Analects*, XX, 3: "He who does not understand words cannot understand people."

of the funerary parks between 40 and 33 B.C. (see Dubs, II, 289-291).

Again the historian is faced with an amorphous, fluid ideological situation, in relation to which sweeping generalizations are bound to create misleading impressions. For instance, how are we to appraise Kung Yü and Wei Hsüan-ch'eng in their rugged common-sense insistence that many of the funerary parks were redundant and should be abolished? Were they being rational, liberal, conservative, superstitious? Read their memorials, and it is clear that they were all four. And what motive lay behind the innovation of having in addition to the High Founder's fane three other comparable fanes dedicated to the great *Tsung* ("Exemplars"), Emperors Wen, Wu, and Hsüan? Was that done because in life they had been such effective individuals that their inspiring influence was, rationally enough, mobilized to the support of the throne? Or was it just fear of their ghostly mana? Further, for all its sentimental idealism, the Han *hsiao tao* was realistic enough in a callous sense. After five generations the tablets of the sacred dead were normally moved into a side room, and there in course of time they became mere decaying lumber.

4. *The Rightness of Loyang as the Capital for True Sons of Heaven*

The poem, getting into its metrical stride with solid rhyme patterns, comes to its first main theme, the rightness of the Loyang site. As might be expected, Chang Heng details the natural amenities of the district and attaches importance to the fact that in the days of old this was made a centre of government. These features are, however, only cited as confirmatory evidence. The basic argument admits by implication that the new capital is less well-guarded by mountain defences than the old capital, but lays down that in the last resort the throne is protected by the good faith (*liang*) of the ruler's subjects. The theme, speaking generally, has a familiar ring to the student of the *Analects* and Mencius, and the reader may be tempted to take it for granted that Chang Heng here enunciates what in principle had been accepted by the scholars. There is room for doubt, since the Teacher is made to draw a sharp antithesis between reliance on passes and reliance on the people's good faith. Pan Ku's Loyang *fu*, for all its eloquence about popular gratitude over peace and plenty, has nothing so explicit as this, and we know from the "Acts of the Emperors" that the Loyang government made full use of the military arm, both for protection and imperial expansion. The general idea was that both *jen* and military efficiency were a *sine qua non* of successful government. That was so in Earlier Han times, and the question about which was more important could hardly arise until the establishment of a less naturally protected capital.

Ancient Chou is presented as the discoverer of the site: King Ch'eng and his faithful servants, the Dukes of Chou and Shao. Although the two Dukes are not mentioned by name until later in the section, they are the master figures in the story, particularly Duke Chou; and the language of the poem where it treats of them is reminiscent of the *Shao Kao* and *Lo Kao* sections of the "History" Scripture where the two Dukes occupy the real centre of the stage. There is, however, in those documents no mention of a *t'u kuei* (measuring table) and calculations being made: they refer only to divining and finding the auspices good. For mention of a *t'u kuei* we have to go to the *Chou Li*, e.g. *Ti Kuan Ssŭ T'u* (ch. 2): "[The officer], using the method of the measuring table, calculates the relative depth of the earth,[3] verifying the shadow of the sun with a view to finding the central point of the land surface."[4] From this and other passages

---

[3] "Relative depth" here refers to the depth of the shadow cast on the *t'u kuei* plate. The reference can only be to the relative proximity of any locality to the four points north, south, east, and west.

[4] The passage continues: "[In the case of] the sun being southerly [in relation to the *t'u kuei*], its shadow is too short and [the locality] has too much heat. [In the case of] the sun being northerly, its shadow is too long

in the *Chou Li*[5] it is clear that the *t'u kuei* was an oblong plate on which fifteen inches (Chinese) were marked in relation to a perpendicular pole of eight feet (Chinese) high. The history of the experimentation from which this table of measurement came to completion is entirely obscure, except for the probability that in Eastern Chou times there was practical need for measuring the boundaries of the 1000 *li* royal demesne (cf. *Chou Li, loc.cit.*). In any case, the discovery was made, so it was thought, that where a horizontal plate placed due north and south with a perpendicular pole eight feet high at its southern end threw a fifteen-inch shadow, there was the centre of "the land." It is not clear whether the rudimentary experimenters took adequate steps to ensure that the pole was exactly at right angles, although they became alive to the necessity of achieving rigidity of position in the pole.[6] Nor is it clear whether they took adequate steps for ascertaining exact horizontality for the plate, e.g. by judging from the surface of a pond.

Here, then, is unmistakable evidence that the genuine

and [the locality] has too much cold. [In the case of] the sun being easterly [? westerly], its shadow has a post-meridional [slant] and [the locality] has too much wind. [In the case of] the sun being westerly [? easterly] its shadow has a premeridional [slant], and [the locality] has too many rain clouds." The Chinese only makes sense, if the author is assumed to be thinking of (1) a standard-ruled *t'u kuei* being taken round to four localities assumed to be south or north, etc.; (2) the operators having with them a clepsydra which registered midday for the summer solstice at the central point. The scholiasts support this interpretation, but they seem to differ in opinion as to whether *"jih tung"* (the sun being easterly) refers to an eastern or a western locality. To me these words do not make sense unless the reference there is to a western locality. The sun in a western locality could not but rise later than in an eastern, and given these ancient Chinese observers had a center-standardized clepsydra, they would see from the post-meridional slant of the shadow on the plate that the sun had not yet reached its meridian. That being so, the experiment must have been in a western locality not an eastern. By parity of reasoning the fourth alternative observation introduced by *"jih hsi"* (the sun being westerly) must have been made in an eastern locality, not a western.

[5] See H. Maspero, *Les Instruments Astronomiques des Chinois au Temps des Han*, Mélanges Chinois et Bouddhiques, VI, Bruges, 1939, p. 220.

[6] See Maspero, *op.cit.*, pp. 218-219 and Tung Tso-pin, *Chou Kung Ts'ê Ying T'ai Tiao-ch'a Pao-kao*, Academia Sinica Bulletin, 1939.

scientific mind was at work, making experiments in an effort to establish earth-space on a mathematical basis of accuracy. The scientific urge in this is the more impressive because— at any rate by Han times—it was realized that the only feasible method was to equate space to time, namely by ascertaining from the movements of the heavenly bodies at what times the winter and summer solstices came in relation to the capital. Thus the invention of the sundial and the clepsydra were stepping-stones in the quest for the accuracy of dial readings. That those would-be scientists were wrong in the assumption that the earth was flat, not globular, was their mistake, as also their assumption that the area of their national habitat contained the centre of the terrestrial world. Thus they were ignorant of the fact that their country lay north of an equatorial global division and was only part of one of two longitudinal hemispheres. But this ignorance of theirs does not detract from the scientific aim of their experimentation, nor from the validity of their discovery that space and time can only be calculated on the basis of their being correlatives.[7]

In the light of the above, what, then, is the evidential value of Chang Heng's reference to the *t'u kuei* in connection with the establishment of the Loyang capital? First, it is significant that, although the *Shao Kao* and *Lo Kao* records of the first establishment of Loyang have no suggestion that any geodetical experiments were made, yet Chang Heng assumed that they *were* made. Since the Scriptures were entirely precise in attaching the fact of that establishment to

---

[7] Maspero (*op.cit.*) had a good deal to say on the final accuracy of the calculations in respect to the *t'u kuei*, and on p. 223 he questioned whether the Chinese constructors of these *t'u kuei* which have survived were so anxious for exactitude. The justice of his critical reflection in those connections is not to be questioned, but I find a particular interest in the fact that archaeological evidence of a *t'u kuei* is obtainable from, for example, the back-blocks of the empire. It points to the extensive use of the instrument and opens the door for the conjecture that some *t'u kuei* were made under insufficient expert supervision. It does not seem to me that the carelessness thus evidenced can be assumed as applying to headquarter experts of the scientific calibre of a Chang Heng.

King Ch'eng and his famous ministers, here is evidence that around A.D. 120 one highbrow was not satisfied with divinatory readings as sufficient proof of the rightness of the site. In his judgement there must have been *t'u kuei* measurements. Also, in his eyes the importance of getting the right site derived from climatic considerations, the avoidance of excessive heat and cold, wind and rain.

Second, there seems no adequate ground for doubting that in the early days of the Chou regime, a royal administrative centre was established at Loyang; and certainly this was later the site of the capital for the East Chou regime. The climatic amenities must in due course have become clear from ordinary year-to-year observation. Yet in Han times this idea of *t'u kuei* observations being a necessary preliminary to the discovery of the site came to be accepted. How could that have happened? There seems only one way, and that the one illustrated in the *Hsi Tz'ŭ* ("Appended Amplifications") to the "Changes" Scripture: the passage in the second part, where the main implements conducive to man's well-being are attributed to discoveries by the sage-kings, and to them being guided by the logic which, it was now maintained, was latent in the diviners' hexagrams. The Han attribution of the use of the *t'u kuei* to Duke Chou is on a par with this kind of reasoning: the decision for Loyang was a sage-like decision, and Duke Chou was a sage, and therefore he used a sage-wise instrument.

Here, then, lies the evidential value of Chang Heng's statement. It brings us near to the new urge towards scientific certainty which came in the mid-Han and Later Han periods. To the questing minds of that epoch the sage-kings of antiquity were not merely mystically inspired by Heaven, but even more intellectually stimulated to explore the rational elements in the physical universe. For further illustrations (apart from those in this book) of this new attitude of mind see the "History of the Later Han Dynasty," ch. 12, e.g. in the thesis there propounded by Pan Ku's contemporary, Chia

K'uei, on the rectification of the calendar. It is that although astrological thinking by no means disappeared there was nevertheless a new class of scientifically-minded astronomers. Chang Heng, it may now safely be inferred, was an outstanding example of this class of men whose conclusions were derived from the use of the clepsydra and the armillary sphere (*hsüan chi*).

With regard to Chang Heng's denunciation of Wang Mang, it is less detailed than Pan Ku's but along much the same line: vilification of a man who tried unsuccessfully to found a new dynasty. On the other hand, there is a very revealing expression: "throughout the nation no one dared have another opinion than his." In the light of what is known about Wang Mang's career, it can hardly be questioned that he was highly dictatorial in temperament.

5. *The New Palaces and Pleasaunces Described and Appraised*

In these forty-two couplets the narrative moves from item to item, the transition marked by change of rhyme and prosodic rhythm. From the point of view of orderly description this section is a masterpiece, true to the genius of double-harness composition. But the narrative is so compressed that there is nothing to show whether any of the buildings specified were administrative offices. Presumably some were, for the Ming T'ang, Pi Yung and Ling T'ai (the Three Yung) were not places where the day-to-day administration was done. Chang Heng's treatment stands in sharp contrast to Pan Ku's, for the latter gives no detail whatever, speeding along to his great emphasis, the noble frugality which inspired Emperors Kuang Wu and Ming. Chang Heng also praises the moderation shown, but, as one high-sounding appellation succeeds another, the seed of a suspicion is sown. One wonders whether a tincture of delicate irony does not permeate the account as a whole.

Finally there is "the laborers labored, the dwellers are

at ease." The T'ang commentator, Chang Hsien, takes these words as conveying the emperor's attitude. Assuming this conjecture to be right, we have to face Li Shan's comment. That cites a story from Chia I's *Hsin Shu*[8] in which a certain king of Ti sent an ambassador to the King of Ch'u. The ambassador, being entertained in a very ornate building, was asked whether his master had any to compare with it. He replied, "The thatch has not been trimmed, the beams not cut to length. Yet my king still feels that the builders have been too hardworked and that the dwellers are too much at ease." The emperor referred to in Chang Heng's passage was Emperor Ming, for he is the central figure throughout the section. That being so, we are faced with the fact that Chang Heng clearly had a genuine admiration for him. Further, the passage in question comes next to the building of the Three Yung. There is no evidence that they were ornate buildings; indeed, it is quite to the contrary. Thus the final conclusion is that our author may well have inserted a delicate probe or two, but it is doubtful whether he wrote in the ironic vein. This conclusion releases our minds to appreciate to the full that this section is no dreary sycophantic recital of the beauties of Loyang. On the contrary the poet was in command of his material, so much so that his wit could flicker into action.

In the main the general appraisal corroborates Pan Ku's, and, as the critique has shown, there is good ground for accepting it as approximately true to the facts. Pan Ku was lyrical about the new architecture, calling it "divine art." Chang Heng more soberly sums it up as "economy not resulting in crudity [*lou*]." Since the two men saw the buildings with their own eyes, it would be of great interest if the archaeologists of today could find evidence pointing to this new motif of restraint.

The mind of our poet-scientist is a study, as it moves from point to point of appraisal. From restraint *not* producing a

[8] Chia I, *Hsin Shu*, ch. 7, "*T'ui Jang.*"

debasement of art, that mind moved—may one say naturally—to the observance of old and simpler standards, and a set goal to be achieved. (Scientists seem to have a proclivity for that kind of thing, definition of the goal and precision in the means for attaining it.) Then comes "Behold, here is *Li*, the right and fitting, in full display." Yes, of course! That was it, *li*, the uplifting of a standard of the spirit, the ethically right and aesthetically fine embodied in a set of harmonious actions. And that range of ideas brought to Chang Heng's mind King Wen, of sainted memory, building his Spirit Terrace ("Odes," III, 1, 8): no driving of the workmen, their task accomplished with a will. That also was *li*, the demonstration of fellow-feeling between master and man, between class and class. It crops up again at the end of the section, and, indeed, is a major theme of the poem, recurring again and again.

With regard to the Ming T'ang, Pi Yung, and Ling T'ai, the order of narration makes them the climax of the building operations. Yet there is no sign of the lyrical fervor Pan Ku felt about them. In plain four-word sentences the bare essential facts about their structure are stated and their respective functions outlined. Emphasis is laid on the elaborate symbolism of the Ming T'ang, its set-up being along the lines of Emperor Wu's *ming t'ang*. That sacrificial rites and recruitment for state service and observation of weather should all come under one generalization needs no comment; but the emphasis on principles does. The yearly routine of the Three Yung was a public demonstration of government at the highest level being by unchanging rules of procedure. That looks suspiciously like recognition of constitutional practice. The Pi Yung rewards scrutiny. The stress is laid on it as the place where the selection of candidates for office took place. In that respect examinational procedure in the Imperial Academy becomes complementary to the development of constitutional government. If the "Record of Education" (*Hsüeh Chi*) in the "Record of Rites" may be taken as having a close relation in time to Chang Heng's age, we can envisage Chang Heng as thinking of those yearly college tests being carried out, and the final test coming after nine years of study. It should be borne in mind that the Pi Yung site included archery butts and proficiency in archery was one of the tests—proficiency in marksmanship as also in courtesy under the strain of competition. To go by the "Significance of Archery" (*Shê I*) in the "Record of Rites," there was more attention paid to physical stamina than has perhaps been recognized so far in Sinological studies.

The treatment of the Ling T'ai makes one rub one's eyes. Here is Chang Heng speaking of his own special field of study, and all he has to say is that the P'ing Hsiang (official) makes observations of evil Yin-Yang weather elements at strife and has intercession made for their removal. This officer's duty seems to have been to keep an eye on the strategic points in the seasons and give warning of threatening changes.[9] Warning being given, the right prayer formula might be used to avert them. Now, why did Chang Heng treat the Ling T'ai theme like that? Was he in revolt against Pan Ku's rosy picture in the ode? Or did the decline in court morale in Emperor An's reign bring the exaltation of minor officials like the P'ing Hsiang and so depreciate the services of the more expert astronomers? The answers to these questions can only be conjectures.

6. *The Empire and Beyond Doing Homage*

Again there is a magnificent piece of vivid description, the swing of it from point to point marked by rhyme and rhythm changes. At certain key points the prosody is irregular—very skilfully so since the irregular lines make a pattern of emphases. For example, the crowning point of the proceedings when the vassals present their tribute and the Son of Heaven

---

[9] For this title, see *Chou Li, Ch'un Kuan, Tsung Po*, where *"P'ing Hsiang"* is mentioned after *"T'ai Shih"* (the Grand Astrologer). No such title occurs in the monographs on the Hundred Officials and on the Calendar in the "History of the Later Han Dynasty."

responds with the properly graded bow. This is marked by an eight-word line followed by a ten-word line, the latter not fitting into a rhyme scheme.

There is vivid delineation of the scene, as if coming from an eye-witness. Yet the special durbar on a grand scale with a large gathering of foreign princes held by Emperor Chang was in A.D. 87; and since our author was only nine years old then it seems doubtful whether he saw it with his own eyes. There were, however, other durbars, for in theory and more or less in practice, the homage of the vassals was due every New Year's day. (Travelling in winter must have been a trying business for those from distant parts in the north.) I assume that Chang Heng's picture was a conglomerate one.

There is not a single word to indicate where the audience was held. Fortunately Pan Ku's account refers to a "Cloud-Dragon Court" and Chang Heng in Section 5 has specified a Cloud-Dragon Gate to the palace enclosure. It was on the east side, corresponding to a complementary Spirit-Tiger Gate on the west side of the enclosure. Since the Emperor on his throne faced south, these two gates presumably lay south-east and south-west of the great audience hall. The difficulty is to envisage space within one courtyard, however big, for "several tens of thousands" of onlookers.[10] Presumably there is considerable exaggeration. However, the account accurately distinguishes between the onlookers and the actual participants in the audience: princes of the blood, foreign potentates, enfiefed nobles, and high officials. They along with the larger crowd are divided into two sections, presumably making a lane for the imperial carriage. We can imagine the

[10] These onlookers should not be taken to be the common people but minor court officers, members of the princes' retinue, anyone who had *entrée* to the palace enclosure. Pan Ku referred to tents being erected in the Cloud-Dragon courtyard, and that may be taken as being so on the occasion of Emperor Ming's smaller durbar. There is no need to assume that for Emperor Chang's great durbar and subsequent ones there were tents for the barbarian guests inside the palace enclosure, or at any rate in the Cloud-Dragon courtyard.

hush as it passed through the throng—broken by the crash of the sound from the drums and bells.

As a piece of pageantry it rivets attention, described, it would seem, from the viewpoint of someone in the main crowd. First the serried ranks of dignitaries, then the bells and drums on their stands, the guards with crossed halberds on the steps to the hall, the imperial carriage filling the porch, the banners a-flutter! Then the torches a-blaze in the audience hall and the crash of the salute with the tremor of the earth! There is the summons to stand apart, as the Emperor alights and enters the robing room. Majesty emerges in full regalia and takes its seat on the throne. Then comes the great moment, the Emperor faces due south, and the audience has begun.

There seem to have been two flights of steps, one where the guards stand, outside the hall, the other inside. According to the commentator Hsieh Tsung, this latter consisted of three parallel flights leading up to the throne, the central flight used by the Emperor, the eastern flight by the inner ring of dignitaries when invited to confer. The odd thing is that no mention is made of the vassals doing obeisance, only of the "hundred princes" entering the hall and there being marshalled in order of rank by the ushers. Was this omission due to Chang Heng, from where he stood, being unable to see the actual kow-tows? He could see the tribute treasures being presented and the Son of Heaven's graded response.

The comparison of this account with Pan Ku's is illuminating. In the first place, although both Chang Heng and his predecessor take the all-subduing power of the imperial *virtus* as their central theme, their treatment of it is almost totally different. Pan Ku was just lyrically enthusiastic about it: "no one on land or water but breathless and trembling comes to pay homage." Chang Heng depicts Majesty on its awe-inspiring throne, and then is content with "How stately, how majestic, [*and*] a spectacle to engage the trust of all the world!" Having struck that note, he proceeds to elaborate: the Son of Heaven calling his high vassals and responsible officers to confer on the "ten thousand *chi*" (lit. "spring-releases") the endless sudden vicissitudes which attend the exercise of government. From that he proceeds to reflect compassionately on the mass of men, and in particular the individual who "has not found his place," i.e. is without a family or any economic niche in society. There were many such displaced persons in Han China, as repeated edicts referring to them show, and in Central Asia a number of displaced tribes. Right along, the stress is on bearing the burden of responsibility. And this linked itself in the poet's mind with that distribution of largesse among nobles and officials which was a prominent feature of these New Year ceremonies. For the Emperor the means to do this, and increase official allowances, were there, not so much in treasure stores as in the public granaries where the real national wealth was held in reserve. Then almost as an afterthought the poem comes to the feasting about which Pan Ku had been so eloquent. It disposes of that in two couplets; but concludes like Pan Ku with the sense of unity stirred to enthusiasm by good food and good wine.

The poem here has nothing on the music at the feast, the national traditional music and the barbarian music, the theme with which Pan Ku had so brilliantly reinforced his rhapsody on unanimity. In its place Chang Heng pictures the Emperor's subjects dispersing happily with a sense of duty done, whilst their sovereign lord bore the burden of continual watchfulness "and unceasing activity." This is significant if only because it seems so clearly to come by revulsion from Pan Ku's picture of the *virtus* spreading so naturally and sweetly among the nations. But there is more to it than that. All through Chang Heng's youth and early manhood Emperors Ho and An had been the reigning sovereigns, and they, on gaining the reins of power, showed themselves both dissipated and irresponsible. Again we sense in our author the purpose of probing the imperial conscience. Yet Pan Ku's sense of a natural victory for the *virtus* is not altogether discarded. To Chang Heng it suggested the *hsüan tê* ("mysterious, numinous *virtus*") and *tzŭ jan* ("self-so-ness") of Great Nature in the Taoist view of life, and he placed the argument on that transcendent level. Nevertheless, he was no starry-eyed mystic. On goes the probing argument to self-examination and to the need for the state to get down to grass-roots and seek out "village incorruptibles" for renewing the highway of the Sages. Only then will "high and low communicate the fellow-feeling, and peace and joy be here."

7. *The Sacrifice to Heaven*

On the first auspicious day in the New Year came the Sacrifice to Heaven, second in the series of ceremonial acts by which the Emperor kept the ship of state on an even keel. The first five couplets emphasize the reverential care and integrity of heart and mind with which the sacrifice should be approached, the last three couplets the central acts of sacrifice, these being preceded by three couplets noting the elaborate accompaniment of music and ritual dancing. In between come twenty-five couplets devoted to the pomp and circumstance with which the occasion was celebrated.

First, it is almost impossible to doubt that Chang Heng saw the proceedings with his own eyes, and that he saw them from the vantage point of the city gate-tower. A whole succession of touches reveal this, e.g. the release inside the city of the rows of carriages at the word of command, the color schemes of the banners, the tossing of draperies on the cavalry horses. From the same vantage point he would hear the drums reverberating on the sacrificial site, glimpse the rows of dancers, and see the flames and smoke rising, but would not descry the Emperor and attendant officers at work.

Second, the suspicion comes again that there may be a satirical intent underlying the account. There is so striking a contrast between the initial emphasis on the necessary moral rectitude and the immensely detailed description of the processional trappings. And we know what little moral rectitude Emperor An showed when he began to get free of the Empress-Dowager Teng.

For the meaning of the term *t'ien* (heaven) in this context our objective is to ascertain what Chang Heng and his contemporaries thought about it. For the wider setting of the problem the student must go, for example, to the *Ku Shih Pien* ("Symposium on Ancient History"), VII, in particular Vol. B (1941), where the various congeries of high ancestors, eponymous heroes, gradually-personalized totems, and sky gods and earth gods of the Sinitic and non-Sinitic tribes are to be seen in process of rationalization by successive steps of mythological interpretation. All this is germane to the main enquiry but cannot be dealt with here beyond this one observation: the Han scholars struggled hard to make sense of it all. One result was the classification of the gods as either *shen* (gods in the sky), or *ch'i* (gods of the earth). This is plain from numerous examples in mid-Han memorials to the throne, as also in the "Record of Rites." The Five Shang Ti were major gods in the one category, Hou T'u ("Ruler Soil") a major god in the other category. Further, the term "*chiao ssŭ* occurs again and again in relation to sacrifices distinct from those made in the ancestral fanes.

The intriguing thing about Chang Heng's use of the term *t'ien* here in this section is that in addition to the general appellation *ssŭ t'ien* for a sky-directed sacrifice he used three other appellations for the object of sacrifice: Shang Hsüan ("Mystery-on-High"), T'ai I ("Supreme One") and Ling Chu ("Spirit Lord"). Now the second of these is not only highly theistic in meaning but also points to the idea of a High God above all the other gods, and on the way to being associated with *T'ien*. That certainly requires scrutiny. We go back to Yang Hsiung and the "border sacrifice" he saw at Kan Ch'üan about 10 B.C. In his commemorative *fu* he also gave alternative names for the major deity worshipped there: Shang-Hsüan and T'ai I, but also Huang-T'ien ("August Heaven"). That would seem to confirm the impression that the term *t'ien* was on the way to being personalized.

Third, with regard to the changing of the T'ai I and Hou T'u sacrifices from out-regions to Ch'ang-an, the "History of the Former Han Dynasty" is most strikingly lacking in informative detail. For instance, Emperor Ch'eng's proclamation in 31 B.C. reads: "We have removed the T'ai I and Hou T'u altars to the southern and northern suburbs." So also in 13 B.C., when he reinstated those sacrifices at their original sites, there is no mention of change of ritual. Yet changes of that sort usually brought with them implementation of new ideas on the meaning of the institution concerned. Presumably there were no striking changes. We can easily believe this, for Emperor Ch'eng, and after him Emperor Ai, were both nervous over what the effect on the two gods would be. This is reflected in the "Acts of the Emperors" round those years. In such a case the man ultimately responsible would feel chary about making provocative alterations. The Wang Mang record is a little more instructive. In A.D. 5 when Wang Mang was in the saddle as "Regent," he returned the two sacrifices to the Capital and boldly claimed that he was "obeying the mind of Heaven." With this move and instructions to Liu Hsin to build a *ming t'ang* at Ch'ang-an for the Five Ti, he ushered in his new dynasty. That *ming t'ang* was erected and used (see e.g., Wang Hsien-ch'ien's *Han Shu Pu-chu*, ch. 99, p. 6a). The new Emperor, being a member of the Wang clan and not the Liu, had a difficulty over the Han ancestral shrines, and had to seek other means for placating their fanes.

The question is: Were changes made in the nature of the T'ai I sacrifice? With regard to the last Former Han emperors, the answer is presumptively No; with regard to Wang Mang, certainly Yes. In what, then, lay the distinction between the two? First, we go to Yang Hsiung's *Kan Ch'üan Fu*, commemorating the sacrifice made to T'ai I at Kan Ch'üan by Emperor Ch'eng (d. 7 B.C.). The description there notes carriages poised so as to roll away of themselves and carry the sacrificial *virtus* to the ends of the empire, the "fiery fragrance offered to T'ai I," "chosen shamans all crying at the gate of [heaven's] Ti, opening heaven's audience hall, inviting a whole host of gods: a medley of helpers bringing down on the altar masses of good fortune, heaped up like a mountain." That was the kind of sky-directed sacrifice which could and did take place in the last twenty years of Former Han. Unfortunately there is no such detailed information about the New Dynasty's[11] method of procedure. There is, however, this: "When he [Wang Mang] knew in himself that he was defeated, he led his ministers out to the south suburb." He there called on "August Heaven" to send down a thunderbolt and destroy him, if he had done wrong. As he did this, he wept to the point of exhaustion.

Throughout four-fifths of the Former Han epoch there was neither a sacrifice to Heaven at the Capital, nor any proposal that that there should be one. Yet when Emperor Wu's T'ai I ("Supreme One") god was brought to Ch'ang-an, we find that the altar set up for him is denoted in Wang Mang's time as an altar to "August Heaven": also that in A.D. 22 the New Dynasty's defeated Emperor abased himself before "August Heaven." Before that regime came into being the main attested site for an altar to Heaven was on the peak of Mount T'ai (where the establishment of new dynasties was believed to have been reported in past ages). There is also this: Kuang Wu, an extremely religious, not to say superstitious man, on the day he consented to ascend the throne, put the propriety of his decision to the test by setting up an altar to Heaven-and-Earth and sacrificing on it. The following year he established it in his new capital, and thirty years later he sacrificed to Heaven in the south suburb and sacrificed to Earth in the north suburb. He also started build-

---

[11] The name of the usurper Wang Mang's short-lived dynasty.

ing a *ming t'ang* for the Five Shang Ti. "Filial Son Emperor Ming" carried on with the procedure, and these rites became established practices of the Later Han court.

In conclusion, there is nothing monotheistic in the whole story. Yet in those stressful mid-Han years something was being engendered, something was emerging, which was in the nature of a religious philosophy—one in which, as the contemporary memorials show, a new term came into use, *t'ien hsin*, the "sky-mind" or "mind of Heaven." The animistic matrix, from whence came the sacrifice Chang Heng depicted, is plain to view. But so also is the rationally questing mind, which in that age sought to extract sense and value out of the mumbo-jumbo of ordinances. As a fragment of the *Po Hu T'ung* puts it, "The sacrifice takes place once a year—so as not to be too intimate with Heaven—at a time when the *yang*-fluid begins to reassert itself." And again, "The King sacrifices to Heaven according to the same principle as he serves his father" (Tjan, *op.cit.*, 653).[12]

8. *Other Ritual Duties and Moral Allegorizing on Them*

Apart from picturing the imperial ritual year, Chang Heng had other weighty matters on his mind (see Sections 12-16). So, having described in detail the pomp of the sacrifice to Heaven, he treated other main functions in briefer fashion. Six of them are dealt with according to their time incidence. For the first three the narrative is clearly demarcated by changing rhyme schemes. In the treatment of the last three this is not the case, although four rhyme schemes mark phases

---

[12] One of the reasons why great caution needs to be used in envisaging purifying innovations in the Later-Han sacrifice is that the *Po Hu T'ung* in no way emphasizes it. It is possible that there was a section on it in the original version of the *Po Hu T'ung* and that this got lost; cf. Tjan, *op.cit.*, pp. 61 and 652. If the sacrifice to Heaven really did not figure in the decisions of the conference, it is possible that there were innovations proposed by the reforming party at court, and the conservative party (whose opinion prevailed at the conference) fought for nothing to be reported either way.

in the narrative. In the circumstances it seems best to divide the section into five subsections.[13] The genius of the descriptive *fu* consisted in the vivid presentation of objects, and accuracy of description took precedence over strict prosodic form. These *fu* are veritable gold mines to the exploring historian. But it must be borne in mind that the pictures are impressionistic and may omit features which the contemporary reader would have had clearly in mind. For instance in this section Chang Heng makes no mention whatever of the sacrifice to Earth at the half-year, a much more important ritual duty than the Emperor blessing the drinking of wine.

A. THE MING T'ANG AND THE FIVE SHANG TI

The critique of Pan Ku's Loyang *fu* left the reader with certain doubts, in chief one with regard to the functional range of the Loyang Ming T'ang. The first question to be faced is whether the proceedings included, as the *Po Hu T'ung* implies, a formal audience of the high feudatories and officers at which governmental policy was promulgated. Chang Heng's account reveals no sign of such an audience, agreeing in this respect with Pan Ku's ode on the Ming T'ang. They speak only of sacrifices, to the Five Ti and to Kuang Wu. Now, if there had been on the notable occasion of Emperor Ming's inauguration of his *ming t'ang* in A.D. 59 so notable a proceeding as a promulgation of policy, then Pan Ku's contemporary evidence is wanting in this important aspect; and Chang Heng thirty years later is found backing his account. Not only so: there is no trace of such a proceeding in the "History of the Later Han Dynasty." Also, the nature of the buildings would make them inconvenient, if not

---

[13] The first three rhyme schemes are a very interesting example of *fu* prosody, for the first and second come to life again in the middle of the third. So far it is prose narrative of proceedings leading up to the actual shooting. The portrayal of that comes under the fourth rhyme, and the poem having done that in one four-word couplet, goes straight to allegorical moralizing and continues doing so to the end of the section, bringing in *en route* the Wine Festival and Entertainment of Veterans. The passage as a whole is, therefore, an illustration of what Lu Chi called *"ch'ing"* "poetic mood").

prohibitively so, for such an occasion—although this would not apply to the presence of a limited number of dignitaries as witnesses of the sacrifices. The only reasonable conclusion is that Pan Ku and Chang Heng are right, and what the *Po Hu T'ung* reveals is the existence of an influential body of scholarly opinion which had other views of what should be done in place of what was done.

Second, with regard to the sacrifices, Chang Heng's language here is even more illuminating than that of Pan Ku's ode. These deities of the Western Ch'in culture are presented in a rationalized form, being identified with the "Five Essences" (*Wu Ching*), i.e. the five constituent forces of the universe.[14] Nonetheless Chang Heng calls them *ling* ("spirits," "gods") and describes four of these *ling* as "energetic" (*mo*) and "loyally warm-hearted" (*yün huai*). We seem to be back in the animist's world. Yet Chang Heng's mind, as we have seen, was by no means naïvely animistic. His idea is, therefore, in the nature of poetic fancy, revealing him as able to stand apart from those solemn rites, indeed think of them in a witty mood. Since "*mo*" and "*huai*" are common in the "History" Scripture in reference to faithful ministers, it may well be that that was just the way in which Chang Heng meant to present them. In any case the picture he presents, with the Han *virtus* of fire specially honored, is one of religious sacrifices conducted entirely with political ends in view. Whether gods or forces of Nature, they must be mobilized by precisional rites in support of the reigning order.

Third, in regard to Kuang Wu, deceased, made *p'ei*, associate god with the Five Ti, Pan Ku had stressed this, and it is stressed in the "Acts of the Emperors" under Emperor Ming's second year. Here, then, in this politico-religious amalgam, old ancestor worship and new filial piety are also to be found at work. King Wu and Duke Chou had long

---

[14] For the "Five *Hsing*" and "Five *Tê*," see Y. L. Fung, *A History of Chinese Philosophy*, tr. D. Bodde, I, 159-169.

ages back done this for their father, King Wen. In recent times Wang Mang as regent in A.D. 1 had had a suburban sacrifice performed in which Emperor Kao was made *p'ei* with Heaven and Emperor Wen *p'ei* with the Five Ti (see *Han Shu*, ch. 12). Thus to elevate Kuang Wu, the creator of Han Redivivus, was a demonstration to gods and men that the new regime had faith in its Heavenly commission and proposed to stand on its own merits.

B. THE ANCESTRAL SACRIFICES

If every culture has its own distinctive rhythms of thought and emotion, then here is a Chinese one. Chang Heng's mind swings straight from the energies of the seasons being controlled by sacrifices; to the ruling geniuses of spring, summer, autumn, and winter; to a consideration of the fervent filial heart of the Emperor moved by the sight of these products so that he takes pious thought of his ancestral manes and the high duty of nourishing them. So he must needs make sure in person that all is duly prepared: the victims and their accoutrements, the succulent meats, the soup, the dances, and the bells and drums, in order that all may be done with "enlightened decorum." Now, the whole passage is conditioned by this initial picture of the "fervently filial heart" and, being so, may be summed up as a typical example of that mid-Han sentimental idealism over filial piety which is so impressive a feature of the "Record of Rites."[15] There are three keys in which emotion is seen at work here. There are the succulent meats presented to those forebears, whose flesh and blood the sacrificers inherit. One of them acts as impersonator and wears his grandfather's clothes, and in his company they now sit down and eat. There is the spirit of potency those forebears possess, so that being well wined they can be counted on to "send down good fortune in masses." And there is the emergent filial-piety strain (the Way of Filial Piety), bursting its ancient animistic bonds

[15] See especially *Sacred Books of the East*, XXVIII, Book 21 ("*Ki I*"), Oxford, 1885, pp. 210-235.

and seeing the filial son serving the dead with no ulterior motive but only because they are the sacred dead to whom life-long gratitude is due.

C. THE PLOUGHING OF THE FIELD OF HEAVEN

Another procession out from the palace and the city is described. The Emperor took the plough in his own state carriage, lying between the driver and the guard on the right. The special carriage with the phoenix bells and the "azure-colored dragon horses" are mentioned in the *Yüeh Ling* ("Monthly Ordinances"), and the same applies. Indeed the whole account is redolent of the *Yüeh Ling*, though no mention is made of the Emperor's toasting the dukes at the end of the ceremony. It is an affecting picture that Chang Heng paints: the Emperor, on the one hand, with his own hands preparing the soil in which is to be sown the grain for the sacrifices, on the other hand, sanctifying and encouraging the toil of his hard-working subjects. Chang Heng apparently had no criticism to make of the proceedings; he was content to let the noble symbolism convey its simple lesson to the far from simple minds of his readers.

As everyone knows, and as, indeed, the classical literature of China amply reveals, there was this sense of community between prince and peasant. There is, also, the other side of the picture, fully documented by the records, revealing the ease with which the peasant could be, and was, oppressed. That Chang Heng himself was fully aware of this side is shown in the prophecies of doom which later sections of the *fu* contain. As for the history of this rite and its connection with a tribal society in which a mana-imbued chieftain or medicine man turned the first clod, that story goes beyond the scope of this enquiry. This much may be said: that just as an insistent urge towards rationalization reveals itself in the Later-Han Ming T'ang and ancestor worship, so also something of the sacramental attitude to life emerges to view in this agricultural rite. The semi-divine Son of Heaven who, as one current saying put it, "served Heaven as father and Earth as mother," can only adequately foster his high-priestly spiritual potency by the sweat of his body—by working the plough in the fellowship of humble labor. As Chang Heng expresses it, "in the supplying of grain in abundance for the high ancestral and suburb sacrifices, there is of necessity [*pi*] a consummation of thought in personal [physical] exertion." Again the *Chi I* ("Meaning of Sacrifice") in the "Record of Rites" is instructive: "Only a sage can entertain the high gods; only a filial son can entertain his parents."

D. THE ARCHERY RITE AND ITS PRELIMINARIES

One or two touches convey the impression of an eye-witness's observations. Since Chang Heng had studied in the Imperial Academy, he would in the ordinary course of events have been able to see the rite being performed, if only at a distance. The most notable feature in his enumeration of the preliminaries is his introduction of four legendary worthies and of Fu Sang, a fairy island—possibly Japan.

In his ode on the Pi Yung, Pan Ku only referred to the autumn use of it for the rite of Entertaining the Veterans. Chang Heng refers to that here, but gives much more attention to the Archery Rite held in the Spring. Neither of our authors refers directly to the fact that the Imperial Academy (*Ta Hsüeh*) was on the Pi Yung site (in the south-east suburb of Loyang, seven *li* distant from the city). Pan Ku's omission is the more curious, since he was eulogizing the Pi Yung as a whole. Chang Heng, on the other hand, was dealing with the ritual year, and the Academy was outside that picture. As a matter of fact, he makes an indirect reference to it in his "advancing enlightened virtue" (see sub-section E), for skill in archery was one of the tests for graduating from the Academy.

The thorny problem of education in the ancient royal capitals does not concern us here, except to this uncontentious extent, that archery unquestionably was part of the Chou system of training for the scions of noble families. Apart from that, the evidence is strong that either King Wen or Duke Chou conceived the political importance of having the feudatories meet together regularly in the capital, there to take part in the royal ancestral sacrifices and engage in archery contests. The rules of these contests were part of a code of chivalry by which was inculcated a sense of loyalty and honor and mutual forbearance. The evidence of the *Analects* is important in connection with the existence of archery contests in Confucius' lifetime. That the tradition survived among the Scholars into Han times is not open to doubt, but there are no references to archery contests or a Pi Yung in early Han records. After Emperor Wu, the idea of a Pi Yung was in the air, not only as a training ground for young aristocrats but with ever-increasing emphasis as the chief training centre for aspirants to the public service. It was, then, with the establishment of the Imperial Academy and the encouragement of the students to practice archery, that the traditional code took on a new lease of life. It became impregnated with the new mystic consciousness of music, whilst the archer's stance and general behaviour became indicative of the qualities required for the imperial service. Both these ideas are strikingly emphasized in the "Meaning of Archery" (*Shê I* in the "Record of Rites").

E. THE MYSTIC ARROW: THE SIGNIFICANCE OF THE WINE FESTIVAL AND ENTERTAINMENT OF THE VETERANS

The introduction of a new and final rhyme marks the swing of the poem's mood from narrative to appraisal—appraisal of the imperial *virtus* in action, and so, by association of ideas, appraisal of the Wine Festival and Entertainment of Veterans. The Son of Heaven is the centre of the picture, and his arrow's striking of the target is represented as stimulating the tender shoots of the grain crop. That statement on the face of it indicates untrammeled belief in mana magic, a mana-imbued king and his shamans able to transmit their mana into a dead implement and transform it into an agent of miraculous power.

We have seen the transformation of the Five Shang Ti into emblems of the five constituent forces in Nature and the sublimation of the Emperor's ploughing rite. Both of these were ceremonies with their roots deep in the soil of primitive animistic belief. In the case of the mystic arrow, we must turn first to the section on archery in the "White Tiger Hall Discussions." There we find this: "Why does the Son of Heaven in person practise archery? To aid the *yang* fluid in stimulating the ten thousand things. In the spring the *yang* fluid is small and weak, and it is to be feared that the [ten thousand] things, meeting obstructions, will not be able to come out by their own strength. Now in archery [the arrow proceeds] from the inside to the outside; it pierces and enters the solid and hard [target], thus resembling the bringing forth of [nascent] things. Therefore, by means of archery they are stimulated [in growth]." This is rationalizing, but rationalizing of that strained, pseudo-scientific kind which characterized the speculations of the Modern-Script school of thought which dominated the White Tiger Hall Conference. So far in our study of Chang Heng's mind we have seen no reason to believe he belonged to that obscurantist wing of scholar opinion, or subscribed to its fantastic logic of symbolism.[16] And here in this passage, having stated the theory of the imperial *virtus* in the imperial arrow, Chang Heng says nothing about the piercing of the solid and hard, but goes straight to "reveals the heart of integrity in a far-reaching parable" (*yüan yü*). A man who had faith in the miraculous efficacy of piercing of a hard target would not have spoken of it as a parable. Further, in the succeeding couplet the pattern of thought is entirely on the moralistic, sublimating level. There too an arresting image meets the eye, "fierce appetites of ravening greed" (*"t'ao t'ieh chih t'an*

---

[16] See Y. L. Fung, *A History of Chinese Philosophy*, tr. D. Bodde, II, ch. 2 and pp. 91-92.

yü). *T'ao t'ieh* were the central mana-inducing patterns on
the Yin bronze vessels. One would not expect a believer in
magic to translate so dangerous a symbol into the language
of fierce moral disapproval.

Any initial suspicion of Chang Heng's rationalism is now
almost gone. But there is still the fact that he introduced
four legendary figures into his narrative, depicting them apparently as actually present and co-operating in the proceedings: to put it bluntly, strengthening the *virtus* of the rite
by their age-old numinous powers. Here we recognize, not
only that Chang Heng's language is entirely precise, but in
the case of Ta Ping and Feng Hou quite extraordinary.
These two legendary figures feature in the Yellow Emperor
legend. On the evidence of *Huai Nan Tzŭ* (ch. 1) they were
fairy drivers who by the power of Tao "rode chariots of
cloud . . . galloped wildly in the dim and distant beyond . . .
crossing frost and snow and leaving no trace, shone on by
the sun and showing no shadow." Yet here they are represented as gentling the Emperor's mettlesome steeds along—
presumably to avoid jarring his muscles. Again it is difficult
to believe that Chang Heng is being pedantically factual.
Rather, it is the imagery of romantic fancy—and witty
imagery at that. As for Po I and Hou K'uei, they figure in
the Yao-Shun cycle as respectively minister of rites and music-
master. They also appear in Table Eight of the "History of
the Former Han Dynasty" as "Men of Wisdom and Understanding."

With regard to the peasants' great feast of the year, Chang
Heng's picture is useful to the historian for two reasons. One
is that in making respect for the aged a feature of the harvest
feast he gives us a date-mark for the infiltration of the filial-
piety motif into the practice of peasant jollifications. The
other reason is that Chang Heng introduces the Emperor
as himself with his bare right arm cutting up the meat for
his aged guests. The Son of Heaven thus demonstrated that
he treated his guests as filial piety demanded a man should
treat his own father and elder brothers. This feature does

not appear in the passages in the "Record of Rites." It does, however, appear in the "White Tiger Hall Discussions," where for the first time in extant Han literature there is the technical definitive phrase "three *lao* ["aged"] five *keng* ["veterans of public service"].[17] It seems clear, therefore, that it was the Later Han emperors who began this nobly conceived ritual act of humble deference. Since in theory what was done at court was a model for the kingdoms and commanderies we get a side-light on the proletarianization of the filial-piety doctrine.

9. *The Later Han Hunt*

Comparison of Chang Heng's account with Pan Ku's reveals a general identity of purpose, namely emphasis on the Loyang hunts being a vast improvement on the Ch'ang-an ones. They may be suspected of partiality in favour of the existing regime, but even so there can be little doubt that the more barbaric spirit of the old sanguinary debauches was purged to a considerable extent. Both our witnesses are so almost naïvely exhilarated by the new spirit of *wen* (refinement) which they acclaim. Their evidence also agrees in making these Later-Han hunts more distinctively occasions for army review, and that with insistence on a high standard of efficiency in timing all sorts of deployment. Chang Heng had nothing to say on the use of cavalry, but then Pan Ku had nothing to say on Chang Heng's central point, the imperial *virtus* reinforcing its power and appeal through the Son of Heaven's demonstration of humanity and mercy. In

---

[17] The term "*san lao*" was current in the Ch'in First Emperor's and Emperor Kao's time, but in a very different setting. Men of over fifty years were selected by the government to take responsibility for the law-abiding behaviour of their respective districts. The term "*wu keng*" seems to have been a later invention. According to Cheng Hsüan (cf. Tjan, *op.cit.*, 479) it, as also *san lao*, denoted one person, the "*san*" and "*wu*" referring to the two men's special qualifications. Ts'ai Yung, however, maintained that *keng* stood for *sou* ("aged") and that there were actually three *lao* and five *keng*. Chang Heng's use of *kuo* ("state's") *sou* strengthens the student in believing (a) that *keng* in this connection indicates veterans of the public service, (b) that two kinds of old men were selected in Later Han times, three on grounds of great age, five on grounds of merit in the service of the state.

this connection, as appeared with Chang Heng's moving picture of the poor escaped pheasant and hare, he reveals a tenderness of heart which is very rare in the classic cultures of the world.

With regard to "three drives," limited in number so that a way of escape was left open, Chang Heng seems to make an association of ideas between that and Sage-King Ch'eng T'ang's net with three closed sides and the fourth left open. What the poem says is "He [the Son of Heaven] admires Ch'eng T'ang's loosened net." One of the Later-Han emperors may well have made an explicit reference to T'ang's net in some order for the hunt, but the language of the poem may just as well represent nothing more than Chang Heng's poetic fancy. The point of the net story comes out in a passage in the third century B.C. *Lü Shih Ch'un Ch'iu* where it is stated that thirty southern countries hearing of the new king's concern for the fish inferred a like concern for human welfare and came and submitted.[18]

The King Wen legend comes in the story of his life in the "Record of History." There it is stated that King Wen, being Lord of the West, attracted the notice of Lü Shang, the great Lord of the East Coast. The Lord of the West went hunting, the oracle being that he would capture neither dragon, tiger nor bear, but capture support for attaining the supremacy. In the hunt the two lords met at Wei Yang and in conversation Lü Shang was greatly pleased with the Lord of the West. It was a handy story for Chang Heng with which to point the moral.

10. *The Driving Away of the Demons of Plague*

The opening words make this part of the Emperor's priestly year, but as a matter of fact he is only in the background, as far as the narrative is concerned—unless by any

---

[18] For earlier evidence of humanitarian feeling for animals, see *Mencius* I A 17, which describes the sympathy of King Hsüan of Ch'i (331-313 B.C.) for a sacrificial ox.

chance the sentences after "Thereafter" should be taken as having him as the unspoken subject. The objection to that is that Chang Heng so plainly is in lighter mood, and it is not likely that he would make His Majesty the subject of those ironical sentences. The impression of irony piles up, beginning with the couplet about the children's shooting and the demons being sure to fall dead. Then in the very next sentence they are racing away into the blue, and our poet piles Pelion upon Ossa with his beheading, braining, imprisoning, drowning, destroying, and exterminating. To crown all, after he has got the two beneficent Tu Shuo guardians on the watch, he says the lictors will see to any demons left over. In a word, when the holes and corners in the houses have been cleaned up, then nothing could be there "which was contrary to right and to rule." Moreover, the treatment is reminiscent of the *Kan Ch'üan Fu* in which Yang Hsiung had described the discomfiture of hostile demons:

> The mountain demons could not propel themselves here; halfway on the long road they fell back.

> One after the other they fell headlong, the bridge of their flight broken, they became a cloud of midges and in a stroke were gone from the sky.

In another part of the poem he wrote:

> The whole tribe of *ch'i yu* bearing fabulous swords and jade axes fled into hiding, racing away belly to earth: all, all of them, jammed together like weeds in an interlocking mass, a rack of stormy clouds whirling away in wild confusion.

> With their ranks joined and overlapping, huddled together they moved like fishes with eyes to the fore, like birds with necks outstretched.

What marvelous descriptive imagery *and* superb irony! And it was for this kind of writing that Chang Heng's compeers had so cultivated a taste.

With regard to the procession through the streets, again it looks as if Chang Heng had been an eye-witness. And this rite of expelling the demons of disease was part of village procedure, so that he may well have taken part in it as a child. This is the rite which Confucius was said to have seen, and which caused him to put on his court robes and stand to sympathetic attention (see *Analects*, X). The parallel is worth noting, for, surely, there is more than irony in those demons being bound to fall down dead. It is the child's process of reasoning: with these thousands of arrows shot into the air, how can the demons fail to get killed!

That pathetic touch and the grizzly list of bogies' names brings home to us the fears which beset the lives of the Loyang populace. Historians know well what the cloacan filth of Paris and London was, even in post-mediaeval times, and the devastating epidemics which resulted. The point here is that one of the functions of government whether at a tribal or at a great-state level, is to take measures with the panic fears which seize a community on these occasions. So here in the poem there is put before us both the mobilization of the city government to deal with the emergency and the mimic warfare of the old animistic rite. The last was necessary, whatever the more highbrow scholars might think about its efficacy. On the other hand, the common sense of hygiene would appear to have been operative in Chang Heng's Loyang as well. Considering what the Loyang temperature in midwinter is now and was then, considering also the babies and old people in the families, the yearly official clean-up referred to in the last line would appear to have been of plain necessity.

11. *The Tour of Inspection*

The Son of Heaven is back in the centre of the picture—how could it be otherwise with the subject what it is, the tours of inspection in state visits to the different parts of the country. Pan Ku had had nothing to say on this, and now Chang Heng fills in the gap: rightly so, since these wide-flung visits were a vital corollary to the *virtus* theory. In terms of the Yin-Yang forces in Nature it was necessary that the sovereign, after gearing them into harmonious operation in the capital, should in person go and stimulate them under the different regional conditions. That a tour should, as Chang Heng's list of items shows, include action in the mystical sphere and on the practical level was of the very logic of the *virtus* theory. The Son of Heaven's influence naturally had to emanate from the capital, but it was necessary that he should also shed the light of his person in every quarter of the realm. That this entailed the labor and discomfort of long-distance travel was supporting evidence of the sage quality pertaining to the imperial government.

It is clear from the treatment of the subject in the "White Tiger Hall Discussions" (Tjan, *Po Hu T'ung*, p. xix) that these royal progresses stood high in public estimation in Later-Han times. The impressive thing in the two documents is the highly bureaucratic nature of the Emperor's program on a visit. For instance, price lists of the goods in the markets were to be presented for inspection (Tjan, *op.cit.*, 496), whilst the poem mentions the planning of the crops, estimation of the harvests, and rewards for industrious surveyance. That there was a disciplinary side is emphasized in both documents, but the dominant motive seems to have been to introduce a debonair monarch among his loyal subjects, exhibiting his all-embracing human-heartedness. To judge from the general history of monarchies, eastern and western, ancient and modern, it has always paid sovereigns and their representatives to advertise and stage these popular occasions. Although in England the curing of the king's evil on a royal progress is a thing of the past, who dares say the launching of a battleship by a royal hand does not contain a lingering belief in a monarchic mana which can bring good fortune in its train? There was good statecraft in Mencius' warning to King Hsüan of Ch'i, when he pictured the king's subjects saying, "If our king does not come journeying, how shall we get blessings? If our king does not make excursions, how can we get help?"

Another feature of the "White Tiger Hall Discussions" is the markedly feudal terminology used in connection with the tours. The intention in this is obvious, to underline the institution as one dating from sage-king practice. There seems no reason to doubt that it did exist in Western Chou times. For example, the retention in Later-Han times of the archaic term *shou* ("a hunt") points to a feudal society in which one of the king's functions was to visit his feudatories and encourage them in the destruction of beasts of prey. There is, however, ground for hesitation in accepting the tour of inspection described in the "White Tiger Hall Discussions" as applying equally to Former-Han times. In the "History of the Former Han Dynasty" the royal progresses do not figure in the early Han reigns as much as they do in the later reigns. Emperor Wu is the key figure here with his passion for traveling and his thirst for sacrificing in all parts of his dominions and so for proving that he had all the gods marshalled in his support. He had no compunction in taking unprecedented lines of action in his sacrifices at Mount T'ai and in the establishment of a centrally-appointed bureaucracy in every kingdom and commandery. The historian, therefore, has to envisage the likelihood that during the succeeding reigns a new type of royal progress came into being, in which more exact methods of inspection were inaugurated. Unification and standardization, we know, became effective watchwords; and from this may be inferred a strengthening of the conviction that the sage-kings had foreshadowed these changes, had, indeed, conducted tours of inspection after the new pattern.

Chang Heng's reference to the comfort of being back home seems a little pointed, particularly as Yang Hsiung in his *Kan Ch'üan Fu* had written:

With the business finished and the merit colossal, we all . . . returned home . . . and took our ease in the Ch'ang Li Palace.

The heavenly quarters were well taken care of, the bounds of earth laid open . . . all the states in the world in peace and amity.

So here, the complacency of the court having been pinpointed, a suspiciously elaborate description of the felicitous omens follows. As a matter of fact, the "Acts of the Emperors" shows that the omens during Emperor An's manhood years were by no means unfailingly auspicious. But Empress-Dowager Teng was surrounded by yes-men, courtiers who might be described, like the *tsou-yü* horses, as docile and "obedient to favors."

The whole section is in fact patently hyperbolic, not least in its triumphant conclusion. There the peaceful *virtus* is represented as a coverlet under which reposed the furthest of far-off lands, Ting Ling in Siberia, Southern Annam, Ta Ch'in (the Roman Empire), and Korea. We have to assume that Chang Heng knew something about the bloody campaign Tou Ku and his generals in A.D. 91 had waged against the Northern Huns, from which sprang Chinese contacts with the Ting Ling people. So also with Pan Ch'ao's plotting and violence in Western Asia, from which sprang contacts with Rome's frontier provinces.[19] It is when Chang Heng is in his particularly hyperbolic vein that the suspicion of irony cannot but assert itself. In this connection it should be noted that this section is the climax of the *virtus* argument on its noble side. The succeeding sections are patently critical. He

---

[19] For details of the Later Han frontier wars and achievements, the memoirs on the barbarians in the "History of the Later Han Dynasty" (*Hou Han Shu*, chs. 75-80) are a mine of information. Cf. E. Chavannes, *T'oung Pao*, vols. 5-8. For contacts with Rome, F. J. Teggart's *Rome and China* (University of California Press, 1939) is useful up to a point. For other works of reference see K. S. Latourette's *The Chinese*, 3rd edn. revized, pp. 140-141 (New York, 1946).

is ironical in a noble, poetic spirit directed at making people face their conventional sentiments in their naked reality.

12. *The People's Argument with the Throne*

The tenor of the poem changes at this point. It becomes more argumentative. With this change Chang Heng's *dramatis personae*, the Teacher and the Nobleman, come more to life, and the two regimes, Ch'ang-an and Loyang, are made by contrast a burning subject of disputation. Teacher Anonymous first lays down the law, enunciating precedents which must be taken as principles of action. The removal of a capital must be after the pattern of the Shang dynasty's removal of its capital to Yin. This, as the *P'an keng* section of the "History" Scripture showed, was done "for the good of the people." So also in regard to luxury versus frugality in the court, the *Ssŭ Kan* ode gave the authoritative lead.

The sacrifices at Mount T'ai and Liang Fu had not been subject to dispute in the *fu* but they had to come in because of their connection with the Yellow Emperor. In the Taoist and to some extent in orthodox mythology, he was the grand exemplar of government by mystic power of personality, and Chang Heng's prime contention is that the Han *virtus* is basically of that nature. That being so, it is not surprising that he uses the purest Taoist language here, particularly as he is not concerned with fiats, as Pan Ku was, but with the Son of Heaven himself. This personal note is struck all through the section, so much so that the Emperor is conceived as communing with himself. Yet it is surprising that the case should be presented in so Taoistic a form even though Confucius is introduced as being of the same mind. Chang Heng was writing for a highly orthodox court to read; and the salient fact is that he did so in this fashion. The *Lao Tzŭ* Book must in Chang Heng's eyes have had considerable authority as a Scripture on the Way and the *virtus*.

Pan Ku's lyrical description of an imperial ban on luxury goods was found to have moderate confirmation in the records. That applied to the reigns of Emperors Kuang Wu and Ming. Chang Heng was writing one to three decades later than Pan Ku; but though there was unquestionably a decline in morale, Empress-Dowager Teng was stiffly puritan in outlook and issued at least one edict against luxury goods (see *Hou Han Shu*, X B). The phrasing in that edict resembles Chang Heng's here, so the question arises whether he had any particular court situation in mind as he wrote. The setting in the poem is curiously suggestive.

First, there is that paean on the Han *virtus* in terms of all within the four seas being transported with joy over its scent "at this very time." Then, "only our sovereign lord can plant the auspicious *ming chieh*," and then, "That being so, then how can the Tao not cherish, how can the [imperial] transforming power not soothe?" The sentiment might easily have come from the sycophantic lips of Emperor An's circle at the time when he was at last free of his domineering regent's will. Equally likely, a good old scholar—indeed Chang Heng himself—could make the same ejaculation, knowing that his sovereign's long minority had increased the sinister power of the eunuchs. But a rhetorical question can sometimes be answered, and it was part of Chang Heng's thesis that the scent of the Han *virtus* had, at any rate in Ch'ang-an days, come to have a very mixed odor. However, all would be well if the Emperor proved himself equal to his opportunity.

The suggestion is made not only because of those particular phrases. There is the poignantly expressed climax, the Emperor communing in his own soul, facing up to his Heaven-given responsibility, and seeing it as integrated with the winds and the life-giving rains. So also he faces the sage-kings. The Han *virtus* as embodied in the Loyang order went beyond anything the Hsia, Shang-Yin, and Chou orders had achieved: it was equal to those of the Five Emperors before them. "Who says we have started too late and cannot overtake Fu Hsi and Shen Nung?"

13. *Sundry Reflections on Emperors and Their Way of Life*

Our attention is arrested at once (a) by the striking of an apologetic note, (b) by the resuscitation of the Teacher and his disputant, the Nobleman, who for so much of the *fu* have not been thrust on our attention at all. Clearly something of special interest is to come, and the author for his part disciplines his thoughts by re-envisaging his *dramatis personae*. As to the apologetic self-deprecation, there are two separate remarks, the one clearly meant to be taken seriously, the other in its Teacher versus Nobleman context construable as an ordinary piece of politeness between two gentlemen in dispute. With regard to the first, since anything approaching to criticism of imperial policy necessitated the use of highly disparaging remarks about one's self, the natural inference is that the "something of special interest" is criticism of the existent regime. Yet on the surface Section 12 was purely eulogistic on the present Han *virtus*, and here in this passage, although there are very pointed allusions to disgraceful incidents at Ch'ang-an, again there is still no overt criticism of the court.

One is at first prepared to accept that Chang Heng had no hidden meaning here. But the passage as a whole has several extraordinary features, notably the zig-zag course along which the argument proceeds. Why should Chang Heng, in contrasting and condemning certain Ch'ang-an vices, have been compelled to jab out this straightforward subject in the way he does? And what had the theme of monarchs in their state carriages to do with those same vices, unless it was that the court Chang Heng knew was extravagant in this respect? In any case he does constructively condemn the court by urging that those immaculately trained carriage horses should be discarded. Working on the basis of that indication, again and again a double scope of reference, past and present, fits neatly to the statement made. Indeed, Emperor An seems to be the person hinted at, as, for instance, in "How much less can the inheritor of the imperial patrimony treat his Heaven-given station lightly." Emperor An was very much under the domination of his favorite eunuchs. Also, one of them, Sun Ch'eng, is on record as being a man of violent temper and on one occasion at an audience "loudly berating those left and right." Compare "So [the lord of] a myriad chariots . . . may yet be intimidated by a commoner." Sun Ch'eng had been ennobled by then, but he was a commoner by birth. Again, "All day he [the Emperor] does not leave his protective entourage—if he makes incognito excursions, where does he go?" True, that cap fitted two Ch'ang-an emperors, and, true, there is no actual evidence of Emperor An making incognito excursions, but in the light of his known weakly, dissipated character, and the Empress-Dowager's sternly moralistic training, what is more likely than that such excursions were made? Again Hsün Tzǔ's theory of education for "the One Man" was that he should be surrounded by exquisite sights and sounds and know no common, vulgar thing, and so have his character fortified against unruly passions. This theory was reinforced in the "Record of Rites" and Empress-Dowager Teng and her doctrinal guide, Pan Chao, had a passion for the strict letter of the ceremonial law. So with regard to monarchs in their carriage and their sheltered rhythmic existence, does not the picture come near enough to a young man trained in the strictest school? Also, compare that picture, one of an exquisite dummy, with the counter picture Chang Heng also created of the Emperor communing in himself about his responsibilities. Compare also his picture of the two great emperors, Kao and Kuang Wu. *They* knew fear of danger, but not the pusillanimous fear of a gilded recluse who had never learnt to face the hard facts of imperial government and took refuge in sanctioning all that his sycophantic, avaricious councillors advized. It remains but to add that when Emperor An assumed his prerogatives he was ruthlessly exploited by that eunuch gang, and when he died, the official eulogy recorded, "The *virtus* [of Emperor An] did not rise: it was [like] unripened grain in relation to our royal standards."

In considering this interpretative suggestion the reader should take into account the contexts to the three classical tags Chang Heng introduces into his argument, two from *Lao Tzŭ* and one from the *Analects*. *Lao Tzŭ* 26 reads as follows: "The sage man goes about all day and does not leave his *tzŭ chung*. Although he has palaces and harem buildings, his mind is aloof from them. How then about the lord of a myriad chariots who in his person treats the empire irresponsibly? If he is irresponsible, then he loses the root: if he is [meaninglessly] active, then he loses the sovereignty." *Lao Tzŭ* 46 reads as follows: "When there is Tao in the empire, then the fleet horses are used to dung [the fields]. When there is no Tao in the empire, the war horses are reared in the suburbs. Of calamities there is none greater than insatiability, of sins none greater than desire for gain. . . ." In *Analects*, XIII 15 Confucius is asked whether one *yen* (remark) can destroy a principality and replies, "Such an effect as that could hardly come from speech, but there is the saying that 'I have no delight in being a sovereign but only that my words are such that no one opposes me.'"

14. *Plain Facts of Social Economy*

The last section was highly poetical—vivid in its imagery, tense with restrained emotion, rugged and yet rhythmic. This section is the reverse: plain statements of plain economic facts, a cool enunciation in formal terms of how peace and prosperity, the rational ends of government, come into being. In English the section may not seem poetry at all. In the Chinese these terse four-word couplets have the balance of poetic diction. There is the ring of their changing rhymes, and twice there is the alternation of rhythm through the use of six-word lines. Thus, although the passage is entirely unrhetorical, it is eloquent, and above all limpidly clear, in all respects a poetic contrast to the passage it succeeds.

This is rather a new side to Chang Heng. Although in his "*Fu* on the Western Capital" he objected to the spawn in the streams being frivolously exterminated, he has not so far shown any particular interest in economic affairs. In point of fact we come here on a characteristic of the classical scholar mind, a marked streak of economic realism which can be traced back as far as Confucius (cf. e.g., *Analects*, 1 5), and which dictated much of Mencius' teaching. It is yet more clearly revealed in the Legalist philosophers, and even appears in the Taoist mystical paradoxes. Leaving on one side the wider historical aspects of this feature as matter more pertaining to the final chapter, what needs noting here is: (a) Chang Heng's competent analysis of economic factors under two heads, natural resources and man power; (b) his emphasis on wise planning, if these two sources of wealth are not to give out; (c) with a flourishing economy the people are prepared to work hard and pay for more prosperity; (d) prolongation of this state of affairs leads to inter-class amity and loyalty to the throne; (e) fair-dealing becomes an established habit, and the ordinary man, illiterate as he is, responds to the appeal of integrity and self-restraint.

It sounds very like the more cogent party speeches in a modern American election, or some of the patriotic appeals made in post-war Britain. In the China of Emperor An's reign this sober facing of facts was made in relation to a definite sag in the national economy. The prosperity of Emperor Ming's time was fifty years back. And the public had reason for suspecting that intrigue and graft in Loyang were perverting the established safeguards of government efficiency.

15. The Nobleman Forced to Face
Unpleasant Facts

In these nine and the succeeding ten couplets the poem reaches its climax, in fact the climax of the whole composition. Since the double-harness mind worked so predominantly in complementary effects, the right line of approach is to take the two sections as complementary to each other, the first culminating in an appeal to the Nobleman on selfish grounds, the second culminating in a general appeal on higher grounds.

The dramatic dialectical setting to the poem is again thrust on the reader's attention: Teacher Anonymous, *alias* the author, versus Nobleman Arrogant. The latter is straightly admonished, and whatever doubt may attach to Chang Heng having the Emperor and his circle in mind in Section 13, there need be no hesitation here in taking the Nobleman as representing a prevalent type among the aristocracy of the time. There is no beating about the bush. A denunciation is made in the form of two equations:

1. The top-dog's oppression of the under dog
   = the under dog's inveterate hatred.
2. The exhaustion of necessary commodities
   = rebellion and nation-wide misery.

In algebraical terms $X_1 = Y_1$, $X_2 = Y_2$, and $X_1 + X_2 = Y_1 + Y_2 = Z$, and Z is a very uncomfortable time in store for "you, Noble Sir" and your friends. The logic of this is driven home, not by citations from holy writ, but by a succession of homely saws (images). The first, about water and a boat, was a current saying in that age. It dated from Hsün Ch'ing, the philosopher, who made its scope of reference doubly clear: as the water bears up and can equally well capsize a boat, so the people sustain the throne and can equally well overthrow it.

The biting force of the other four images comes out when Chang Heng's sense of time is examined: time past, time present, time future, an ineluctable process. From his point of view it was a mechanically operative nexus of cause and effect in relation to human affairs, although when an effect would become operative was incommensurable. Thus, a hundred years earlier, disastrous as Wang Mang's wicked usurpation had been, the mysterious forces at work had taken time to mature, and it was twice nine years before the bogus regime crashed. So too with the mysterious but regular changes in the seasons; it is not till you wake up one morning and find frost on your shoes that you know hard winter is at your door. On top of that, the force of human nature must be taken into account—human nature with its natural proclivity to blind laziness.

The quotation "If [you] rise at dawn . . . how much more . . ." comes from the *Tso Chuan* (Duke Chao, third year). These words were inscribed on a famous sacrificial tripod, and "how much more" was followed by "if daily [you] refuse to reform, [you] cannot endure [in the land] for long." Chang Heng cut out that trite moralistic warning to his noble readers—they knew it well enough as coming in the Scriptures. Instead, he aimed at the aristocrat's sense of bodily comfort and class superiority, accustomed as he was to robes cut regardless of expense. The day of economic distress will surely come when a gentleman will perforce cut his cloth to a penurious pattern.

16. *The Final Word from Teacher Anonymous*

If the reader is expecting the eloquence of an impassioned appeal, he will be disappointed. Chang Heng's mood was otherwise. That the idea of eloquence occurred to him is evidenced by his reference to Ssŭ-ma Hsiang-ju and Yang Hsiung and their *fu* poems on the Ch'ang-an hunting park, in Chang Heng's day the applauded patterns of torrential eloquence. He glanced at that, recalling perhaps those of his friends who could smack their lips over the literary virtuosities and gently blink the appeal to action. He forces their attention to that by quoting the two poets' words, Ssŭ-ma Hsiang-ju appealing for the park to be given to the peasants to cultivate, Yang Hsiung calling for game preservation; and he crowns this by declaring that even if those measures had been taken, they would have been of no avail. Ch'ang-an was doomed, by reason of its ingrained vices. It did not matter who ruled there, a descendant of Emperor Wu or a wicked usurper. Neither did it matter that it had strong passes to protect it. The day came when at the Han Valley Pass the government troops were beating their drums, and at that very moment the people's army was sacking the seat of government.

In a very real way this presentation of hard facts here is linked to the argument contained in the simile of the water and the boat. The people sustain the throne, and the people can overturn it: they did so a hundred years ago, opening the door for our glorious Loyang regime. Here is material for the historian. In the eyes of a Chang Heng the decline and fall of all-conquering, resplendent Ch'ang-an was the major fact in the country's history. That he used this fact at the climax of his appeal to the throne and its advisers and the nobility and scholar world demonstrates that it was for him the strongest ground of appeal. In other words, in their eyes, as to some extent in his, Later Han was so vastly superior to Former Han that, although there might be blemishes, the ship of state was travelling safely on its keel of enlightened rule and order. All through the *fu* Chang Heng has eulogised that enlightenment, and here he pins his hopes on being able to awake a commensurate enlightenment of mind in the guardians of the *virtus*.

It was self-complacency he had to break up, in a blasé young Emperor, in successful careerists enjoying very comfortable emoluments. "It is human for the mind to think that what it has learnt is right, for the limbs to be comfortable in habitual postures" ("but actually—I, Teacher Anonymous, challenge you to deny it—there is a pungent smell about, and if you were not so used to it, you could not but be revoltingly aware of it"). On top of that thrust, the more caustic because of its market-place vulgarity, comes the reference to the *Hsien Ch'ih*, the most refined of images in scholar minds; for of all the court musical dramas which had come down from antiquity[20] this was in theory the most purifying in its effects; and without music even *li*, the code of outward form, could not attain its ends. One of the hall marks of a scholar and a gentleman was that he responded to the *Hsien Ch'ih*'s passion-subduing influence, as in his deportment the measured chiming of his jade girdle-pendants signalized a nobleman's dignity and honor. What did Chang Heng say? He said in effect: "You, Noble Sirs, are well aware that the court are bored with the *Hsien Ch'ih*, and would rather listen to the croaking of frogs, the base, libidinous music of Cheng which Confucius hated, as he hated those who with covetous mouths overturn states and families" (*Analects*, XVII 18): "the great Music Master K'uang of such noble repute, he had a different mind, had he not: is he the only one?"

The critique assumes that that question of Chang Heng's was both a rhetorical one and a genuine one. It was rhetorical since orthodoxy laid it down (see Tjan, *Po Hu T'ung*, pp. 387-391) that from the Emperor down fine ritual and fine music were essential to them if they were to govern successfully. The question also was a real one, for Chang Heng's hope was that every reader would take it to heart for himself. To the modern reader, peering through the long centuries at that patriot figure, brush in hand, his final appeal in this form may seem stilted and artificial, little calculated to strike home. It may be, for after all the appeal failed and the vices of that generation became worse vices and Chang Heng's warning of doom was most miserably fulfilled. On the other

---

[20] I take it that the historian can accept the evidence of the extremely learned Liu Hsieh (6th century A.D.), in *Wen Hsin Tiao Lung*, ch. 7. He refers there to the music of the Yellow Emperor and his immediate successors as being "unascertainable for discussion." About what date did that and other antique music become obsolete and forgotten? In other words, is Chang Heng's peculiar reference to the *Hsien Ch'ih* music evidence that it was already on the way to being obsolete? It seems safe to assume that very antique musical dances were carefully transmitted, only with variations introduced by a succession of talented court producers. Cf. the tradition that Yao expanded the Yellow Emperor's *Hsien Ch'ih*, made originally to purify his court of drunken and licentious orgies.

CRITIQUE

hand, he knew his age, as he also knew the limits of the pressure an unennobled scholar might exert, and this was the form he chose. As has been emphasized above, sinners in high places were regarded as more likely to reform if skilfully encouraged to prod themselves.[21]

17. *The Nobleman Repents*

The lack of an elegant peroration to the Teacher's discourse has been noted. The poem as a whole has, to be sure, been amply eloquent, even bombastic in its Section 12. The remarkable thing is that here, after deploying his dry, caustic attack on blind self-satisfaction, Chang Heng continues his ironic line in the first couplet, turning his wit against himself and his prolixity, and then lets loose his eloquence in a picture of penitence. He gives a portrait of a proud man tortured by the realization that he has both behaved badly and made a fool of himself. (One is reminded of the Hebrew poet's Job when brought face to face with the All-Righteous.) It was in this fashion that this Later-Han scholar and patriot, avoiding a vulgar display of his own fine sentiments, compelled his courtly readers to face their own souls. He could do no more, the rest was in the hands of fate—of Heaven that had brought Han and Later Han into existence for the good of the people, of the Yin-Yang cosmic forces which in man and nature unceasingly made the new old and so opened the door to recreation, with the wicked man destroyed in his wickedness.

[21] In *Chuang Tzŭ* (ch. 4) Confucius is presented as arguing with Yen Hui when the latter wanted to go and convert the arrogant and self-willed Prince of Wei. The sage warns the earnest young man against the danger of "forcing rule-of-thumb speeches about moral ideas upon violent bragging men." The well-meaning people who do that, said the Master, are rightly called calamity men, for they bring calamity on others as well as on themselves. Cf. E. R. Hughes, *Chinese Philosophy in Classical Times*, Everyman Series, 1954 edn., pp. 186-189.

Chapter XI

GENERAL APPRAISALS

◇◇

1. *The Value of Pan Ku and Chang Heng as Witnesses*

I HAVE BEEN TRYING to achieve a vignette of Han history through the study of two minds, related to each other by the fact that the two men lived for most of their lives in the same city, that one was born fourteen years before the other died, and that they both spent a great deal of energy in writing lengthy poems on the same subject. Since these two writers are my prime source of information, my first task is to appraise their value as witnesses. That is a question of relative intelligence and relative honesty. To my readers and myself who are in this case a panel of judges in a court of inquiry, a pair of muddled-headed, unobservant witnesses would be useless; their respective stories would neither corroborate nor contradict each other. A couple of self-interested liars might be of some use, if we should be clever enough to get at the facts behind the misleading impressions they were out to convey. If, on the other hand, they were men of real intellectual acumen, with sharp eyes and attentive ears for what was going on around them, and if, better still, they had a habit of discriminating about what they learnt, whether it was fact or fiction, they would be invaluable; and the mere fact that at certain points their testimony disagreed might throw yet more light on the matters they describe. It is necessary, of course, to look out for signs of *tendenz* in their personal idiosyncrasies, their opinions as members of a class, and their unconscious assumptions as men of a particular age and particular cultural environment.

In the foregoing chapters of critique, attention has been paid from time to time to these matters, and there is, in one way and another, a considerable body of data. A summarization works out as follows:

(1) Pan Ku's record in regard to his *Han Shu* ("History of the Former Han Dynasty") has been dealt with in Chapter II. Certain signs of critical intelligence in that work are noted in the critiques. On the whole he is seen more at his judicial best in his historical work. In his two *fu* on the capitals he is more the prejudiced witness, not so much untrustworthy about the bygone regime, his life-long field of study, but uncritically enthusiastic about the regime under which he lived, and to be suspected of not telling all he knew about the concomitants to imperial policy on the far western border.

(2) Chang Heng, a mathematician and a deviser of precision instruments, when he came to matters within the field of history showed himself about as penetrating as Pan Ku in his judgements on the past, and more trustworthy in regard to the political and social complexion of his day between twenty and forty years after Pan Ku's, when signs of a moral decline had begun to appear.

(3) Both men were conscious of the unreliability of hearsay evidence, but both were not always consistent on this point when it came to universally accepted stories about the sage-kings of antiquity. Whether they accepted them literally or symbolically is not clear. If symbolically, then we need to remind ourselves that the history of thought is filled with instances of symbols achieving an aura of factuality.

(4) Both men had a naturalistic philosophy, which to a considerable degree was superimposed on their inherited animistic beliefs, transforming them somewhat but not dislodging them entirely.

(5) Both men's outlook was more cosmopolitan than nationally restricted, although both were persuaded that their own civilisation was fitted by its enlightened moral, social, and political principles, its cultured manners, its learning and literary genius, its command of resources and extension of

communications, to rule not only a greatly enlarged dominion but also all the lesser breeds without the law.

(6) The four poems show a high level of literary competency. The authors were able to express subtle distinctions of meaning, to build up series of cogent propositions, to show genius in their use of apt and pithy illustrations, and to communicate nuances of mood by the skilful placing of one revealing word. The four overall pictures they produced are composed of lucid representations of very complicated objects of sense-observation, and of their discriminating reflections thereon. In addition, whereas Pan Ku followed one order of consecutive portrayal and Chang Heng followed another, in all four cases the results reveal mature powers of coordinating effects and achieving artistic balance. And these qualities of the mind were shared, to some extent at any rate, by the circle of readers for whom our authors wrote. The outburst of literary production which Pan Ku's Preface so vividly depicts was accompanied by a new and excited consciousness of literary talent as one of the highest products of advancing civilization. Both Pan Ku and Chang Heng themselves, products of the new birth, were well aware of the critical minds that would study the fruits of their labors.

(7) They both had a sense of humour, more of the urbane than the bucolic type, although Pan Ku could get near to slapstick. Chang Heng's command of irony was nothing short of masterly, so informed with wit, so straight to the mark, for the most part so free from the bludgeoning malice of wounding satire.

(8) They both had powers of sensitive discernment in regard to emotional moods and physical disturbances, as, for example, the dizzying effects of flights of stairs (Pan Ku), and the intolerable ennui caused by a surfeit of routine entertainment (Chang Heng). They were familiar with the symptoms of mental confusion arising, for example, from nostalgia for a supposedly pleasanter past, or from conventional ideas making the unmistakeable evidence of one's senses

unbelievable. Chang Heng, at any rate, could appreciate why the peasant's kind of life made him satisfied with simple pleasures and then, when frivolously deprived of the necessities of life, made him blindly destructive in his hatred of the oppressors.

(9) Although, therefore, their philosophic acumen came short of a modern logician's idea of precision thinking and Chang Heng's highest attainment in mathematics did not go beyond a faulty attempt at a more accurate reckoning of π, yet along the main thoroughfares of human endeavour to achieve clarity of thought and precision of expression, to apply cause and effect on the cosmic scale and in the realm of ethics and social order, both Pan Ku and Chang Heng pass a general test of intellectual acumen.

(10) As for their honesty of speech, this is more difficult of appraisal because of the sophisticated conventions of their age and the court they lived in. As the reader will have noticed, I have had my doubts about Pan Ku on the score of flattering his masters. But we have a double check on him in this. His comparatively low rank at court and his thirst for recognition were one thing: his trained eye for fact-finding was another. Of Chang Heng we get an impression of deeper sincerity. Faced as he was—in a way Pan Ku was not— with an ominous decline in court morale, he had a greater strain put on his sense of honor. His value as a witness is that much the higher because he nobly took the risk of exhorting his imperial master and reproving the powerful nobility. Yet he also used the terms of conventional adulation. We are, therefore, more able to appreciate the iron compulsion of the code of manners and to avoid depreciating Pan Ku as a mere sycophant. Thus Pan Ku may be counted as medium honest: Chang Heng as superlatively so.

The evidence from our two witnesses is, therefore, trustworthy to a high degree, and even where it proves untrustworthy, generally succeeds in being clear and precise. In a word, these two voices from the past communicate to us. For example, as we have scrutinized Pan Ku's and Chang Heng's reactions to their environment, we have been able to appreciate those reactions. They make sense, in spite of the fact that the ideological values of Han China are in certain respects alien to our dominant values. We are encouraged to compare: to compare their "that" with the other "thats" of the world's cultural history and the "this" of our present experience.

As for the relevancy of Han China to modern man with his need of usable knowledge, that is another question, one which can only be answered by surveying the data which the four critiques have assembled. Since politics and religion are two major fields of interest, they take pride of place.

2. *The Body Politic Set-up: An Autocracy? A Theocracy?*

There is no attempt in the four poems to give a complete picture of the governmental set-up either in relation to Ch'ang-an or Loyang. Pan Ku comes nearest to it in his description of the old capital, but even that account is sketchy in relation to the chief administrative offices. From Chang Heng all we learn is that there was a practice of officers by rotation taking duty at night. About Loyang even that amount of detail is lacking. Pan Ku's description of the palace area is purely general, and Chang Heng's named list of buildings there leaves the historian groping in the dark as to which of them were government offices. In point of fact, both narrators were concerned with something else, not with the set-up but the source from which it derived its powers: the something-else which *might* gear the machine to effectual working, or on the contrary *might not*. That was the Han throne, in their eyes a unique institution, unparalleled in the history of the race. In the first phase of its existence it had ended in calamitous failure. Only in its second phase was it a real success.

The basis of comparison was the Loyang monarchy. To both our witnesses it was a beautifully articulated institution which in dealing with Heaven and the gods, the Yin-Yang forces, the manes, the *Chu Hsia* (Sinicized peoples) and the whole world, gave for the first time free vent to the true *virtus* of government. Under that conviction the two poets wrote their respective Ch'ang-an poems. In those poems, after depicting the military impregnability and prolific economy of the city and area, they devoted their powers to pillorying Emperor Wu and his later successors. These are portrayed in general as irresponsible autocrats, free to indulge their megalomaniac and libidinous impulses. A special Han *virtus*, brought into existence by the plebeian Emperor Kao Tsu, was evidenced by the continuity of authority and extension of sovereign power. But it was cribbed, cabined, and confined, unable to maintain efficiency and prosperity. How could the *virtus* be fully efficacious with vast expenditures and state sacrifices of unbridled luxury and determined by the hocus-pocus of shamans, and with the disciplinary side of government characterized by the cruel holocausts of the hunts? As Pan Ku emphasized, much of the Ch'in virus was at work in the body politic.

I have argued that Later Han was essentially a theocracy, Former Han an autocracy. If to some modern minds this seems a distinction without a difference, what the critique has urged is that the Loyang theocracy was accompanied by features which suggest what we moderns call a constitutional monarchy. It should be noted then that the Vatican is the outstanding example of a theocracy in the West, and it also has over the course of the centuries developed a remarkably complete set of routine procedures. These are to all intents and purposes the constitutional law under which His Holiness the Pope exercises his theocratic prerogatives. In other words, his effectual authority depends on his discharge of his ritual and administrative duties and his recognition of the historic rights of the Catholic hierarchy.

It is the ritual of government which requires attention, for one of the surest ways of discovering the nature of society and its government is by examining its state rituals. In them is revealed in dramatized form the nexus of relationships which binds the society together. Now, the impressive thing about those Loyang rituals is that they represent so complete a combination of interlocking divine and human relationships: the Son of Heaven in compact with Heaven and Earth and the Yin-Yang forces, the Emperor on his throne in consultation with his high vassals, the filial son serving the numinous dead, the monarch and the peasant in the fellowship of the sweated soil, the arch-governor and his scholars in the comradeship of training for service, the exalted younger brother serving the nation's veterans. And Emperor Ming's reign was the first occasion on which all these symbolic acts were collectively performed in the capital for all men to note.

The unifying principle which seems on all counts to combine these rituals into a coherent whole is that of the sovereign's duty and responsibility. Emperor Kuang Wu had rights as a descendant of the High Founder and as the man of merit who had conquered all his competitors and brought peace. In him and his filial successor as occupants of the Han throne reposed all the time-honored prerogatives attached to it. Their word was law. On the other hand, they elected by the evidence of these rituals to exercise those prerogatives for the good of all their subjects. This was the Son of Heaven's bounden duty in the sight of Heaven and man; and, to judge by the sage-kings and all the dynasties of antiquity, this was the only basis on which a dynasty could survive.

That these rituals do not evidence the existence of a constitution is clear; but it is equally clear that such impressive year-by-year symbolic affirmations of principle point to there being something of the sort. So also does Emperor Kuang Wu's acknowledgement of economy as a cardinal rule for expenditure at court and among the aristocracy.

The main evidence of constitutional procedure is to be

looked for in the field of government service and the method of recruitment for it. One of Kuang Wu's first acts was to follow his Han predecessors in establishing a corps of Erudites, fourteen in number. When peace came, the Pi Yung was built to house teachers and students, and the graduates were taken into government service. At the same time recommendations of "the filial and upright" were obtained from the governing officials throughout the empire. Any man, however humble his birth, could count on his learning and ability being tested, and once his foot was on the ladder could rise to any height. For all this there was Former Han precedent. On the other hand, with regard to the hierarchy, the first picture of a comprehensively standardized bureaucracy comes to us from the Later Han records, namely Liu Chao's (*Hou Han Shu*, chs. 34-38) version of Ssŭ-ma Piao's "Monograph on the Hundred Officials." It is a most instructive document, covering as it does the whole gamut of imperially commissioned officialdom, at headquarters and throughout the empire. Every office, its title, duties, grade of emolument, is specified. Not only so: Liu Chao's foreword reveals Kuang Wu's reforming zeal at work, tightening up the service and establishing *ch'ang hsien* ("abiding rules of procedure"), whilst his commentary makes pregnant comparisons with Former Han.[1] Add to this the enormous pride taken in Later Han in its enlightened *li* (the code of manners) by which one official recognized the rights of his superior and inferiors and their duties towards him. In these circumstances no other hypothesis fits the case except that of a bureaucratic state functioning with a nexus of reciprocative rights and duties, in fact a constitution.

---

[1] The weighty nature of the evidence contained in these five *chüan* has not, as far as I have been able to discover, received the attention it deserves from modern scholars. Ssŭ-ma Piao (240-306) lived at a time when those court records which survived the Tung Cho incident in 190/1 were still *in situ*, and he had easy access to them. Liu Chao, living in that remarkable Liang Dynasty (502-556), seems to me to have had exceptional opportunity for attaining a sound historical perspective, and to have used his opportunity to most illuminating effect.

The question now is whether, in spite of Pan Ku's and Chang Heng's insistence that the two regimes were so vastly different, there is ground for believing that in Former Han times there had come to be much the same state of affairs. At first sight it seems that by Emperor Hsüan's reign (71-49 B.C.) there was something very like a constitution in operation. Thus Dubs has recently urged that there was a "virtual constitution" and adds an eloquent plea based on the throne's recognition of "Confucian" principles.[2] Here it is, first of all, necessary to recognize that all or practically all of that round of rituals which Chang Heng portrayed had its prototypes in Former Han. That principle of the sovereign having duties and responsibilities to his subjects had since the days of Confucius and then of Mencius been part of the mental furnishings of the Lu State and Ch'i State *Ju*. Also Emperor Hsüan, and long before him Emperor Wen, had been admirable examples of *jen* and *i* (human-heartedness and justice). As for the bureaucracy, there is no evidence, that I have been able to discover, to show that Kuang Wu made radical changes in the system which had come down to him.

There is this to be said for the Pan-Chang thesis. First, there is no question but that the Han emperors inherited the Ch'in ethos of government. As Ssŭ-ma Ch'ien said, "the Ch'in

---

[2] Dubs (*History of the Former Han Dynasty, II, 8*) refers to a "fundamental unwritten constitution" as existent when Emperor Wu ascended the throne, and urges that he made changes in the direction of autocratic rule. That the first Han reigns saw the development of precedent in procedure is of course to be accepted on general grounds, if on no other; no governing on a wide scale can continue without deliberately or undeliberately moving in that direction. But I have considerable doubts whether in so overtly a Legalist state as Former Han such a trend could have attained any settled proportions in sixty-odd years. The high officers of state knew that they were scrappable tools, and that masterful woman, Empress-Dowager Lü, held the reins for fourteen years. I grant, of course, that the disability of her sex led her to take the line of high consultation, but surely there was no guarantee of dynastic precedent about that. So I take it that Emperor Wu ruled as he had a perfect right to do, not only in general but in particular in relation to his private secretaries and their controller. The hallmark of an autocracy is that anyone who has the ear of the monarch can stir him to override any and every precedent of procedure. Cf. Louis XIV's famous remark "L'état c'est moi."

emperor lost his deer, and everyone went hunting it." The High Founder caught that deer, and it was his personal property, to do with as he willed. To his successors the empire was the sacred patrimony passed down to them for safe keeping. All through Former Han this was the unfailing theme, and although the idea of a mandate from Heaven of course came to be zealously preached, it was the only one amongst all the other religious struts to the throne founded on the Legalistic ground, right of conquest. Second, the Han Fei Tzŭ school of Legalist theory emphasized statecraft, so that the rulers' ministers were nothing but his tools, to execute his commands, and, if the results were bad, to take the blame. Always the ruler must appear as the sole fountainhead of honors, rewards, public largesse, spurring his subjects to meritorious efforts, as by his published penalties and ruthless justice he destroyed the contumacious and drove the lazy and incompetent to increase the wealth of the state. This also is writ large on the pages of Former Han history. In A.F.P. Hulsewé's *Remnants of Han Law* (vol. I, Leiden, 1955) it can be studied in detail.

Third, as to those religious struts to the throne, that array of time-honored high places where the Former Han emperors did periodic sacrifice, there was, as the critiques have stressed, the most intimate connection between them and a chieftain or ruler's achievement of mana authority. Here also the right of conquest, of possession of the soil on which the altars stood, is to be seen at work, not on the ground of any Legalist theory, but according to deeply entrenched tradition. The animistic mind was in command: the gods must be placated, could be placated, and indeed, as the Former Han emperors saw it, demonstrably *were* placated and acted in their favor. If calamities occurred, suitable measures were available for restoring good fortune. Then, however, came Emperor Wu and that vast expansion of empire. Nothing is clearer than that the situation demanded sacrifices of more extensive potency, and that Emperor Wu acted entirely according to his autocratic will. His Ming T'ang sacrifices at Mount T'ai and the T'ai I sacrifice at Kan Ch'üan, etc., were a series of experiments, and from the point of view of his successors, on the whole successful experiments. As filial descendants entrusted with the imperial patrimony, they continued to serve these altars, but with such alterations as they came to think were advisable for the buttressing of the throne.

The alterations made were at first of little if any theological significance, since the dominant incentives to action were economy, the convenience of the emperors in sacrificing, and a superstitious hope to increase the prestige of the Ch'ang-an administration. The struts to the autocratic regime needed strengthening, and these were the means adopted. On the other hand, to Wang Mang scheming for a throne it was of the utmost importance to placate influential opinion, in particular the scholars. Hence, with a mixture of motives including a belief in his own divine commission, his emphasis on the south-suburb sacrifice as one to August Heaven. This move was attended by success both with influential scholar circles and in the good omens attendant on the sacrifices. The result was a claim on his part to exercise untrammeled theocratic authority.

To sum up, it is clear that on its autocratic basis of the right of conquest the Former Han monarchy in time developed some constitutional procedures in haphazard, uncoordinated fashion; also that all along there was a deep-seated theocratic element in the whole monarchic idea. To Kuang Wu and his supporters the problem was how to reinstate Han authority in a viable form, the autocratic kind of monarchy being completely discredited by both gods and men. Here, I submit, the Pan-Chang evidence throws light where the extant historical records leave the historian bemused. In particular, Pan Ku's emphasis on the establishment of the basic human relations "for the first time" gives the essential clue: man bound by the very structure of his Nature-and-Man cosmos to live in a community of mutual service. The idea was not new. It was there to be found in certain Scriptures, tentatively explored in certain Han pronouncements, but not for the first time solemnly affirmed as the foundation on which society rested. By this the throne pledged itself to constitutional practice.

It may be argued that this spelt the triumph of "Confucianism."[3] Rather, it is to be urged, that out of the Han maze of animistic beliefs and naturalistic logic, of autocracy tried and found wanting, there emerged a coherent view of the Great Society, man governed by a theocratic sovereign, and that sovereign pledged to constitutional practice.

3. *The Fact of Empire and Its Effect on Men's Minds*

Were it not for Pan Ku's statement about the imperial hunts intimidating the barbarian world (Western Capital *fu*, Section 9), the reader of the two Ch'ang-an poems would hardly realise that the earlier regime did enormously extend the sphere of China's power and prestige. Of course those exotic birds and beasts in the palace grounds and those blood-sweating horses from Ferghana were incidental indications of the expansion of empire. Also, there was no need for Pan Ku or Chang Heng to stress the facts with which their scholar readers were familiar, e.g. Chang Ch'ien's diplomatic mission to Bactria and Li Ling's and Ch'en T'ang's resounding military exploits. Nonetheless the silence is noticeable, since it contrasts so emphatically with the lyrical exuberance of the Loyang poems in their depiction of the later world-enthralling *virtus*. Take also Chang Heng's sole reference to empire in his "*Fu* on the Western Capital." His Nobleman in his summing up refers not to the Former but to the Later Han emperors as having "covered the whole world and made one family."

I submit that this contrast is of far-reaching significance, that after due deduction has been made for Pan Ku's and

---

[3] See H. H. Dubs, *History of the Former Han Dynasty*, II, pp. 341-345.

Chang Heng's flattery of the court they served, there still remains a residual fact; and that fact is that in their eyes whereas the Ch'ang-an court viewed the barbarian peoples as there for its greater glory and wealth, the Loyang court had a more far-sighted, more ethically statesmanlike view. It conceived of a comity of all peoples knit together under the Chinese aegis, their intertribal feuds composed, their barbarous customs refined, the light of knowledge, technical as well as mystical, enriching their minds, above all participating in the Son of Heaven's embodiment of the Will of Heaven and felicitous ordering of the seasons. The sublime code of *li*, with all that it meant in pious sacrifices and the ordering of human relations, this was the possession of the Central State, and by the sharing of this inestimable treasure peace and plenty would ensue for all.

The question is how this change of outlook came about. It has already been urged that the prestige and power of the Scholar bureaucrats in the last reigns of Former Han did not signify so definitive a doctrinal change of outlook as at first appears. At any rate the government's policy in relation to the barbarian peoples showed no sign of being activated by that code of reciprocal human relationship which Confucius had done so much to consolidate on an ethical foundation. It is necessary, therefore, to look for less doctrinaire factors in the situation. This search involves, first, a clarification of the component parts of the empire as it came to be in Former Han, second, an investigation of the emotional effect of the loss of empire concomitant with the fall of that regime.

The spread of the Chou era's cultural influence is still a confused and somewhat indeterminate story. Yet it is clear that in its later phases some degree of Sinification of the tribes in the north and of the Yangtze Valley states, Ch'u and Yüeh, had taken place. Then came the First Emperor's expedition to the far south, reaching to about latitude 25°, and those great areas came onto the map of men's minds. It was not until Emperor Wu's time that such far-flung conquests excited imperial ambitions, but from its early days the Ch'ang-an court was committed to establishing its authority over the surrounding semi-Sinicized areas.

The pattern of control can be traced in outline starting with protectorates and resident Chinese advisers and leading on to full incorporation in the empire with the organization of commanderies with Chinese governors and officials, locally trained troops, statistical reports, and regularly imposed taxation. Also there were schools for the training of local talent as minor officials. It was from these areas, stretching from the Ch'eng-tu plain (Szechuan) to Kweichow and Kwangtung and reaching out in the north-east to Korea, that the Ch'ang-an government derived the main part of its unprecedented wealth. North, south, east, and west this inner empire, for all its variety of climatic conditions and natural products, was uniformly agrarian; and it was here that the Scholar officials were able to use their inherited wisdom to the greatest effect. Defects there were of course, cases of peculation and oppression, but in general the public good was the officials' good; and where serious difficulties such as crop failures occurred, the central government was there to ameliorate the situation.

In the north-west, the Hun area of influence and beyond, the situation was almost entirely different. There was very little scope for intensive agriculture, the indigenous inhabitants living at the pastoral level, and the Huns in particular well able to contest Chinese interference with their traditional way of life. Indeed, in its earlier days the Ch'ang-an government had bitter experience of their power to devastate the "Land within the Passes." Thus there was no peaceful penetration to the north-west. Either there was intrigue to set one barbarian faction against another, or great armies operating over terms of years, inducing temporary submission. There could be no consolidation of empire, nor any reliable income from tributary potentates. There was money to be made if the oases on the long roads communicating with Western Asia could be guarded, and this was the Ch'ang-an policy, never more than partially successful. Barbarian the regions were and barbarian they remained, enemies to be forced into homage to the Son of Heaven. A special class of officials came into existence, not Scholars of the *Ju* type but men from the border families and experts in barbarian politics, civil and military.

What, in this milieu of empire building and the extension of hegemony, of the *Ju*, the Scholars of the middle tradition who became so deeply engaged in governing and training men for the services? Again the historian finds a confusing situation, one in which a rigorous belief in Scriptural author-ity went hand in hand with violent controversy over the authenticity, meaning, and importance of any one text. Some light comes from Tung Chung-shu's (second century B.C.) synthesis of the "Spring and Autumn Annals" view of history with the Yin-Yang cosmology. That satisfied the minds of both Emperor Wu and the *Ju* as giving a rationale to "Great Han" in the world of peoples under the sky. A hundred years later came the Szechuanese thinker, Yang Hsiung, protesting against the fantastic speculations of the dominant school, yet himself indulging in abstruse calculations. In the last resort, however, his desire to enlighten took the form of a call to go back to Confucius, the real source of light on Nature and Man, for Yang Hsiung the sage of all sages to whom Great Han owed the Scriptures which it so meretriciously professed to obey. His *Fa Yen* ("Categorical Sayings") is the first solid indication coming from a known Han writer of devotion to the ethically minded Confucius of the *Analects*. His poetical writings reveal a profound disillusionment over the govern-ment of his day and their moral is unmistakeable: the Ch'ang-an *virtus* was not the *virtus* of the sage-kings or the Scriptures, nor suited to world empire.

It is the Pan-Chang evidence on which the historian must mainly rely for belief in a widespread sense of dismay at the malfeasance of the dynasty; but Wang Mang's efforts to commend his new regime add confirmation. Most of the Scholars were anxious to be reassured and took office. Nonetheless, who could be sure that this was Heaven's decree? Only time could show, and what time did show was the crumbling of empire, ever increasing economic distress, and finally the sack of Ch'ang-an, the real idol of the Scholars' adoration. Then came the crisis: was the country of the sages and the Scriptures to sink back into the a-moral, suicidal disunity of the Warring States period, or was it not? It was a Kuang Wu who tipped the scale, and established what was essentially a new dynasty in a new capital.[4] Whether he approximated to Pan Ku's eulogistic description of him or not, there can be no doubt that he played for the Scholars' support and won it, nor that, when his throne finally became secure, he had the homage of the inner empire and of some regions of the outer. That he won this by the might of his military machine is unquestionable, but on the other side stands the evidence of his purified sacrifices at his Altar of Heaven and above all his enunciation and enforcement of Confucius' great principle of economy. This he applied to himself and his harem, his court, and his nobles, and to all who drew emoluments from the public purse. This doubtless had high propaganda value, but it was the foundation on which ethical statesmanship could alone be built and applied to all peoples in the empire.

Again what of the Scholars? Kuang Wu's Erudites, as far as we know, remained chained to their omens and prognostications, and indeed their master was as anxious about this as they were. On the other hand, amongst the Erudites whom he appointed was Fan Sheng, a master in the *Analects* and the "Filial Piety Scripture," and in spite of the revulsion against Wang Mang's use of the Ancient Text Scriptures,

[4] In Kuang Wu's struggle for power part of the trouble was the size of the peasant hordes which were in the field. Equally portentous were the rival claimants belonging to the imperial Liu and other clans. See Hans Bielenstein, *The Restoration of the Han Dynasty*, Bulletin of the Museum of Far Eastern Antiquities, No. 26 (1953). The longest resistance came from semi-Sinicized Szechuan.

the Emperor insisted on having a chair for an expert in the *Tso Chuan* (see *Hou Han Shu*, ch. 66, *Fan Sheng* biography). His intention was finally blocked, but the biographies of Cheng Hsing, Ch'en Yüan, Chia K'uei and Chang K'ai reveal that these devotees of the *Tso Chuan* and Ancient-Script texts did not hesitate to raise their voices at court. A new leaven was at work, something which Pan Ku acclaimed in the Preface to his two *fu*, something which inspired educated men apart from the arid fields of textual controversy. The fact that stared men in the face was that "Great Han" had died, ignominiously, and "Great Han" was now alive again, gloriously—not next door to the capital of the Ch'in despots, but in Duke Chou's city of Loyang. What he effected on the smaller scale among the feudatories could now be effected on the grand scale of empire. What was there to prevent the gospel of cultured manners and *noblesse oblige*, of music taming unruly passions, of a law of magnanimous justice winning its way throughout the barbarian world and by this means bringing world dominion?

The happy re-incarnation of "Great Han" in the new capital and the return of the border peoples to allegiance synchronized with an awakened sense of a mission to the barbarian world. The Yi, Man, Jung, Ti were not just enemies to be warred down and made a source of profit, but fellow humans needing the grace of the *virtus* to save them from the misery of intertribal strife and barbaric custom. As for the government's actual methods in Central Asia, it is doubtful whether this principle was put into practice to any effective extent, but as far as the inner empire was concerned the work of integration went on. Year-to-year Sinicization was effectually accomplished in a dozen new commanderies; and, when after a century and a half Later Han fell and its empire became three, one was centred in Szechuan and another near the delta of the Yangtze. Both were centres of vigorous and enlightened scholarship. The noble scholar family of Lu was a southern product: Lu Chi (d. dur. 196-220), the mathe-

matician, Lu Hsün (183-245), the great administrator, Lu
Chi (261-303), the author of the immortal *fu*, "The Art of
Letters." And, going to the southern limits of the Han empire, there was that brilliant expounder of his Buddhist faith,
Mou Tzŭ (flor. A.D. 200), a native of Chiao Chou (Annam),
who said of himself, "I studied the Scriptures and Amplifications and the Philosophers. I was a lover of books both
great and small."[5]

4. *Concerning Later Han Levels of Self-conscious Reflection*

The above two problems have been explored as a try-out
in this task of appraisal; they seemed to stem directly from
the main Pan-Chang thesis and to promise well-defined conclusions. They have, as problems, proved difficult to solve,
and the validity of the conclusions is affected by incon-
gruities in the evidence at our disposal. The outstanding
difficulty lies in the apparently complete divorce between
what our two witnesses affirmed with such noble eloquence
and what absorbed the attention of the scholars and politi-
cians of that time. Yet, when we compare the language forms
of the *Po Hu T'ung*, for example, with those of the four *fu*,
we find that the persons concerned were all products of much
the same education and avowed devotion to very much the
same sacred writings. The temptation is to label the Erudites of the Modern-Script school as obscurantist and Pan
Ku and Chang Heng as either sycophantic or wildly idealistic. Resisting this temptation—as indeed a historian must on
all counts—the task of appraisal drives him to closer consideration of this tangled and paradoxical situation.

First of all with regard to Pan Ku and Chang Heng, the
critique arrived at the conclusion that although their minds
were stuffed with legends whose root and essence was purely
animistic, they manifestly took those legends with a grain

[5] See the Foreword to *Li Huo Lun* in *Hung Ming Chi*. There is a translation of *Li Huo Lun* by P. Pelliot: *Meou-tseu ou les doutes levés*, T'oung
Pao, XIX (1920), 255-433.

of salt. This did not apply to the sage-kings, but then those stories had been rationalized and ethicized long before our two poets' day. They were hearsay, but hearsay guaranteed by special proofs. Nonetheless for all the dominant rationality of both our authors' minds, there were still pockets of incongruous animism lurking in them. This feature, the commonest of phenomena in the history of the world's advanced cultures, represents the sub-conscious influence of ancestral lore in the would-be rationalist; and it may in certain circumstances denote a restricted range of stimuli to self-consciousness, no more than simple powers of introspection. That kind of judgement, however, cannot apply to Pan Ku or Chang Heng, or to their more intelligent contemporaries.

The four *fu* have revealed the clarity of imaginative vision and pungency of discriminate language of two first-class minds. What, then, of the second-class, third-class minds who produced the mammoth Woof-Scripture literature? On its numerological side as also in its passion for lists of omens, this literature was the expression of a determination to link every kind of phenomenon, physical and psychological, human, animal, vegetable, geographical, cosmological, into a coherent system of which the naturalistic Yin-Yang and Five Hsing (Elements) were the binding principles. The very extravagance of their numerological theories denotes a conviction that the world and everything in it can be reduced to mathematical calculation; and the correlation of portents was based on the belief that human conduct, being either ethical or contra-ethical, must have repercussions in the world of nature.

There was, therefore, no fundamental dichotomy between the Pan-Chang type of mind and that of the less intelligent scholar-minds of that period. Both kinds could have existed side by side. Both exemplify the stimulating impact of "Great Han," unique Han, on their powers of thinking. Where the two types differed was that Pan Ku and Chang Heng, being able to exercise themselves in the freer atmosphere of poetic conception, looked for a gospel of world salvation. The main

[239]

bulk of the *Ju* had theological minds. They were dogmatizers, fitting their new world to a jig-saw pattern of Scripture proof-texts; they wasted their ingenuity in a mass of technical detail. Learned scholars *can* do that sort of thing, *and* see themselves as fighters for truth and the highest ethical standards.

5. *Concerning the Humanitarian Ethic and Its Origins*

For final appraisals it is not enough to allow a measure of Pan Ku's and Chang Heng's claim that the Loyang culture was a humanitarian one. For one thing, rightly or wrongly, we moderns are unable to accept the theory of a divinely arranged succession of sage-kings operating from the beginnings of the race. For another, the humanitarian ethical idea is an ingredient in the great tradition of Chinese political philosophy, marking it as somewhat unique in the history of ancient cultures.[6] It is the ABC of Sinological knowledge to recognize this as one of the supreme achievements of China's classical era. Since Chang Heng's "*Fu* on the Eastern Capital" represents a high-water mark of this ideological achievement, the problem here may well be envisaged in his language: "the dew of mercy is extended to bird and beast and insect, and the far-off places of the earth are saved" (Section 9). The astonishing leap of his imagination from one affirmation to the other, and the astonishing fact that he should hope for some readers in the Loyang court to take the statement seriously!

The historian's difficulty here, over origin and development, is that although the "ancient Scriptures" are explicit

---

[6] It might be claimed that this achievement was unique, but there were certain features in Ancient Rome of the Caesars which bear a close resemblance; e.g. there was Hadrian's view of Roman citizenship as open to all dwellers in the empire, a view embodied in various codes. Also, imperial Rome envisaged itself as having a mission to serve the world. In the Jewish culture there is the humanitarianism of the Book of Deuteronomy, and in the later chapters of Isaiah the consciousness of a world mission to enlighten the nations with the Torah. In both these cases the approach is on a different footing from the Chinese.

enough, there was that enormous gap of Former Han in which, according to our two witnesses, there was at most only fitful government recognition of mercy to men and the very reverse of mercy to animals. As a matter of fact, as all Later Han *Ju* recognised, the gap extended back into the period of the Warring States, an age in which the policies of all the states were flagrantly contrary to the example of the sage-kings. Further, not only have Chinese thinkers and writers subscribed to this view but also modern critical study has not produced any grounds for doubting that that age was a time of ruthless oppression and of great misery for the common people. On its positive side research has thrown new light on the causes of this state of affairs. In briefest summary, the mid-Chou era saw an increasing command of agricultural techniques and increasing accumulations of wealth in the hands of ambitious feudatories. The result was, first, a number of swollen fiefs, achieved by conquest and absorption of neighboring fiefs, second, the ruling of large bodies of serfs unattached by any traditional bonds of mutual services and mutual benefits. Right through the period of the "Spring and Autumn Annals" this process continued so that by the Warring States period North China consisted of competitive independent states. The only feasible method of government was by rigid rules of taxation and published codes of legal penalties for crimes against the state. With the fierce competition that came between state and state, there was no room for a humanitarian ethic of government, whatever might have been the case in dead-and-gone feudal times.

For the Chou feudal order in its heyday the evidence is almost entirely what is to be found in the "Odes." As a book this is riddled with interpretational conundrums, yet in its mass effects it is unmistakeably delineatory of the society which produced these three-hundred-odd poems. In them the harsher side of feudalism comes plainly to view: so also does that personal relationship between lord and peasant which is characteristic of a feudal order. It was a relation of patent inter-dependence, each party rendering services vital to the existence of all.

This "Odes" collection of tribal songs, rural courtships, festal odes, personal laments from castle and cot, and temple chants was put together by Confucius in the last generation of the "Spring and Autumn" period. Confucius was a *Ju*, a member of that intermediate class between lord and peasant. They were not Scholars in the full Han sense, some of them no more than shamans, but all of them repositories of tradition. Somewhere in the traditions they guarded there was enshrined that consciousness of a personal bond between lord and peasant, each needing to be respected for the indispensable services he rendered: the lord to be honored and obeyed as the tribal chieftain had been, the peasant to be encouraged at his tasks and saved in his times of distress.

At the end of the sixth century B.C. this was a live memory, the ancestral way. For the young *Ju*, Confucius of Lu, it took shape in his mind as the divinely-ordained key to his country's problems, as in sober fact the way King Wen and Duke Chou had elected to rule. The only remedy to the strife and disorder in the states was to "go back to Chou." The Master spent his life working to this end; and whether his vision of Duke Chou's benevolent statecraft was a figment of his imagination or not, is a question to which today there is no sure answer. In any case in his old age he realized that he had set himself an impossible task: the power-holders and power-seekers in Lu and elsewhere would have none of his dream. For his intimates, the younger men who entrusted their hopes of a career to his powers of training, it is impossible to say how many were under the same firm conviction as their teacher. Clearly they often had difficulty in grasping the full significance of his language. Yet unquestionably he had power in the minds of some of them, and through the dark centuries that followed their disciples treasured the memory of his sayings. This "Way of *Jen*"—that vague inclusive term of his which included all humane thought beyond the conventional demands of family and clan relationships—became enshrined as the "Way of the Sage-Kings," and those small bands of *Ju* who cherished the Confucian tradition exalted him to be the last of the sage-kings, the "Uncrowned King." By early Han times that was part and parcel of the *virtus* residing in his name; and, since the concept of him thus became half-myth, the essential virtue of his teaching was the more subject to the *parti-pris* theorizing by the various schools of the Han *Ju*.

Whether this reconstruction of the Confucius of history be sound in every detail is not to the point here. The appraising contention is that with regard to the high and holy duty of rulers to rule primarily for the good of the whole nation and with humane concern for the common man, Confucius of Lu was its main author and source of inspiring appeal. That, I submit, is not open to doubt. I also submit that Ch'ang-an saw itself as far removed from the days of simple feudalism. In a bureaucratic and legalized state there was little room for Confucius' dream. Loyang, also a bureaucratic and legalized state but born in a time of blood and tears, was for a time more responsive, and it was possible to envisage the dream as at least one indispensable foundation of world empire.

6. *The Filial Piety Strain*

As a concomitant to the humanitarian ideal there stands in the four poems what has been described in the critiques as the eudaemonistic strain. That strain stands counter to what may be called the puritan type of ethic, the subscription to a moral standard solely because it is right. Mencius shows evidence of this, although not to the exclusion of the eudaemonistic type. The combination is, indeed, a feature of that intellectually lively and in so many ways progressive age, the last century B.C. It was part of its interior consciousness of the individual and his emotions, of the influence he can exert in his community, and of the austerity of personal discipline by which the man of breeding and a sense of honour must cultivate himself. Along with this went acute consciousness of the pleasures of the table together with a studied delight in music and the beauty of all forms of art, including that of courteous behaviour. Nowhere does this appear in more subtle form than in the "Way of Filial Piety" (*Hsiao Tao*), that distinctive achievement of classical Chinese culture.

At first sight the Pan-Chang evidence would cause us to minimize the part that the *Hsiao Tao* played in the motivation of the Former and Later Han folk. The same applies to ancestor worship. In Pan Ku's "*Fu* on the Western Capital" there is no reference to filial piety and only one to ancestor worship, and that is just by the way. Chang Heng's "*Fu* on the Western Capital" has no reference whatever. In Pan Ku's "*Fu* on the Eastern Capital" there is a bare reference to the seasonal sacrifices to the imperial ancestors. Chang Heng, in his calendar of the year's sacrifices, includes the one in the Loyang ancestral fane; and later he notes the routine autumn visit to Ch'ang-an to sacrifice in the High Ancestor's fane. He starts the former account in good filial-piety terms but winds up with what looks like an ironical touch on the blessings to be expected.

To infer from this scarcity of reference that Pan Ku and Chang Heng were not conformist ancestor worshippers and staunch filial pietists would, to be sure, be wrong. So also would be any inference, from the exclusion of ancestor worship from not only the Ch'ang-an and Loyang palace areas but also from inside the city walls, that these rites were not of central importance to the emperors. High-brow Scholars of the Pan-Chang calibre may have felt critical of the animistic beliefs preserved in the rituals of ancestral fanes; they would not doubt the essential rightness of these memorial practices in the ancestral way. The problem that comes to mind here is that of relating Chinese ancestor worship, a type form of ancestor worship all over the world, and that special Chinese discovery of *Hsiao Tao*. It cannot be ignored in the task of appraisal, for, of all the blessings of civilization which Later Han was persuaded it could impart to barbarian peoples, the cult of filial piety was unquestionably the chief.[7]

Although the two phenomena are so intimately connected, it is confidently assumed that they are strikingly disparate, standing on very different levels of ethical aspiration. Ancestor worship is impregnated with the fear of the dead and never succeeds in breaking away from the rudimentary logic that the tasty dishes the living enjoy will also be enjoyed by the ghosts of the dead, even though it be only by the smell. Thus the mana of the "old man," so potent in his lifetime, whether in favor or disfavor, must be even more potent after his death. The same applied a fortiori to the "grand old man"—the original progenitor of the tribe or clan. That this kind of mentality was in Han times vigorously alive in all ranks of society is completely evidenced, particularly with regard to the emperors and their entourage. The long and highly emotional struggle over the keeping or not of all the funerary parks demonstrates this for mid-Han times. On the other hand, the markedly mid-Han production, the "Record of Rites," contains works which are impregnated with a totally different attitude to the dead. In that group of three very freshly written dialectical essays (*lun*), the *Chi Fa, Chi I* and *Chi T'ung*,[8] the great argument of appeal is that the sacrifices to the dead are made out of pure love and reverence, the filial son passionately longing for some sign that his adored parents are near. There is no

---

[7] The *Chi I* ("Principles of Sacrifice") in the "Record of Rites" has the passage: "Tseng Tzǔ said, 'Exalt filial piety, and it includes heaven and earth; broaden it, and it encompasses the Four Seas; hand it to future ages, and morning and evening it will expand. . . .'"

[8] The *Chi Fa* has no distinctive exposition of piety in relation to the sacrifices. It is entirely concerned with the proper rituals for the sacrifices to Sage Kings and other great figures of high antiquity. Nevertheless, it betrays the same kind of rationalizing mind as the other two *lun*, and in its final section asserts the principle of grateful remembrance of those who had long ago rendered outstanding service to man. The other two *lun* are vital for an understanding of Later Han filial piety.

better evidence of the cogitational acumen which the enquiry of this book has brought into clearer perspective.

The history of the emergence of this *Hsiao Tao* is beyond the scope of this enquiry; it goes back to the early days of the Chou regime, and began to undergo some quite startling developments in Confucius' generation. Confucius' emphasis lay on serving parents when alive in homely acts of service. His disciple Tseng Ts'an went much farther, inculcating life-long remembrance of the dead. The tendency towards extravagance in funeral rites became more and more marked. Indeed, in the Warring States age only the wealthy could figure as filial sons. The downtrodden peasants had no ancestral fanes, and often could not afford coffins at their parents' death.

It is submitted that the final downfall of the Warring States entailed the ruin of their rulers' ancestral fanes and the proletarianization of their remaining descendants. Those of them who were literate maintained as best they could the aristocratic ritual tradition. With the rise of prosperity under Han the scene was set for a popularization of the *Hsiao Tao*, the *Ju* taking an active part in teaching the right forms for mourning and daily service. Then came the rise of the *Ju* to power, the establishment of schools in the provinces and contemporaneously the intensive study of the traditional rites. With the return of prosperity in Later Han and further diffusion of education, the moral teachings of the *Ju* penetrated more into village life, turning the hearts of parents and children to noble acts of ungrudging devotion. Pan Ku's eulogy of Emperor Kuang Wu speaks of the "Five *Lun*" (basic human relations) as his act of creation. Although sometimes in Han writings the relation of sovereign and subject comes first in the list, the dominant practice was to make the relation of children to parents the chief duty of man. Filial piety became the categorical imperative. *Pu Hsiao* (stark contravention of the filial piety code) became the worst of sins—

an accusation of which made the most hardened sinner blench, from the Emperor on his throne to his meanest subject.

7. *The Spread of Educational Facilities*

It may seem to some readers that the Pan-Chang evidence on education is of no great significance. That, as the critique on Section 6 of Pan Ku's "*Fu* on the Eastern Capital" has pointed out, is not the case. The statement there, the only one in the four *fu* which refers to education as such, is remarkable for a double emphasis: (1) on the empire-wide establishment of schools; (2) on the village school as a centre for community sacrifices and feasts. In that connection the critique has made two possibly fanciful conjectures as to what lay behind Pan Ku's words. Apart from them, what he very explicitly did have in mind was to depict these gatherings as a channel through which the imperial *virtus* flowed out to "all within the four seas." The village people, old and young, "tread the measure of *tê* and chant of [the goodness of] *jen*," i.e. they learn the code of *li* and are imbued with its concord-engendering power. It is the same process at work which has been described above in relation to the proletarianization of filial piety. Here this power is ascribed to the *hsiang* (high schools in the provincial centre) and *hsü* (village schools), to the ever wider extension of education throughout the incorporated regions of the empire.

In view of the remarkable cultural influence exercised by China over the medley of tribes east of the Himalayas, it is necessary to see this proletarianization of education not as a figment of Pan Ku's imagination but as a process which did in some measure actually take place.[9] The question then

[9] For confirmation of this view see the *Po Hu T'ung* (Tjan, *op.cit.*, pp. 487-488) and take into account that according to the *Ju Lin Chuan* foreword (*Hou Han Shu*, Biog. 69A) there were about A.D. 146 "35,000 *yu hsüeh* students" going from one teacher to another. The "Notes on Education" (*Hsüeh Chi*) of the "Record of Rites" gives tantalizing glimpses of provincial schools, but its main interest is in the higher education in the capital. Arguing from the general tone of the document and the incentive there was for commandery and kingdom high schools to ape the

is whether this advance must be dated as taking place during the Later and not the Former Han dynasty. A strict interpretation of the Pan-Chang thesis would lead to the conclusion that it did, since the Ch'ang-an court became too besotted with its own grandeur to be able to release the power of the true Han *virtus*. The evidence, however, does not warrant so wholesale a conclusion. The most that Pan Ku and Chang Heng could have meant was that the Loyang emperors had vastly increased the momentum of this development in education. It is urged that this actually was the case.

The first major steps towards popularization of education must have synchronized with the implementing of Emperor Wu's policy of having better trained government servants and larger numbers of them. It became increasingly necessary, if a "filial and upright" candidate for office was recommended from the provinces, that he should prove on examination to be reasonably well grounded in the Scriptures. That meant years of preparation under competent teachers, and—so the critical historian inevitably surmises—the formal distinction between higher grade and primary schools became more or less recognized. With the establishment of the Ta Hsüeh (Imperial Academy) in Ch'ang-an and the employment of the most famous *Ju*, the Erudites, as teachers in it, a new standard of scholarly competency was set up. Within fifty or sixty years there came to be on the one hand those Ch'ang-an street-corner Scholars "splitting hairs and dividing the muscles [of Scripture] asunder," and on the other hand the litterateurs, excited by the unexplored possibilities of ordered expression. As early as Emperor Wu's reign there was Ssŭ-ma Hsiang-ju, educated in distant semi-Sinicized Szechuan, but able to electrify the court by his literary brilliance.

---

methods used in the capital, it seems likely that passages in the *Hsüeh Chi* refer to those provincial establishments. It also seems likely that if one of those *yu hsüeh* students was obliged to take charge of a provincial school, he might easily be guilty of the faults of "teachers today" as described in the *Hsüeh Chi*: "humming over the tablets before them and propounding knotty problems. . . ."

What, then, of the first hundred years of Han? To what extent were schools to be found scattered about the central states? The evidence is scanty in the extreme, and the existence of scholastic centres is mainly by inference from the fact that there were famous Scholars and competent administrators. That they were really literate is obvious, although there is the teasing question what difference the new script had made to teaching method and how far Scholars were at home in it. Chia I of Emperor Wu's reign clearly had mastered it, but presumably when he went to Ch'ang-an he read the *Li Sao* in the old script. Altogether the situation is very much blurred and in no way clarified by the fact that the Ch'in First Emperor used a large number of clerks in running his government offices. They must have learnt to read in the old script; but what standard of proficiency did they reach with its clumsy and variable forms? Did they learn the new script easily? Did the Emperor himself learn it? Was the merchant Lü Pu-wei competent in reading and writing? To all such questions there seems to be no answer for the historian today. All we know is that most teachers of the time were accustomed to using copies of one scripture or another in their possession. How complete those copies were we do not know, but by the end of the Chou dynasty no *Ju* could achieve repute as a teacher unless he possessed some tablets—tablets on which were recordings of traditional lore, ritual notes, divining oracles and reflections thereon, statements as to regulation behaviour for government servants, etc. The more lively-minded among the teachers would write down their own reactions to the teachings they knew by heart, whether in the central *Ju* tradition or the Taoist or Legalist or what. The *Ju* of Lu State and Ch'i State were famous in late Chou times, and the authors of the *Tso Chuan*, *Kuo Yü*, and *Chan Kuo Ts'ê* must have used the services of quite a number of scribes. Away south in the Yangtze area Ch'ü Yüan could pour out his burdened heart in 374 impassioned lines. At the same time it was easy to find "vulgar

[249]

Ju," pretentious men in big hats and voluminous gowns, with little understanding of what they had been taught.

The Warring States period is forever famous for the galaxy of highly individual thinkers whose (more or less) orderly thinking took literary shape and was preserved by disciples. There were also those academies where these philosophizers could meet and argue. There was also Hsün Ch'ing, who seems to have first discovered that vital literary form, the discussion of a particular subject under its particular title. Hsün Ch'ing's theory of human nature drove him to see the necessity for an artificial disposition to be cultivated by continued practice in courtesy and unselfish renunciation, and his essays are found quoted at length in the "Record of Rites." Plainly, he was the father of the movement which brought the proletarianization of *Li* in mid-Han times. In view of these well-attested phenomena no one can doubt that the lamp of literacy was well alight. In terms of thought and communication, the age that could produce the Mencius book and the more clearly original parts of *Chuang Tzŭ* was gifted with a mind which was well started on its climb to mature powers of ratiocination. Yet it is a far cry from that age to the intellectually more sophisticated age of Pan Ku and Chang Heng. It is not merely a matter of men of humble origin rising to be high-rank bureaucrats and being ennobled, but also of recognized ethical standards backed by a subtle understanding of the individual-in-society.[10]

Again, it is quite a far cry from Hsün Ch'ing's time back

---

[10] To illustrate this development, T'i-wu Lun's career (see *Hou Han Shu*, Biog. 51) shows how a talented man of peasant origin could in Kuang Wu's reign be advanced from local office to high station. Nothing is recorded of his education, but his home was in the Ch'ang-an regional government area, so that a handy village school may be credibly assumed. From the other angle of social approach, Chang Heng had a rather younger contemporary, Chang Kang (see *Hou Han Shu*, Biog. 46), who came of a long-established noble family, and whose father, a man of outspoken character, held high office. Chang Kang wore plebeian clothes and modeled himself on Confucius in taking part in village confabulations. On one occasion he won over to law and order the rebels of a district in revolt against their avaricious official. Such a man would foster village education.

to the days of young Confucius as he embarked on his career. There is no record of who his teacher was or what he, belonging to a *Ju* family, had learnt from him, or of what sets of tablets he inherited, no record of other contemporary teachers and their pupils. It is triple-guarded tradition that, although he was never a state archivist, he had access to Lu State records and composed the "Spring and Autumn Annals." But with all his genius as a teacher and his passionate concern for his followers he never took stylus and wrote down what he would have them to remember. The only possible conclusion seems to be that the idea of an individual on his own initiative expressing himself in cool and collected prose fashion had not occurred to anyone at that time. There is much to indicate that writing was still invested with a numinous aura, so that not till Confucius was dead did his followers feel they could and must write his sayings down. The rider to that conclusion is that formal education in that age could only have reached a rudimentary stage.

To come back to Later Han, the spread of education meant for our two witnesses the spread of *wen*, i.e. civilized modes of living. They themselves are incontrovertible evidence of these more advanced cultural standards, mental, moral, and artistic. Their poems reveal a refinement of sentiment and principle which is unmistakeable. They also show the inspiring effects on—at any rate some—intellectuals of "lifting up their eyes to the ends of the earth." And theirs was the age in which the *Li Chiao*, the code of manners and morals, intensified its hold on society, developing into a philosophy of *Li* in which old and new observances were compounded into one massive structure. To the *Ju* it was the very embodiment of *wen*. Yet to the modern mind, the more it is examined in detail, the more it appears as a restrictive, perverting influence, fostering a pharisaical, hypocritical spirit. Whilst admitting some truth in this—a truth applying to all social codes of behaviour, ancient *and* modern—the Pan-

Chang evidence drives us to explore the opposite aspect, the enhancement of the individual and the means by which there is effected the alignment of practice with principle. The exploration of this subject is beyond the scope of this final chapter, but two illustrations may be given to show the immense possibilities in this line of enquiry.

The first is taken from Book X (init.) of the *Analects.* We find there illustrations of behaviour at court, and at first sight it is a fantastic picture of the *Li Chiao* at work. It is urged here that actually the author of those anecdotes was depicting absorbed self-expression in the conduct of duty. The second illustration is from the "Great Learning" (*Ta Hsüeh*) in the "Record of Rites." At the outset there is a prime emphasis on the "cultivation of the self as the root process"; and this is linked with the "development of knowledge" and the "investigation of things," i.e. natural things. Any reader going through the "Great Learning" will discover that this text-book of *Li Chiao* philosophy is concerned from first to last with the flowering of a noble personality.

It is, therefore, assumed with some confidence, that the *Li Chiao* of Later Han set up standards of personal honor in all ranks of educated society—standards which survived the severest tests of later anarchy and disruption. On the other hand, there was one class of person in Later Han on which the *Li Chiao* failed to exercise its ennobling influence: the class of the emperors. A young heir-apparent—always, it must be remembered, on approval—was subjected to a severe scholastic discipline into the results of which the reigning Emperor would enquire. Yet, having been nurtured in his early years in the imperial harem, he was imbued with its enervating influence. As Emperor he was shut away from contact with the outside world, as Chang Heng's muffled dummy in the imperial carriage brings home to us; and all the time he was surrounded by flattering career-mongers. There was the endless routine of ritual duties in which he figured as a public god. Psychologically speaking, a man of outstanding character could rule circumstances to his will, a weakling could not. Hence, that dereliction of imperial authority which characterized the last fifty years of Later Han. From A.D. 89 on, the nine successive emperors all ascended the throne when they were boys or even babes in arms.

8. *The Sage-Kings*

The enquiry and appraisal here, it is hardly necessary to say, is limited to Han, to what ideas the Han intelligentsia before A.D. 120 had about the sage-kings. Since it was in that era that the Chinese people moved so vigorously out of their ancient northern environment and spread their dominion so widely, and in that era that their intelligentsia set their minds so methodically to work on the nature of legitimate sovereignty, they could not but face up to their sacred past and rationalize it to the best of their ability. To what extent old legend became new myth or alternatively old myth became new legend, in relation to this or that sage-king, is probably one of the test questions in this field, but even that temptation is resisted in the discussion here.

There are two points to be made about the references in these *fu* to the sage-kings. One is that there are no references to them at all in the two Ch'ang-an *fu*, but only in the Loyang *fu*, notably the references in V, 2 and VI, 12 which, if taken at their face value, point to both Pan Ku and Chang Heng believing in the whole series of sage-kings back to Fu Hsi. The other is the admirably logical emphasis Pan Ku laid (V, 2) on Kuang Wu as out-doing all the sage-kings put together, an emphasis paralleled in his own way by Chang Heng (VI, 12). All three features are surprising according to particular angles of consideration.

First, how was it that, whether by intention or by inadvertence, the creators of the two protagonists for Ch'ang-an omitted any reference in their speeches to the sage-kings? One weighty answer is, of course, that the Pan-Chang thesis about Ch'ang-an was that it embodied the true royal *virtus* much more in *posse* than in *esse*. On the other hand, both authors knew perfectly well that in Emperor Wu's reign the much admired Tung Chung-shu had used his best reasoning powers in demonstrating the march of history under the compelling power of cosmological forces, and that in his scheme the Han throne with its *wen* (high civilization) was in due succession to Hsia, Shang, and Chou, the regimes inaugurated by Sage-Kings Yü, Ch'eng T'ang, and King Wen.[11] Also, Pan Ku at least was familiar with the fact that in the official eulogy in the "History of the Former Han Dynasty" Kao Tsu was represented as claiming descent from Yao. (Yet Pan Ku refers to Kuang Wu, not Kao Tsu, as linking his regime to Yao.) It looks very much as if in Pan Ku's day his divergence from Tung Chung-shu's theory in postponing the revelation of the sage-king succession to Later Han, was accepted by the legitimist theoreticians. The point really is whether that theory could be and was adapted to present facts. There can be little doubt that it was. Thus, for example, in curiously illuminating fashion, Tung Chung-shu in his *Ch'un Ch'iu Fan Lu* (his only work which has survived) shows no interest at all in any particular *virtus* of any sage-king. He is merely concerned with getting the succession right, and in doing so he goes no further back in antiquity than the Hsia regime. True, he mentions Yao and Shun, but only in passing, and for the earlier sage-kings has only a tag reference, "Five Ti and Three Huang" ("August Ones"). None of these plays a part other than as links in his dynastic scheme. That was one type of rationalization, and a very prevalent type in mid-Han, incidentally throwing

[11] One striking feature of Tung Chung-shu's theorizing was to include Confucius in the dynastic series as inaugurating a sort of half-in-Heaven, half-on-earth sage order of rule. One may suspect that he had in mind the bridging of the gap between Chou and Emperor Wu, but the connection is not clear. One thing is clear, that he was thinking a good deal in terms of the class "sage," whether ruler or not, and the influence of this generalization should be borne in mind. It comes out very prominently in the *Po Hu T'ung's* chapter "On Appellations" (see Tjan, *op.cit.*, 232/6).

light on Wang Mang's use of the sage-kings in advancing his claim to establish his New Dynasty.

It is submitted, therefore, that there were a large number of stories current about the sage-kings, as about other heroes of antiquity, and that not only Pan Ku and Chang Heng but many other scholars, too, sat rather lightly to them as a whole. Some legends were more credible than others which contained miraculous elements such as were told of the Yellow Emperor, the part-Taoist, part Middle-Tradition hero. In either case many of the *Ju* were, like Tung Chung-shu, not seriously interested in them as individuals. They were eponyms, attached to this regime and the other, or, as the "Changes" Scripture affirmed, the semi-divine discoverers of society's civilized inventions. The paramount consideration was the procession of dynasties like the order of the seasons. If that were the case, then Chang Heng's reference to "the Five" and "the Two"[12] is not to be taken as expressing his conviction that these far-off beings had actually existed. They were convenient pegs to which he could pin his argument and enforce his appeal.

As for the romantic details of this and that sage-king, e.g. Yü who by his labors "wore the hair off his calves and shins" and passing the door of his house heard the cry of his new-born child but stayed not to see him—who knows whether Yü was originally a god or a man, whether myth was piled on legend or legend on myth? Whatever the substratum of factual event, if any, it may have passed through a dozen transformations before it reached the final form we know, with its lesson that government is for the sake of the common man. Can the specialists trace any such intervening stages? But for this appraisal the question is a more clearly definable one. Take Chang Heng's *Ssŭ Hsüan Fu* with its endless recital of gods and goddesses whom he contacted round the world: did the poetic force of those sage-king

---

[12] I have no theory to propose as to why Chang Heng substitutes "the Two" for "the Three," the formula common after Tung Chung-shu's day.

images so appeal to him that their vigorous aptness made for him a sufficient substitute for actual historicity? The question may be unanswerable, but there is this to be said: since, whatever philosophers may argue, the images created by words so much are symbols of what they are supposed to represent, what was there to inhibit so scientifically minded a man as Chang Heng from adopting a highly poetic symbol as near enough to the actual truth? The dice were heavily weighted in the direction of such a belief. No one can read the "Changes" Scripture and then go on to Yang Hsiung's extension of its philosophy of symbols without realizing how profoundly an intelligent *Ju* was imbued with this quite arguable theory. After all, the Taoist Scriptures which Chang Heng knew maintained that the ultimate fact about the universe was a mystery, from man's angle of approach, a nothingness from which sprang somethingness as a relative image. Along that line of speculation, what was the truth about the sage-kings: a faltering balancing of evidence, or the living image which struck an echo from your mind?

9. *Concerning Han "Confucianism" and the Scriptures*

The critique discovered grounds for questioning the appropriateness of the Western Sinologists' term "Confucianism" for the "Great Tao," the "Middle Way," which gradually took shape in Han times. Then earlier in this chapter something more approaching the real teaching of Confucius of Lu was discovered as an unprecedented feature of the new Later Han political set-up. For the final appraisal here it must be confessed that no delineatory answers can be given to the questions which clamor for answers. For the historian the situation is one sown with paradoxes, as, for example, the fantastic conglomeration of ideas found in the report on the White Tiger Hall discussions and the fact that its official reporter, Pan Ku, burst out in his Loyang *fu* in fulmination against the Scripture proof-text mongers who dominated that conference. That the court's decision, some eighty years after Pan Ku's death, to inscribe the Scripture on stone pillars and its subsequent encouragement of Cheng Hsüan's commentaries point to a more intelligible situation may be true, but is beyond the scope of this enquiry. The only suggestion I venture to make is along the lines of generally accepted opinion today, namely that these developments point not only to the growing strength of the Ancient-Script party among the *Ju* but also to the central importance, in the eyes of the Scholars and the government, of getting the Scripture texts authoritatively fixed and their meanings authoritatively defined. There was no suggestion of this kind in the Pan-Chang age—and yet the plenary authority of the Scriptures as a whole was the main plank in the platform of *Ju* beliefs.[13] In view of our relative ignorance of what the said Scriptures did or did not contain at that particular time, it is submitted that there is a pronounced *x* quality to the term "Confucianism." If we turn to Confucius of Lu as our main guide to its meaning, we may be able to advance up to a certain point, but then we are faced with the question as to which "Confucius" is the really historical one: the Confucius of the *Analects*, the Confucius of the *Tso Chuan*, of the "Changes" Scripture, of the biography in the "Record of History" (*Shih Chi*), of the Modern-Script school with its emphasis on the "Kung Yang Amplification," of the "Filial Piety Scripture," or of the "Record of Rites," where he appears in so many passages discoursing at far greater length than he does in the *Analects?* Here again we are faced with a formidable *x* quality in the evidence at our command.

---

[13] This statement, true in general, must not be taken as referring only to the "Five Scriptures." The *Po Hu T'ung* contains a quantity of citations from other books of near-canonical status (cf. Tjan, *op.cit.*, pp. 180-194). Among these the "Woof" (*Wei*) Books must be taken into account. They also figure as lending authority to the opinions recorded. Clearly some of these "Woof Books" were held in such esteem that their advocates, the Modern-Script party, were able to get near-Scripture recognition of them. The natural inference from that fact is that the "Warp" (*Ching*) Books did not constitute a closed canon in A.D. 93.

The historian today has one source of encouragement. It is that the patient work of critical scholarship has confirmed the *Analects* as the most nearly reliable account we have. It is second-hand evidence, third-hand, or even fourth-hand evidence, but its imperfectly correlated format and general coherence of portraiture puts its value in a class by itself. Arguing from this angle of approach, one mid-Han and Later Han belief becomes highly questionable. It was that Confucius by his sage wisdom came to see that the records of sage wisdom of antiquity must be preserved for a more enlightened age when the scholars could prize them at their full value. Hence in general terms he was the transmitter of the Scriptures. With the strong backing of the *Analects* we can accept the "Odes" as a collection owing its existence to Confucius' enthusiasm. That, however, is a different proposition from believing that he regarded his collection as a Scripture in the Han sense. That he took a number of Chou court historical records—the Modern-Script and Ancient-Script devotees violently disagreed as to which and how many—and put them into final shape for the future as a "History" Scripture is hardly credible. That he in his last days was devoted to the "Changes" (as it was then) and added the amplifications of the "Wings," this has become more and more open to doubt. As for the "Rituals," specified in Later Han times as the *I Li, Chou Li*, and constituent parts of the "Record of Rites," the grounds of the belief are dubious at every point. Not that Confucius was not a master of the *Ju* lore of ritual in his day, or that he did not possess tablets of notes on ritual practice. However, that he passed on an *I Li* Scripture as a whole, much less a *Chou Li* or any recognizable parts of the "Record of Rites" is definitely not credible. As for the "Spring and Autumn Annals," although the *Analects* stresses his insistence on the rectification of terms, it knows nothing of such a work. Yet in Mencius (III B, 9) Confucius is stated to have been the inspired author and as saying "Those who know of me, will it not be through the 'Spring and Autumn Annals'!" The problem is completely baffling, particularly because as an existent book it vanishes from sight until in Emperor Wu's reign it comes to light as a Scripture. It was acclaimed as such at the instigation of Tung Chung-shu, and along with it, *with very little delay*, the *Kung Yang Chuan*. The astounding thing is that Scripture status was claimed for this amplification, and for its rival the *Ku Liang Chuan*, and then later for the *Tso Chuan*, a very different kind of book. For this last it was claimed that its author was a direct disciple of Confucius in his old age and assistant to him in composing the "Spring and Autumn Annals" (a very dubious proposition).[14] This direct link with "the Master" was not claimed for the two previously contested amplifications.

It stares us in the face, this passion of the mid-Han *Ju* for a corpus of infallible Scriptures. It is as if amid all the Scholars' rivalries and controversies that was the fixed point in their minds: that insofar as Confucius came into their arguments he was a convenient pawn to be moved here and there in support of a main contention. Also, taking the Five Scriptures together, we realize that the scope of their combined ideologies goes far beyond what any *Ju* of the Spring and Autumn era could possibly have envisaged, even though he were one of Confucius' pre-eminent calibre. Also, through Pan Ku's and Chang Heng's eyes we have seen how profoundly the *Ju* had been impressed by the achievements of the Han monarchy, and how firmly they backed the new order of unity and headquarters control. That monarchy and order had to be buttressed, i.e. authenticated by metaphysical proofs. Those proofs were to be found in the tablets by means of which the teachers of the administrators and the learned had inducted them into the illuminating mysteries of learning. Thus the Scriptures guaranteed the authenticity of the throne, and the throne guaranteed the authenticity of the

---

[14] See B. Karlgren, *On the Authenticity and Nature of the Tso Chuan*, Göteborg, 1926.

Scriptures. By the same logic applied to antiquity, the Scriptures authenticated the sage-kings, and the sage-kings authenticated the Scriptures.[15] To our modern intelligence this may be outrageous logic: to the Han dogmatist, a theologian in grain, it was doubly fortified reason.

The question arises whether this Scripture-centric belief was a religion. To that this appraisal has but two suggestions to offer. One is the emphasis that Han religion and politics were indissolubly interrelated. It is urged not only as a peculiar feature of the Scholars' religion-cum-politics but also as a universal characteristic of all cultures, ancient and modern. The other suggestion is that although the Scholars' religion had such strikingly mundane elements, there was also a transcendent, mystical streak. This comes to view in Chang Heng's Loyang *fu*, where Scholar Anonymous expresses himself in markedly Taoistic terms.

The first impression in Western Sinology was that "Confucianism" and "Taoism" were basically antagonistic views of life and reason and that the glaringly superstitious Tao experts in Former Han times degraded Taoist beliefs and discredited them in the eyes of the scholars, and so Confucius' more rational views became the Great Tradition of the Chinese people. More recent scholarship has discredited this over-simple view. Not that Emperor Wu's shamans did not disgust the more intelligent scholars, nor that the *Chuang Tzŭ's* socially nihilistic philosophy of the individual did not strike them as unpractical. But there was a magic in the pure transcendentalism of the *Tao Tê Ching* and the *Chuang Tzŭ* which the more sensitive *Ju*, those less obsessed with ambi-

---

[15] This kind of reasoning is seen very clearly in the *Lun Heng*, e.g. ch. 28, c. 1 (A. Forke, *The Lun Heng, Philosophical Essays of Wang Ch'ung*, vol. I, Kelly and Walsh, 1907, p. 452). There we see Wang Ch'ung himself under this influence, although at the same time he maintained that the Scriptures had suffered irreparable damage, i.e. had been recovered in Han times in very imperfect condition. In ch. 28, c. 2 (Forke, *op.cit.*, vol. II, p. 238) he unintentionally reveals the dominant belief: "Supposing that the Five Scriptures had come undamaged from Confucius' disciples; then they might be said to be a perfect whole and could be trusted."

tion, could not resist. One key to the mid-Han attitude is to be found in Liu Hsin's Catalogue, where the Taoist section is placed next to the "Confucianist" section of the philosophers' works, and that and the other succeeding sections are all appraised as contributory to the elucidation of truth. Here again is a sign of the belief in the power of the written word, a semi-sacred word, throwing light, if only by contrast, on the completely sacred word of the Scriptures. So when we turn to the central theme of the four *fu*, the Han imperial *virtus* and its mystic life-engendering powers, it is plain that Later Han *Ju* beliefs owed much to Taoism.

10. *Suggestions for Systematic Research*

The critique has been at considerable pains to estimate the intelligence quota of Pan Ku and Chang Heng, and to analyse out their respective thought processes. At the beginning of this chapter an attempt was made to estimate the results. Since both authors succeeded in being remarkably self-revelatory, there is ground for the hope that the results, patchy as they are, may be of use to Han historians and even inter-cultural historians. On the other hand, the actual sphere of observation has been so restricted that obviously further studies on a wider basis are needed. In the case of Pan Ku there is the field of enquiry afforded by his eight other works in the *Wen Hsüan*, none of them of importance comparable with his "*Fu* on the Two Capitals," but nonetheless needing more careful scrutiny than I have had time and energy to give. Also, there are various old and new studies of Pan Ku's worth as a historian, particularly by Chinese critical scholars. From these, owing to my recent more narrowed conditions of study, I have been unable to profit.

With regard to Chang Heng, in the *Wen Hsüan* there are four other items, including his "*Fu* on the Southern Capital." A preliminary study of this left me with surprise at its lack of significance, and it dropped out of view in my later studies. His *Ssŭ Hsüan Fu* is of supreme importance for the understanding of him and would vastly repay the most painstaking study, both in relation to the sage-kings and to his world outlook. There are also various items in Yen K'o-chün's compendium *Ch'üan Han Wen* ("Complete Literature of the Han") which are necessary for the clearer understanding of Chang Heng's attainments as a scientist. Both Pan Ku and Chang Heng need to be rediscovered as products of the conventional Scripture-based education combined with the inspiration of the mid-Han literary up-rush.

Then for the sociological and ideological anthropologists surely there are valuable data in that great *virtus* theory which Pan Ku and Chang Heng, the historian and the scientist, make the central theme of their poetic discourses: the concept of *tê*, reaching so far back into the dim yet turbulent life of early animistic tribal society. Here it appears in all its glory of civilized, ethical application, the key to Later Han's consciousness of a world mission of peace and friendly cooperation under the guidance of Heaven. Does it not in its lights and shades stand in ancient history on a par with Constantine's espousal of the Christian religion and Asoka's espousal of the Buddhist cause?

As to that literary up-rush, it above all requires the most painstaking investigations. It is off the main line of historians' researches today and seems to be regarded as a very specialized arcanum into which only rather antiquarian-minded literary critics of the purest water need to probe. Yet one plain fact about those momentous two centuries of Former Han was the acceptance of the First Ch'in Emperor's experimental new script. The experiment was a success, both for governmental purposes and as a tool in the hands of the nation's educators. Apparently all parties took to it and proceeded to make themselves highly proficient in it. The pre-Han literature, including the Scriptures, such as they were, were reinscribed in it, so that by the time Liu Hsin's Catalogue was made, scrolls occur in it for new as well as old manuscripts.

The significance of this revolution can only be realized

in the light of modern studies in the ancient script and phonetics. With much that still remains dark and uncertain there are two features of the end-of-Chou age which may be taken as sufficiently clear and certain. One is that in the Chou centuries the substitution of the phonetic principle for the original pictographic and ideographic principle had slowly but surely come to pass. The other is that this process was not autocratically regulated, and when the rival states (including Ch'u in the then far south) came to their full power, strong divisive cultural influences were at work. That script, the *hsiao chüan* ("small seal" script, or whatever it may have been), was subjected to regional variations. To that was added the confusion of specialized new meanings to old script forms, a process enhanced by the lively schools of radical philosophizing. The written language was altogether in bad shape, in addition to which the stylus and the wooden tablet were clumsy laborious media of communication.

The Ch'in First Emperor by brute force substituted his rule for the effete Chou hegemony, and he and his prime minister Li Ssŭ realized that without a universally recognised script universal government could not but be hampered at every turn. They promptly made a new and simpler script. What mental processes activated Li Ssŭ and his assistants must in the absence of evidence be largely a matter of conjecture, stimulated by the patient collection of indirect clues. But the main fact is clear that their new script, being aimed at producing clarity of communication and speed in writing, did achieve this end, and that it did so by enlarging the scope of the Chou phoneticizing trends. The greater use of phonetically based terms was coupled with the use of phonetic loans (*chia chieh*).

It is impossible now to trace what struggles teachers and students had over this new departure in the written word. There is, however, one significant item in Liu Hsin's Catalogue. It is the assumption that from the beginning of written works of public interest, an imprimatur had to be issued by some department of state. That would seem to indicate that in Former Han some sort of headquarters pressure was exercised in obtaining conformity in the use of terms, i.e. of scribal conformity. In any case, by the end of the Former Han Dynasty the ancient awe over the written word with its mana-imbued symbols had changed into intelligent appreciation of *wen* (patterned language) as a noble art of the mind (*hsin*). A sharp distinction was drawn between *pi* (rough notes) and the studied expressions of considered thought. From this angle of approach Tung Chung-shu's seventeen *chüan* of philosophizing in his *Ch'un Ch'iu Fan Lu* becomes an exciting document, a dated example of literary capabilities on the way. Ssŭ-ma Ch'ien's "Record of History," a document of slightly later date, running to 130 *chüan*, is even more exciting from the literary angle, for by his mastery in sentence progression and chapter division literature on the grand scale is on the way, and the door opened for Pan Ku's masterly advances in the writing of history. Even more exciting, as a contemporary event to Ssŭ-ma Ch'ien's achievement, is Ssŭ-ma Hsiang-ju's amazing revivification of the old *fu* genres. He transformed the patterned forms of Ch'ü Yüan's impassioned introspection, of the *Ch'u Tz'ǔ*'s animistically-inspired reflections, and of Hsün Ch'ing's and other Scholars' didactic poetry, converting them into a medium for delineating large-scale objects of observation, and he did this in an overall vein of irony strengthened by the use of *dramatis personae*. There is no need to cite Pan Ku's other instances of the new literary capacities exhibited in the later Ch'ang-an court. It is enough to cite Pan Ku and Chang Heng, the architects of those four grandly conceived poetic structures revealing the discriminate features of the two Han capitals and regimes, to realize what heights of communicative power that recreated script made possible.

The whole field of dateable mid-Han literature requires reexamination from the angle of this central idea—the prose as well as the poetry, the state papers and reports of conferences, the memorials and warnings (probings), the encomiums and bewailing condolences, not omitting the styled products of courtly badinage and riddle-making. Anywhere may be found grist to the explorers' mill. In particular, since it was in the period that the Yin-Yang cosmology really asserted its power over Scholar minds, stirring them to all sorts of ratiocination, close attention needs to be paid to the emergent forms of speculation. For example, from it stemmed a rationale of history, of what ancient history must logically have been: extremely convincing to minds under the sway of ineluctable processes, birth, growth, decline, and death. Also its effect on language awaits more rigorous investigation: the growth of dioptic expressions, "looking up . . . looking down," "the inner . . . the outer" (point of view), "referring to the past . . . referring to the present." They reveal an analytical consciousness in regard to angles of consideration on a subject of reflection. They are the more impressive because the same ability is disclosed in relation to the aspects of Nature, heaven and earth, summer and winter, the curved and the rectilinear, the dark and the light, the fine and the rough. Also the same complementary distinctions were worked out in relation to man, man in the family, man in society and the nation.[16] Whether the distinctive qualities of the new script aided or retarded the development of these new powers of the mind is awaiting research, and along with that must go research into the effects of the Yin-Yang mind on the structure of sentences and the tightening of discourse.

Finally, evidence of this power to drive the mind in double harness may seem to be forthcoming from late-Chou literature, evidence at any rate of rudimentary forms of it. There is, however, the inescapable doubt whether we can be sure

[16] For further ideas on this subject, see my paper, "The Epistemological Method in Chinese Philosophy," in *Essays in East-West Philosophy*, University of Hawaii Press, 1951. A good example of "double-harness" reasoning is to be found in Liu Hsieh's *Wen Hsin Tiao Lung*, ch. 1, a translation of which appears as Appendix 2 in my *Art of Letters*, Bollingen Series, New York, 1951.

of any such book having come through the Han era without undergoing some change, even if only a small one. To refer only to Liu Hsiang and his colleagues, they took their duties of redaction very seriously, and we know that they had difficulties. There was also the transcribing of old-script documents into the new script, and we know that many mid-Han Scholars had a passion for demarcation of the text, as also for composing amplifications, elucidatory of the meaning as they saw it. The doubts thus created cannot be entirely resolved by citation of recorded instances of Erudites and others being severely punished for tampering with sacrosanct writings. Modern critical scholarship, stirred by the Ch'ing Dynasty learned questionings, has continued on the long road of linguistic and stylistic enquiry. The suggestion here is that from more detailed, more exact knowledge of the new styles of language selection and sentence structure which spring to life in mid-Han times there might emerge new powers of discrimination in relation to the Scriptures. In particular it is urged that the most likely Scripture to produce results from the application of this technique is the "Record of Rites," known as a compilation of mid-Han *Ju*. That the intricate weaving of old and new material in many of its books and passages would, of course, create problems, in some cases insoluble ones, would naturally be expected. But the new style, the "contemporary style," very much laid its hands on time-honored phrases and disciplined them into line with its passion for short clear-cut clauses and sentences in which one statement is made to impinge sharply on its fellow statement. By this means the twisted cue of Scripture studies might be untwisted somewhat, the cloth untrue be levelled in some texts, and the wobbling ellipsis of dating documents become more amenable to direction.